T0340154

Advertising Organizations and Publications

Advertising Organizations and Publications

A Resource Guide

EDITED BY

JOHN PHILIP JONES

Sage Publications, Inc.
International Educational and Professional Publisher
Thousand Oaks ▪ London ▪ New Delhi

For information:

Sage Publications, Inc.
2455 Teller Road
Thousand Oaks, California 91320
E-mail: order@sagepub.com

Sage Publications Ltd.
6 Bonhill Street
London EC2A 4PU
United Kingdom

Sage Publications India Pvt. Ltd.
M-32 Market
Greater Kailash I
New Delhi 110 048 India

Library of Congress Cataloging-in-Publication Data
Main entry under title:

Advertising organizations and publications: A resource guide/ ed.,
John Philip Jones.
   p. cm.
   ISBN 0-7619-1236-3 (cloth: alk. paper)—ISBN 0-7619-1237-1 (paper: alk. paper)
   1. Advertising—United States. 2. Advertising. I. Jones, John
Philip.
   HF5813.U6 A654 2000
   659.1—dc21   99-050479

This book is printed on acid-free paper.

00 01 02 03 04 05 06 7 6 5 4 3 2 1

Acquiring Editor:	Harry Briggs
Editorial Assistant:	MaryAnn Vail
Production Editor:	Astrid Virding
Editorial Assistant:	Nevair Kabakian
Copy Editor:	Linda Gray
Typesetter:	Danielle Dillahunt

This series of handbooks is dedicated to David Ogilvy (1911–1999).

This photograph, taken at Chateau Touffou in 1994,
shows David Ogilvy and the editor, John Philip Jones.

"Last summer the Queen asked me what I did for a living. When I said ADVERTISING, you should have seen the expression on her beautiful face— a mixture of horror, incredulity, and amusement.

"I can only plead that whatever you do in life, however humble, is OK if you do it right."

David Ogilvy, 1986
The Unpublished David Ogilvy

Contents

Advertising Publications

Postlude

CHÂTEAU DE TOUFFOU
86300 BONNES

12 September, 1995

Dear John

I cannot believe that you are going to dedicate your series of handbooks to me. A <u>sublime</u> compliment.

When will it be published?

Will you send me a copy?

It must have been infernally difficult to <u>organize</u>.

How many volumes?

I trust that the piece about SUBLIMINAL is exposed as a hoax, as its author finally admitted.

You must have worked your head off. Hero!

Yours ever

David

This letter is David Ogilvy's response to the news that the handbooks were being dedicated to him.

In accordance with David Ogilvy's request—

"Subliminal" Advertising

Of all the common misconceptions about advertising, the most delightful is the notion of "subliminal" effects: the supposed ability of advertising to sell (a) by flashing words or images onto a cinema or television screen so rapidly that the viewer's eye cannot pick them up or (b) by hiding potent symbols in the illustrations in print advertisements. This "technique" was first described in an article in the *Sunday Times* of London in 1956 and given wide publicity in the United States by Vance Packard in 1957.[1] This article described a supposed experiment in a New Jersey cinema, an experiment that became very famous indeed. Interest in the subject has not flagged during the past four decades, and the notion of "subliminal" effects has become all but universally believed by the public.

At an early stage in the history of "subliminal" advertising, skeptics—notably Walter Weir, an experienced practitioner—pressed its proponents for evidence of its effectiveness. Under scrutiny, it was discovered that the original "test" of "subliminal" advertising in the New Jersey cinema never in fact took place. Indeed, the cinema in which it was supposedly held never existed. The whole thing was a journalistic hoax, a minor "Piltdown man."

The volume of *Proceedings of the 1987 Conference of the American Academy of Advertising* contains a perfectly serious paper on "subliminal" advertising, which includes 50 footnotes referring to papers on the subject in academic journals. In 1994, a less fanciful paper by Stuart Rogers was read at the annual conference of the American Academy of Advertising.[2] This paper describes exactly what "subliminal" advertising is.

Wilson Bryan Key, who has written two widely selling books on the subject, claims that "every major advertising agency has at least one embedding technician in its art department. The technique is taught in most commercial art schools." My 27 years of professional experience in the advertising agency business and my 19 years of advertising consultancy and teaching the subject at an American university have made it quite clear to me that Key's claims cannot be described as exaggerations. They are total fantasy.

Notes

1. Vance Packard, *The Hidden Persuaders* (Harmondsworth, UK: Penguin, republished 1979), 41-42.

2. Stuart C. Rogers, "Subliminal Advertising: Grand Slam of the Twentieth Century" (*Proceedings of the 1994 Conference of the American Academy of Advertising*).

Introduction

John Philip Jones

This book is the fifth and final volume in a series devoted to best advertising practice. The following works have already been published:

How Advertising Works: The Role of Research
The Advertising Business: Operations, Creativity, Media Planning, Integrated Communications
How to Use Advertising to Build Strong Brands
International Advertising: Realities and Myths

Unlike the earlier volumes, this present work is composed of a large number of mainly short articles: pieces that give essential information about the many organizations and publications whose purpose is to improve professional practice in the advertising field.

Of the 81 articles in this book, 78 are directed to the main substance of the work: 65 dealing with organizations and 13 with publications. And of these 78, 51 are American and 27 are foreign-based.

I have tried very hard to make the coverage of organizations and publications in the United States as comprehensive as I can. However, my coverage of foreign countries is much more selective. The criterion I have used is not whether the organization or publication in question does a useful job in its native country. I have looked for more by including only organizations and journals whose work is useful in a broader setting, being of demonstrable value also to international advertisers and in particular to advertisers in the United States. In other words, the selected organizations and publications must in some way contribute to our *overall* understanding of advertising and how it works.

The majority, although not all, of the organizations and journals that appear in this volume are run on a not-for-profit basis.

Like the earlier volumes, this present one is the joint effort of a number of authors. Sixteen identified authors have written articles covering topics of which they have specific knowledge and experience. The remaining chapters have been written by me, using data in every case supplied by the organization or publication I am describing.

As mentioned, 78 of the 81 articles are concerned with the main substance of the work. The remaining 3 articles comprise this Introduction, plus two pieces indirectly connected with David Ogilvy, the justly celebrated advertising practitioner to whom this series of books is dedicated and who died at the age of 88 when the copy for this manuscript was being finalized.

When I had told him in 1995 that I was going to dedicate this series to him, David Ogilvy, besides being rather pleased, was anxious that I should say something about "subliminal" advertising—a subject invariably treated as a joke when it is discussed in professional circles. It is in truth a subject best totally ignored because there is the real danger that people outside the advertising business might treat it seriously! But David Ogilvy was rather disturbed by the credence given to the fanciful notion of "subliminal" effects, and I have therefore written a brief essay on the subject, and this forms part of the dedication.

From an early stage in the enterprise, I had felt that the whole work should conclude with a tribute to the Founding Fathers of advertising. I have therefore included as a postlude an article on the 10 personalities who I think did more than any others to make the advertising business what it is today. The last of these 10 figures is David Ogilvy himself. The discussion of his career therefore makes a very fitting conclusion to this multivolume work.

In a second and rather important sense, this description of David Ogilvy's life and career also marks another *finis*. He is almost certainly the last major figure to make a really powerful personal impact on the advertising business—or rather, on the business *as we know it.* His contribution therefore signals a full stop in the development of current advertising practice. Advertising will continue to exist and will remain important in the business world, but I believe that it will change organically—and perhaps rather rapidly—as targets for marketing efforts become narrower, as advertising agency services become substantially unbundled, as advertising activities become integrated with other marketing stimuli, and as measurability of response acquires a totally new importance.

These developments, which are well under way and widely discussed in professional circles, all have a place in these handbooks and each is discussed in more than one chapter.

This is not quite the end of this Introduction, because I must describe a little further these five books and say a few words about the people who have contributed to them.

The five volumes comprise a total of 210 separate contributions: 129 chapters in the first four books plus 81 articles in this last one. There are in total 2,050 printed pages and well over 800,000 words. This is the most substantial work of its kind ever published on advertising. It is not written as a simple descriptive textbook. The 129 chapters in the first four books are analytical, and they are all devoted to ideas, always "state of the art" and generally controversial. When I started to plan the project, I aimed to put together the most extensive and indeed the best work on advertising ever published. Only the reader can judge whether my hope and expectation have come even remotely close to realization.

I wish to thank a number of people who have worked with me. First, the authors of the chapters and articles: Their names are a roll call of many of the most distinguished figures on the world advertising scene during the last quarter of the 20th century.

Second, at Sage Publications, I must mention Harry Briggs (acquisitions editor), Judy Selhorst and Linda Gray (copy editors), Ravi Balasuriya (designer), and Astrid Virding (production editor). They and their colleagues have throughout been helpful, positive, rapidly responsive, and unfailingly cheerful. These are the qualities that authors and editors value most.

Third, in Syracuse, my thanks go to Peter Moller and Ed Voytovich, who have contributed in a substantial way to my wife's computer literacy and who have solved many many problems—all urgent ones. Scott Bunting, of Industrial Color Labs, Syracuse, was responsible for the more than 190 superb computer-generated diagrams.

Fourth, my greatest thanks of all go to my wife, Wendy, who has lived with this project for 8 years. She has typed on a computer every word of the manuscript, plus many preliminary drafts. She has single-handedly administered the enterprise, including all the complex and prolonged correspondence with the authors. She has policed the quality and timing of all five volumes from beginning to end. She has looked upon the whole endeavor as a professional challenge, and she has responded magnificently. Over the years, there were many occasions on which she expressed her rather trenchant opinion of the books and their editor. And when the work was completed, she felt satisfaction and relief—but none of the nostalgic sadness that Edward Gibbon experienced when he had finished the manuscript of *The Decline and Fall of the Roman Empire!*

Advertising Organizations

Advertising Archives— The University of Illinois

Diane Foxhill Carothers

The Library of the University of Illinois at Urbana-Champaign has been the recipient of three outstanding advertising collections that either are now or will later be made available to scholars and other investigators. The Advertising Council Archives are housed in the University Archives in the Main Library building and contain material dating back 50 years. The D'Arcy Collection, donated in 1983 by the St. Louis advertising firm D'Arcy, MacManus & Masius, now D'Arcy Masius Benton & Bowles, is part of the Communications Library and consists of slightly more than three quarters of a million newspaper and magazine advertisements, primarily from 1890 to 1970. It is probably the more heavily used of the two collections, and reproductions of its ads have appeared in scholarly research journals, books, and magazines. The largest and most recently acquired is the Woodward Collection of Advertising, an unprocessed collection located in the Archives Research Center and serviced by the Communications Library staff. These three collections are supplemented by other holdings related to the history of advertising that include 25 years of

International Harvester tractor and truck ads, the papers of ad agency/screenwriter Samson Raphaelson, and various advertising and journalism departmental publications and photographs.

Whereas the D'Arcy and Woodward Collections extensively illustrate commercial advertising in America during the 19th and 20th centuries, the Advertising Council Archives tell the story of public service advertising since the early days of World War II. This nonprofit organization was formed in 1941 primarily to use advertising to promote the public good. Known during World War II as the War Advertising Council, it worked in conjunction with the Office of War Information (OWI) to create public service messages that supported the war effort. Its function was to create campaigns and disseminate information inducing people to take "actions necessary to the speedy winning of the war." Using a volunteer campaign manager and someone to oversee operations, a task force from volunteer agencies worked in concert with OWI and whichever government bureaus needed similar assistance. Their campaigns were circulated to advertisers by means of committees of sponsors that donated space and air time for public service messages. Among the major campaigns during the war years were those concerning working women, conservation projects, war bond sales, the Red Cross, anticipated peacetime problems, and forest fire prevention.

After the war, the council shortened its name to the Advertising Council and began serving private organizations not connected with the government. Individual citizens with an interest in public issues constituted its Public Advisory Committee, later renamed Public Policy Committee, to consider requests for council assistance. It drafted criteria requiring all requests to be in the public interest, potentially successful through advertising methods, timely, noncommercial, nonpartisan, nonsectarian, and not designed to influence legislation. An Industries Advisory Committee advised the council about projects under consideration that involved business, suggested new projects, advised the board of directors, helped to develop greater public understanding of democratic government, and obtained contributions of time and space from the media estimated to total over $800,000,000 in 1984. (The Advertising Council is described in this volume.)

Television advertising was begun in 1948, and since then, the council's messages have focused on national problems—drunk driving, drug abuse, racism, child abuse, the use of seat belts, AIDS awareness, mental illness, the United Negro College Fund, and so on.

The Advertising Council Archives contain examples of thousands of such ads from magazines, newspapers, radio, television, billboards, and posters. In addition, the nearly 110 cubic feet of documents constituting that collection include office files, board and committee minutes, and other working documents. These show how such advertising materials are produced and outline how individual ad campaigns were developed and presented to the public. The materials have been used also by scholarly researchers studying American cultural history and the effects of advertising. A special exhibit based on the Advertising Council Archives was mounted at the Smithsonian Institution's National Museum of American History in 1992. The collection is now available to users through a historical file series containing a record of every advertising campaign.

In addition to the Ad Council Archives, the University Archives now have the papers of two well-known academic advertising leaders: Charles Sandage and S. Watson Dunn. These two collections are not yet completely processed for access to the public, but the archival staff can provide help to those who want to view the material.

The D'Arcy Collection is believed to be the only one of its kind and size in a public institution and is unusual in that it encompasses products advertised by many agencies rather than just one. Although almost all the ads are from newspapers, magazines, and trade journals, there are a few in other formats, such as brochures, signs, programs, coupons, contests, photostatic copies, direction sheets for use of the products, and some correspondence. The material is generally in excellent condition, although many of the newspaper clippings are now yellowed and brittle. The advertisements range from approximately 1 × 2 inches to full-page newspaper size. The majority of the ads are dated and their sources given, but there is almost no identification of either the creator or the agency responsible. However, some of the advertisements for General Tires, Cascade Whiskey, and Coca-Cola that were actually created by the D'Arcy agency are identified by a small D with an arrow going partially through it; the agency also used arrows in its illustrations for a short period of time. These are particularly evident in Coca-Cola and 3-Minute Oat Flakes ads from about 1920 to 1925.

The collection is housed in a secured, locked area in the Communications Library and is contained in 166 legal-sized steel filing cabinet drawers. It is arranged in alphabetical order by product, brand name, and date. The Communications Library has recently acquired an additional 107 boxes of clippings from the D'Arcy agency. These ads appear to be primarily from 1983 and 1984, although they have not yet been processed and logged. Many well-known contemporary products and brands are represented, but there are a number of ads for obsolete items, such as spats, fallout shelters, razor straps, and Prohibition. Included also are organizational and governmental advertisers such as the American Red Cross, the North Atlantic Treaty Organization (NATO), New York City's Lincoln Center, and various states promoting tourism.

A grant of $84,000 was awarded by the National Endowment for the Humanities to preserve the D'Arcy Collection on 35-mm microfilm. This film has been catalogued and circulates through interlibrary loan. Although the actual collection has restricted access, the microfilm has been heavily used by students, faculty, and extramural researchers. Arrangements can be made to have the original ads photographed for use as illustrations for books or articles. Selected ads have been cited and/or used as illustrations in books (e.g., *The Branding of America, The Inventive Yankee, Technology and Women's Voices*), professional journals (*Best of Business Quarterly, European Journal of Marketing, National Trial Lawyer, Science News*), magazines (*Our Century, Playboy*), exhibits (Hudson River Museum, American Advertising Museum, German Postal Museum in Frankfurt am Main), and by the City of New York Law Department for a court case.

An article in the 75th anniversary issue of the D'Arcy, MacManus & Masius house organ, *Between Us,* recounts that William D'Arcy founded his agency in 1906 in St. Louis after he had worked for Western Advertising Company, one of the first such agencies in the city. He initiated the collection in 1920 when his staff started clipping ads from newspapers and magazines for company use. For a period of time, two copies of *Harper's Bazaar, Life, Time,* and *The Saturday Evening Post* were received and every ad removed and filed. Single copies of other magazines and trade journals were acquired and their ads retained. In addition to St. Louis newspapers, eight big-city dailies were subscribed to at one period, and other newspapers were scrutinized sporadically. Once the staff had created a contemporary file, they began a retrospective search of old issues of trade journals and general magazines. Clipping by the agency staff continued until June 1983 when the job was transferred to a national firm that furnishes specific clippings on request.

The advertisement that has been identified as the oldest is dated 1869 for Gorham silver, and ads for H. W. Johns's asbestos materials and Union Pacific Railroad are from 1870. Other very old ads are for Travelers Insurance (1877),

Baker's Chocolate (1878), *Ladies Home Journal* (1880), Beeman Chewing Gum (1882), Durkee Cooking Oil (1886), Pro-phy-lac-tice Brushes (1887), Hires Root Beer, and Richardson & Boynton Furnaces (both 1888). Coca-Cola, one of William D'Arcy's original clients in 1893, became a bellwether for his new agency and was one of its longest-running accounts. Another early client was Anheuser-Busch, as D'Arcy created ads for its Malt-Nultrine, a liquid food tonic containing 1.9% alcohol, and Bevo, its nonalcoholic soft drink. There are at least 1,000 ads each for more than 50 different brand names. Campbell's Soups, General Tires, Goodyear Tires, and LaClede Gas Company have over 3,000 ads apiece, and Coca-Cola has 6,000. Shoes, railroads, mortgage and loan companies, and alcoholic beverages are some of the subject categories with the largest number of ads.

The vast majority of the ads in the collection are in English, but there are a few in foreign languages. Lucky Strike cigarettes were advertised in Japanese in *Asian Weekly* in 1964. Hastings Piston Rings ("tough but oh so gentle") used the same slogan in a 1942 Spanish version ("duro pero tan suave") in *El Automovil Americano.*

A detailed listing of products and brands has been prepared for the D'Arcy Collection that shows the range of years of advertisements held for each, the number of ads, and the appropriate microfilm reel number for use with interlibrary loans. Cross-references have been included to make the material more readily retrievable. In addition, a detailed index of product and company names has been created that is particularly helpful when a company manufactures more than one product—for example, corporations such as General Electric, Smith Corona, International Harvester, and Fleischmann's. Publication of this index is not yet arranged.

The newest acquisition to the Communications Library is the Woodward Advertising Collection, a gift of Chicago businessman Garry Woodward in 1989. It is similar to the D'Arcy Collection but much more comprehensive. It is contained in approximately 1,000 filing drawers and boxes. The library staff is making an inventory at the present time of the collection and is creating a Web page of categories in the collection that will show brand, category, and date. An estimate has been made that puts the collection at between 4 and 5 million advertisements.

According to personal correspondence with Woodward, this collection was started by Reginald Vance Coglan, a creative director for the advertising agency of Ruthrauff and Ryan. He was a friend of John Breck who offered his several thousand magazines in which the Breck Girl Shampoo advertising ap-

peared. Coglan separated all the magazines, compiled and collated the advertisements, and began a service organization offering historical copies of ads,
usually covering the whole product category or multiyear history of a brand
and so forth. Coglan subsequently subscribed to various national magazines
and newspapers and clipped advertisements for approximately 40 years; the
collection goes through 1984.

These collections form the nucleus for probably the nation's leading center
for the study of the history of advertising.

During 1999, the acting communications librarian mounted a special advertising exhibit in the university's main library showing color copy versions of
ads found in the D'Arcy and Woodward Collections. A Website of the exhibit
is available to viewers through the Internet at http://www.library.uiuc.
edu/adexhibit.

The collections are held at two University of Illinois sites:

University of Illinois at Urbana-Champaign
University Archives
19 Library
1408 West Gregory Drive
Urbana, IL 61801
Telephone: (217) 333-0798   Fax: (217) 333-2868
E-mail: illiarch@uiuc.edu
Website: http://www.library.uiuc.edu/ahx

Communications Library
122 Gregory Hall
810 South Wright Street
Urbana, IL 61801
Telephone: (217) 333-2216   Fax: (217) 333-9882
Website: http://www.library.uiuc.edu/cmx

Advertising Archives— Other Collections

American Advertising Museum
5035 SE 24th Avenue
Portland, Oregon 97202
Telephone: (503) 226-0000   Fax: (503) 226-2635
Website: http://www.admuseum.org

Center for Advertising History
National Museum of American History
Mail Code 601
Washington, DC 20560
Telephone: (202) 357-1648   Fax: (202) 786-2453
Website: http://www.si.edu/nmah/archives/d-7.htm

John W. Hartman Center for Sales, Advertising, & Marketing History
Duke University Library
Box 90185
Durham, NC 27708-0185
Director: Ellen Gartrell
Reference Archivist: Jacqueline Reid
Telephone: (919) 660-5836   Fax: (919) 660-5934
Website: http://scriptorium.lib.duke.edu/hartman

Museum of Broadcast Communications
Chicago Cultural Center
Michigan Avenue at Washington Street
Chicago, IL 60602-4801
Telephone: (312) 629-6025   Fax: (312) 629-6009
Website: http://www.mbcnet.org

Museum of Television & Radio
25 West 52nd Street
New York, NY 10019
Telephone: (212) 621-6800 (daily information); (212) 621-6600
    (all other information); (212) 621-6845 (archives)
Fax: (212) 621-6700
Website: http://www.mtr.org

State Historical Society of Wisconsin
816 State Street
Madison, WI 53706
Telephone: (608) 264-6460   Fax: (608) 264-6486
Website: http://www.shsw.wisc.edu

Strong Museum—Documentary Artifacts
1 Manhattan Square
Rochester, NY 14607
Curator: Nicolas Ricketts
Telephone: (716) 263-2701, ext. 241   Fax (716) 263-2493
Website: http://www.strongmuseum.org

University of British Columbia
History of Advertising Archives
Faculty of Commerce and Business Administration
2053 Main Mall
Vancouver, BC
Canada V6T 1Z2
Curator: Professor Richard W. Pollay
Telephone: (604) 822-8338   Fax: (604) 822-8521
E-mail: richard.pollay@commerce.ubc.ca or
   pollay@merlin.commerce.ubc.ca

The Advertising Association (AA) (United Kingdom)

Andrew Brown

The Advertising Association (AA) is a federation of 26 trade associations and professional bodies representing advertisers, agencies, the media, and support services in the United Kingdom. It is the only body that speaks for all sides of an industry worth over £14 billion.

Thus, its remit concerns the mutual interests of, or threats to, the business as a whole. It operates in a complementary way with the perfectly proper vested interests of its members who have specific roles for their individual sectors.

The AA speaks as "the common voice" for all in the following ways:

- Combating unjustified restrictions and all outright bans on marketing communications for freely and legally available products or services
- Promoting public understanding of, and respect for, advertising and its role in promoting competition, innovation, and economic and social progress in society
- Upholding standards and the principles of self-regulation
- Providing information, research, and statistics about the advertising business

The AA exists to provide a coordinated service in the interests of its members' member organizations—that is, the individual companies that make up this large, diverse, and competitive business.

Its objective is summarized this way: "To promote and protect the rights, responsibilities and role of advertising in the UK." This is in line with Article 10 of the European Convention on Human Rights, which recognizes commercial freedom of speech as a right, alongside political and artistic freedoms of speech.

The AA is a non-profit-making company, limited by guarantee and funded by a combination of subscriptions, donations, and revenue-raising activities, such as seminars and sales of publications.

The AA is directed by its members. They learn about, review, and direct its activities at every level—(a) in Council, which is the legal and representative body; (b) in the Executive Committee; and (c) in the various committees and task forces operating within specific remits.

It is imperative that all parts of the business are represented in the development of AA policies and actions, and thus, membership of these groups is drawn from both trade associations and key individual practitioners.

This ensures the setting of priorities, maximum effectiveness and minimum duplication of effort, and a constant readiness to respond to changing contexts and issues as they arise.

The four key officers of the association—the president, chairman and two vice chairmen—are always well-known and respected practitioners from the business, representing the advertiser, agency, and media sectors.

The AA produces the official U.K. advertising expenditure statistics and also, in conjunction with the Advertising Information Group (AIG), produces the official European advertising statistics. These statistics are made available to the advertising business and the general public through various publications. In addition to the published statistics, the AA organizes, in conjunction with AIG, the World Advertising Statistics Symposium. This symposium brings together the international organizations that produce advertising statistics with the aim of harmonizing the data and improving the quality of statistics available.

Advertising Association
Abford House
15 Wilton Road
London SW1V 1NJ
United Kingdom
Telephone: +44 (0)20 7828-2771   Fax: +44 (0)20 7931-0376
E-mail: aa@adassoc.org.uk
Website: http://www.adassoc.org.uk

The Advertising Council

Founded just 3 weeks after the attack on Pearl Harbor in 1941, the Advertising Council is credited with creating the category of public service advertising. The organization began as the War Advertising Council, with a mission to place the resources of advertisers, advertising agencies, and the media at the service of the government. Early council campaigns recruited merchant seamen, urged Americans to buy war bonds, and encouraged women to work in important factory jobs during the war. Overall, the council produced more than a billion dollars worth of advertising between 1942 and 1945 to help the war effort. And the campaigns were successful. For example, the War Advertising Council helped raise $35 million in war bonds, and recruited 2 million women to work.

Just before he died, President Franklin D. Roosevelt asked the council to carry on after the war. At the end of World War II, the council continued with a new name and a new mission: to identify important public issues and to develop advertising campaigns on those issues that will help stimulate action.

The Ad Council continues its mission today as a private nonprofit organization headquartered in New York City. The council unites private nonprofit bodies and federal government agencies with volunteer advertising agencies who create campaigns to educate the public about important social issues. The Ad Council coordinates the production and distribution of campaign materials to the media. The media, in turn, donate time and space for the public service announcements (PSAs).

Over the years, more than 1,000 campaigns have been created by the Ad Council. Although many people are not familiar with the Ad Council name, most know of its work. The 50-year-old Smokey Bear, born of the wartime necessity for wood and cellulose products, is one of advertising's most famous icons. McGruff the Crime Dog, another Ad Council creation, has been urging Americans to "take a bite out of crime" for 15 years. The United Negro College Fund's "a mind is a terrible thing to waste," one of the more memorable Ad Council slogans, has become part of American vernacular.

Ad Council campaigns are not only highly visible; they are enormously successful. The Recruiting New Teachers campaign led to 800,000 calls to an information hotline and has resulted in more than 40,000 callers becoming teachers. A 1991 study of the effectiveness of an Ad Council colon cancer commercial proved that with a sustained effort over a period of 12 months, public service advertising changes attitudes and stimulates action.

Such success has led to more inquiries for assistance than the council can possibly handle. The council receives about 400 requests from nonprofit groups about campaign support each year, but, on average, it can accept only 3.

Each application is reviewed by the Ad Council's Proposal Review Committee. To be considered by the committee, the campaign must be proposed by an accredited organization, and its goals cannot be commercial, political, or denominational. The issue to be addressed must be significant and national in scope yet of concern to all Americans.

Once a client is accepted, the American Association of Advertising Agencies assigns a volunteer ad agency to develop the campaign, and a volunteer campaign coordinator (a corporate communications professional) is appointed by the Association of National Advertisers. The client organization and an Ad Council campaign manager oversee the campaign development to ensure that the advertising is geared toward the solution of the problem being addressed.

Donated media time and space are key elements of the Ad Council's success. In 1993, the council was the 19th largest advertiser in the United States with more than $612 million worth of donated media time and space from 22,000 outlets nationwide.

With the rapidly changing media environment, the Ad Council continues to explore new avenues for its PSAs. Computer bulletin boards, taxi tops, and stadium and arena scoreboards have all been used to extend Ad Council messages to the American public.

In addition, as the makeup of our nation's population evolves, the Ad Council has begun to create campaigns for specific audiences. Over the past several years, six campaigns have been targeted to the Hispanic community, and one has been targeted to the Asian community. In addition, whenever possible, campaigns are localized to list a nearby source of help to increase further their impact on individuals in local communities.

Over its lifetime, the Ad Council's job has gotten more difficult. Convincing people to plant victory gardens during World War II was a little easier than ending racial discrimination or preventing domestic violence—issues addressed in current Ad Council campaigns. But with the unique combination of support between advertisers, advertising agencies, and the media, Ad Council campaigns have helped to save lives, have educated the American public about current issues and concerns, and have helped to make America a smarter and healthier country in which to live.

The archives of the council are at the University of Illinois at Urbana-Champaign.

The Advertising Council
261 Madison Avenue
New York, NY 10016-2303
Telephone: (212) 922-1500   Fax: (212) 922-1676
E-mail: info@adcouncil.org
Website: http://www.adcouncil.org

The Advertising Educational Foundation (AEF)

Paula A. Alex

The Advertising Educational Foundation (AEF) is a nonprofit, operating foundation supported by one-time contributions from ad agencies, advertisers, and media companies. Created in 1983, the foundation is dedicated to building a better understanding of advertising and a greater appreciation of its social and economic roles in society.

The AEF mission acknowledges that advertising is a vital and highly visible force in American society. Thus, a realistic understanding of how advertising is created, how it works, and what it contributes to our social and economic life is important—for liberal arts students as well as students of advertising and marketing—and for all who play active roles in our complex society.

In 1999, the AEF updated its mission. Beginning immediately, the AEF will serve as the industry's clearinghouse, repository, and distribution force for educational information and materials to improve the perception and understanding of the social and economic role of advertising. The foundation's main priorities are two:

1. To support advertising education in any academic context through on-campus visits and the World Wide Web

2. To help attract the highest level of talent to the industry

Three major programs address the AEF's updated mission:

1. The ongoing *Ambassador Program* at college and university campuses across the country is designed to provide a forum in which the advertising/marketing professional can discuss all facets of the industry, including the issues associated with advertising, and respond to student and faculty questions and concerns. Members of a corps of 200 seasoned advertising and marketing executives volunteer their time away from the office to visit small liberal arts colleges as well as large universities and graduate business schools to discuss and debate current industry issues, such as free speech, ethics, regulation, manipulation, gender issues, cultural diversity, and global advertising, as well as the creation of advertising. Over 150 colleges and universities participate each academic year.

2. The *AEF Website* will be expanded to establish the AEF as the preeminent on-line advocate of advertising's social and economic benefits. With this expansion, the foundation hopes to increase awareness of the AEF within its target audience and within the industry. In addition, the site will serve as a way to facilitate learning among students and professors in the liberal arts and professors of advertising and marketing/communication, and to build partnerships with key AEF supporters on both the agency and client sides, in addition to leveraging partner resources to advance the AEF's mission.

3. The *Educational Materials Collection* is designed to help professors with their daily classroom work and corporations with their training programs. At present, the collection consists of the highlights and complete study results of two major AEF-sponsored research projects—*The Miscomprehension of Televised Communications* and *The Comprehension and Miscomprehension of Print Communications*—and four video cassettes that cover public service advertising, self-regulation, the creative process, and advertising research. The AEF offers these materials on free loan and for purchase at a nominal fee. Discussions are underway to update existing videos and to expand the topics offered.

Advertising Educational Foundation
220 East 42nd Street, Suite 3300
New York, NY 10017
Telephone: (212) 986-8060   Fax: (212) 986-8061
Website: http://www.aef.com

The Advertising Federation of Australia (AFA)

Helga Diamond

AFA Members

For the past 25 years, the Advertising Federation of Australia (AFA) has been the voice of the Australian advertising industry. The AFA's role is to protect the business and professional interests of its members, to encourage best practice in advertising, and to promote the value of advertising to business decision makers.

Membership in the AFA is open to companies whose principal business is advertising, including strategic planning and marketing, media planning and buying, direct marketing, on-line marketing, and sales promotion. The AFA also welcomes associate members from related businesses and university departments. The one thing all our members have in common is a passion for communicating and a commitment to the success of our business.

The AFA's Role

Full membership in the AFA comes with a substantial range of benefits for agencies' businesses.

Promoting the Value and Effectiveness of Advertising

One of the AFA's key functions is marketing the value of advertising to business decision makers. The AFA Advertising Effectiveness Awards and casebooks are an important part of this marketing program. The AFA also conducts a series of seminars featuring winning campaigns with the people who made them work.

Managing Agencies' Business and Improving Margins

Current industry data are collected in three valuable annual benchmark surveys: Agency Income & Cost Analysis, Salary Survey, and Agency Remuneration. The surveys help members with the financial management of their agencies.

A Remuneration Policy Committee is focused on promoting the AFA's perspective on remuneration to agencies and clients.

Protecting Agencies' Business

The AFA provides practical advice to agencies on issues such as copyright, agency remuneration, industrial relations, talent contracts, tax, understanding new legislation, and advertising codes. These and many other issues are also covered through regular information bulletins, publications, and the AFA Website: http://www.afa.org.au.

Protecting the Advertising Agency Industry

As the voice of the advertising industry, the AFA provides representation in areas such as commercially workable intellectual property rights, advertising to children, advertising on the Internet, and advertising codes. This representation is maintained through strong relationships with government, the media, unions, advertisers, and other communication industry bodies.

The AFA has a national structure with a Sydney-based secretariat and a presence in all mainland states through state-based executive groups. Special program committees manage activities such as the AFA Effectiveness Awards and Education. The National Board of 10 member representatives covering all states and up to 3 National Directors endorses the AFA business plan and oversees members' financial contributions.

The AFA's Strategy

The AFA has produced a set of objectives called the Three Es strategy. The AFA stands for *ethics, education,* and *effectiveness.*

A World First in Advertising Ethics

The AFA Statement of Ethics and Code of Practice is a first for advertising anywhere in the world.

The Statement of Ethics sets out the values and principles to which all AFA members have agreed to subscribe, and the Code of Practice addresses relationships with advertisers, media, colleagues, and suppliers. Together they aim to encourage the highest standards of ethical behavior and best business practice in the industry. They also establish the levels of professional practice advertisers can expect when they deal with an AFA member.

An Education in Advertising

The AFA provides an extensive range of educational services to keep members informed on the issues that affect them most.

Information on issues such as remuneration, legislation affecting advertising, managing business, and improving margins is regularly distributed through surveys and bulletins to members. Educational seminars and events are also available to associate members.

The AFA also makes a considerable investment in the education of talented young people through AdSchool, the Graduate Trainee Program, and its Mentoring Program.

Nothing Works Like Effectiveness

The Advertising Effectiveness Program, which includes the Advertising Effectiveness Awards held every 2 years, is the AFA's flagship. These awards have become the industry benchmark in terms of advertising effectiveness and have earned the rare distinction of being widely respected by agencies and advertisers alike.

The awards generate substantive case histories that provide convincing evidence of the power of advertising to create commercial value for advertisers. The winning entries are published in the AFA Effective Advertising casebooks. The series of these represents a unique set of reference material that is widely being used in tertiary education by advertising and marketing practitioners. Statistical and research data accompany the case studies, which describe the contribution made by a campaign in marketing a product or service.

The best campaigns receive gold or silver awards in the following categories:

- Consumer goods—established
- Consumer services—established
- New products and services
- Retail, leisure and tourism
- Commercial, corporate, social, and government

The overall winner of the Gold Pinnacle will be one of the category winners above. Another four categories also receive trophies and publication:

- Integrated "through-the-line" communications
- Integrated use of interactive communications
- Innovation in media strategy
- Ingenious use of small budget

The winners are published in the AFA Effective Advertising casebooks.

Jhonnie Blampied, chairman of the AFA Advertising Effectiveness Awards, says this:

The AFA Advertising Effectiveness Awards, which have been running since 1990, are established as one of Australia's pre-eminent award schemes, probably because they are unique in what they set out to achieve:

1. To demonstrate the potential value of advertising as an accountable business investment.
2. To promote a deeper understanding of what makes advertising more effective.
3. To provide a detailed record of Australia's most effective advertising campaigns.
4. To raise the level of professionalism in the way advertising is created and evaluated among both advertisers and agencies.

Advertising *is* an accountable business investment. Whether you choose to view advertising as a cost or an investment, in both cases you expect a return.

Primarily, agencies are paid to build brands. We get paid to add tangible value to a business's profit and loss account. Our responsibility doesn't end with the booking of a media schedule or the shooting of an ad. Our responsibility to create a positive impact on the health of our client's business is ongoing. Creating advertising that works is the most important challenge for the industry. Perhaps the truth in this statement is what explains the record levels of support and patronage the awards have received. The issue is one that unites advertisers, agencies and researchers. And that is where these awards can return real value to all the stakeholders. Advertisers are undoubtedly conscious of the significant cost that advertising represents to their business. Issues such as the amount of money spent on production relative to media and the commercial value of creativity can be addressed with the benefit of some real live case studies. Similarly, agencies can be encouraged to explore less traditional ways of doing things. Whether it is maximizing the impact of a small budget, or devising integrated communication solutions.

The awards raise the level of professionalism in the industry. They are tough. In today's competitive markets it is tough to create effective advertising. It is tough to find measurements that isolate the effects of advertising. Tough to write an entry and even tougher to win an award. However, agencies and advertisers that have invested time in marshalling a case will have found it worthwhile, because the evaluation of advertising is one of the most critical stages of the creation of advertising. The more rigorous we are as an industry the more effective our work will be. Consumers have beliefs about how advertising affects them. How often have you heard someone in a research group say "That wouldn't make me buy that brand?" Similarly, the industry can make snap judgements about what is a "good" campaign or a "bad" one; what is likely to be effective and what is not. Another value of these books is that some of the cases challenge our subjective assumptions about campaigns. The provision of an objective argument about why a campaign has been effective challenges these assumptions and can lead to new insights and new ways to evaluate work.

How the Campaigns Are Evaluated

Marks are allocated on the following criteria:

Outcome of campaign	50
Credibility of case	30
Originality of thinking	20

In assessing the outcome of the campaign, the judges are asked to consider the following:

- The degree of difficulty of the task
- The strength of evidence
- The scale of the result
- The return on investment

The judges need to be convinced "beyond reasonable doubt" that the campaign was effective. Beyond being convinced that any impact was not the outcome of some other element of either the marketing or communications mix, a clear link between the advertising and the outcome has to be made. "We advertised and sales went up" does not prove a causal relationship.

In assessing the *originality of the thinking* of the campaign, the judges are asked to consider these criteria:

- The cleverness of the strategy in answering the challenge of the task
- The extent to which the campaign contributes a lasting impression
- The extent to which the advertising breaks new ground in adding new knowledge to the ways in which advertising works

The last criterion was added because of the real value of the awards in contributing to the industry's knowledge bank of how advertising works. As reference material, they provide important learning that can contribute to the creation of more successful advertising in the future. Advertising that was created overseas, but that has run in Australia, is not excluded from entering. However, it is less rewarded for originality of thinking than a domestically created campaign.

The Judges

The judges are all independent. It has been a policy set by the organizing committee of the first AFA Advertising Effectiveness Awards as a means of ensuring the absolute integrity of the awards. It has also been a policy to invite leaders from the fields of advertising as clients, management consultants, advertising researchers, and marketing academics.

Judging the awards is a very demanding task because the judges each have to evaluate the entries. Through their efforts, we have a bank of exceptional case studies that will provide a small stimulus for us all to find new ways of creating more effective advertising in the future.

Sponsors and Official Supporters

The awards are open for "official supporters" in the guise of advertisers, market researchers, and advertising agencies to lend their support to the awards. There is a high level of commitment and enthusiasm from the industry, with the level of sponsorship and the number and quality of entries increasing with each award.

Seminars

Effectiveness Seminars bring the winning case studies to life and give the audience an opportunity to look behind the scenes of some of the most successful campaigns in the country. The seminars are open to advertisers, researchers, academics, and students, as well as to member agencies.

Casebooks

AFA Effective Advertising casebooks are available from the AFA secretariat or its Website.

Jhonnie Blampied, chair of the AFA's Effectiveness Awards, has been Chief Executive Officer DDB Sydney since 1995. Having started his career in marketing and subsequently market research, he entered the field of advertising as a strategic planner. His background and passion for creating advertising that works made him a natural choice to take over the chair of the awards. He previously won the Golden Pinnacle Award in the AFA's Advertising Effectiveness

Awards for the Wrigley's "Extra" case study, and he subsequently won another AFA Golden Pinnacle Award for McDonald's. He has also written the AFA's AdSchool Strategic Planning Course. He has a BA honors degree in business studies as well as diplomas from the Institute of Marketing and the Market Research Society.

Advertising Federation of Australia
Level 1, 201 Miller Street
North Sydney, NSW 2060
PO Box 166, North Sydney, NSW 2059
Australia
Telephone: +61 (0)2-9957-3077   Fax: +61 (0)2-9957-3952
E-mail: afamail@afa.org.au
Website: http://www.afa.org.au

Advertising Industry Awards

Awards for outstanding campaigns are given by the following organizations. The organizations and the awards are all described in the articles devoted to the organizations.

The Advertising Federation of Australia
The Advertising Research Foundation
The American Advertising Federation
The American Marketing Association
British Design and Art Direction
The European Association of Advertising Agencies
The Institute of Canadian Advertising
The Institute of Practitioners in Advertising
The International Advertising Association
The International Advertising Festival (Cannes)
The One Club for Art and Copy
The Point-of-Purchase Advertising Institute
The Promotional Products Association
The Radio Advertising Bureau

The Advertising Research Foundation (ARF)

Jim Spaeth

F ounded in 1936 by the Association of National Advertisers and the American Association of Advertising Agencies, the Advertising Research Foundation (ARF) is a nonprofit corporate membership association that is today the preeminent professional organization in the field of advertising, marketing, and media research. Its combined membership represents more than 400 advertisers, advertising agencies, research firms, media companies, educational institutions, and international organizations.

The principal mission of the ARF is "more profitable marketing through more effective research." It seeks to accomplish this in the following ways:

- Promoting the highest-quality business and consumer marketing, advertising, and media research by developing guidelines and standards and by providing objective and impartial technical advice and expertise
- Expanding the knowledge base by developing new research tools, meaningful research studies, and training programs

- Providing opportunities for all industry segments to discuss issues and exchange ideas
- Communicating and promoting this research and knowledge through publications, conferences, seminars, an information center, and by other means

Throughout its history, the ARF has demonstrated a strong tradition of leadership within the research history by developing landmark studies providing practical solutions to some of the industry's most persistent problems and challenges. Some of the most significant of these are (a) establishment of the first standards for fieldwork verification, (b) designing the first syndicated multimagazine and multinewspaper audience studies, and (c) demonstrating the potential of cable television for split-market advertising research through the use of a controlled advertising research facility using cable television.

More recently, the ARF in the past decade alone has completed the following list of research achievements, which represent more than $4 million worth of primary research:

- *The Copy Research Validity Project:* A definitive analysis of the validity of measures of copy testing, which redefined the area of copy testing
- *The ARF/AMA Marketing Practices Survey:* A review of current trends and methods
- *The ARF Qualitative Research Market Survey:* A survey of qualitative research methods, practices, and incidence of use
- *The ARF Research Providers Study:* A study of issues and opportunities for advances in research techniques
- *The CEO Study:* A study of top management's perception of the contribution of research
- *The Effect of Interview Attempts on Survey Results:* A study of how and whether the number of attempts to complete an interview affects survey results
- *Toward Global Guidelines for Television Audience Measurement:* A sweeping review of TV ratings practice worldwide
- *Research Guidelines for Evaluating Special Radio Programming:* A study to aid media buyers in evaluating special and long-form radio programming for which audience estimates from a regularly published radio rating service are not available

Dedicated to a role of industry leadership, the ARF advocates the importance of cooperation and communication within the industry by joining forces with other associations, both nationally and internationally, to launch important new initiatives. Some of the industry organizations that the ARF supports financially or with which it is actively involved in joint ventures such as conferences, symposiums, research projects, or industry surveys, are these: the Council of American Survey Research Organizations (CASRO), the Marketing Research Association (MRA), the American Marketing Association (AMA), the Advertising Council, the Marketing Science Institute (MSI), the European Society for Opinion and Marketing Research (ESOMAR), and the Japan Marketing Association. The ARF has been leading the development of audience measurement techniques for the World Wide Web through the Future of Advertising Stakeholders Group (FAST) and the Council for Advertising Supported Information and Entertainment (CASIE).

The ARF publishes the important bimonthly magazine the *Journal of Advertising Research.*

Advertising Research Foundation Awards

The ARF has established three important advertising awards: the David Ogilvy Award (1993), the ARF Richard L. Lysaker Prize (1994), and the Michael J. Naples Research Industry Leadership Award (1998). These awards represent an important step toward the goal of establishing advertising awards based on campaign effectiveness determined by objective criteria rather than on aesthetic considerations.

The David Ogilvy Award

The David Ogilvy Award was initiated by the ARF in 1993, and the winners of the first year's competition were announced at the 1994 annual conference. Clearly, the award filled an industry need. "New David Ogilvy Award takes research out of hiding," said the *Wall Street Journal,* and the newsletter *Inside Research* cited the "fascinating presentations by the three top finalists."

Winners were selected based on the best demonstrations of the way in which well-conceived and well-executed research—by advertiser, agency, and research company working together—affected the creation and success of an advertising campaign. Specifically, entrants were required to document the manner in which research was linked to one or more of the following creative or marketing steps:

1. Uncovering new or emerging product opportunities or users
2. Shaping the underlying strategy
3. Developing the executions
4. Gaining management approval to run the executions
5. Guiding media exposure to product or service prospects
6. Demonstrating marketing success

The first-place trophy went to the research operations of AT&T as the advertiser and N. W. Ayer as the advertising agency for AT&T's "You Will" corporate campaign. The second-place winner's certificate was awarded to Nabisco (advertiser), FCB Leber Katz Partners (agency), and ASI Market Research (research company) for Oreo Cookies' "Unlock the Magic" campaign. The third-place winner's certificate was garnered by Goodyear Tire & Rubber Company and its agency J. Walter Thompson, Detroit, for the Goodyear Aquatread Tires "Demonstrations" campaign.

The ARF Richard L. Lysaker Award

Originally launched as a best-paper competition in 1992, the Lysaker Award has been recently (1999) reformulated to promote the best media research design. It was first awarded in 1993 in honor and memory of Richard Lysaker for his major contributions to the development of techniques for measuring media audiences and other approaches for evaluating media. The purpose of this award is to stimulate and encourage further development of improved measures and evaluations of media. The winning research design is put into the field and the investigation carried out. It is funded by the Sponsorship Committee, chaired by Audits & Surveys Inc., where Dr. Lysaker served as president from 1978 to 1991.

The Michael J. Naples Research Industry Leadership Award

This award was created in 1997 by the ARF's Board of Directors to honor Michael J. Naples, president of the foundation from 1981 to 1997. During that time, he rejuvenated the importance, the contribution, and the leadership of the ARF to the marketing, advertising, and media research industry. The ARF's board believed it only fitting that the prodigious impact of his leadership be recognized in kind by granting, in his name, leadership awards to others who have benefited the industry. The object of the award, therefore, is to recognize a single individual each year who stepped beyond the bounds of his or her daily business to move the research industry forward through personal leadership.

Advertising Research Foundation
641 Lexington Avenue
New York, NY 10022
Telephone: (212) 751-5656   Fax: (212) 319-5265
Website: http://www.arfsite.org

Advertising Seminars International (asi)

Advertising Seminars International (*asi**), a company established in 1991, organizes pan-European conferences on advertising and media issues. It also publishes *Commercial Communications: The Journal of Advertising and Marketing Policy and Practice in the European Community.* The publication is sponsored by Directorate General XV (Internal Market and Financial Services) of the European Commission.

In 1991, the plan for the establishment of the Internal Market was nearing completion, and companies were preparing to take advantage of the opportunities that would be afforded. There was little understanding, however, of the difficulties the advertiser and marketer would face when seeking to engage in cross-border commercial communications activities.

Advertisers, agencies, and media owners were facing a dramatic shift in marketing and geographical perspectives. In this increasingly competitive environment, a wealth of new opportunities presented themselves, together with

*This acronym is always lowercase.

attendant problems, on a European and global scale. It seemed, and seems, increasingly important for all players to share their experience in a rapidly evolving marketplace. It was equally important for them to do so at a European and broader international level.

In Europe, the media structure of each of the markets had evolved in very different ways. Whereas the United Kingdom had a highly developed and mature commercial television market, Germany's commercial television market was in its infancy, and in much of Scandinavia it was nonexistent. Many other European countries had deregulated their television markets in the recent past. There was much to gain from shared experience.

These changes to the European media landscape not only had an impact on media planning and research; they also had profound implications for advertising research. Until now, this also had been dominated in the main by the United States and the United Kingdom—that is to say, the mature commercial television markets. In this area, too, there were many benefits to derive from shared experience.

From the outset, *asi* believed that it would seek to provide in its programs a means by which advertising, marketing, and media practitioners could gain a clearer understanding of the contribution made by research. Equally, the programs would seek to provide the research community with a better understanding of the business needs of their clients. It was felt that "pure" research conferences, where researchers talked with other researchers, clearly had a great value. However, *asi* attempts a style of program that brings the business practitioners and the research community together. This should not mean that the research issues are simplified, although more sophisticated technical questions would appear as a technical appendix to an *asi* paper rather than in the paper itself.

The company operates in six main areas:

1. It organizes a number of international advertising and media conferences over 2-3 days: the European Television Symposium, the European Print Media Symposium, and the European Advertising Effectiveness Symposium.
2. It also organizes 1-day seminars in specific subject areas: audience targeting, advertising and marketing in Europe, satellite and cable broadcasting, sponsorship, TV buying and selling, integrated marketing communications, and the regulation of advertising, marketing and media in Europe.
3. It organizes cooperative conferences. Because of the company's experience and knowledge of these areas it was chosen in 1993 by the European Commission to

organize a series of seminars. These highlighted major issues and offered the opportunity for industry to consult with the commission ahead of the Green Paper on Commercial Communications in the Internal Market.

4. It also mounts in-house training programs across the fields of media and marketing. These range from 1 day to 2 weeks, with from 6 to 30 participants. The courses are modular and are adapted to meet particular needs.

5. It arranges conferences for third parties. This service can be purely administrative, although the company will provide detailed consultancy on all aspects of the event if required.

6. It also participates in publishing.

The founding company directors have a wide range of experience in different advertising and media disciplines.

Mike Sainsbury, chief executive, has a publishing background, most recently as publisher of *Media International* and *Admap* (with considerable experience of conference management). Previously, he was for several years publisher of *MediaWorld* and was a founder director of the on-line media planning service MediaTel. He is a graduate in English and American Literature and lives in Tavistock, United Kingdom, with his wife and three daughters.

Peter Todd, nonexecutive chairman, was previously director general of the Market Research Society, chief executive of the Poster Audit Bureau, and assistant managing director and media director of the advertising agency Davidson Pearce (now merged into BMP-DDB Needham). He has held a number of British advertising industry appointments—as chairman of the Technical Committee of the Joint Industry Committee for National Readership Surveys (JICNARS) and as a founding board member of JICCAR (Joint Industry Committee for Cable Audience Research). He has served also on the Council of the Institute of Practitioners in Advertising (IPA) and is a past chairman of the Media Circle.

Advertising Seminars International
111 Whitchurch Road
Tavistock PL19 9BQ
United Kingdom
Telephone: +44 (0)1822-618-628   Fax: +44 (0)1822-618-629
E-mail: asi@dial.pipex.com

The American Academy of Advertising (AAA)

Robert L. King

The American Academy of Advertising (AAA) is the nation's premier professional association of university-level advertising academicians. Its nearly 700 members are located throughout the United States, Canada, and more than 20 other countries. The academy's objectives are as follows:

- To provide an organization through which all persons interested in advertising education may coordinate their efforts to advance academic and professional advertising
- To assume leadership, especially in academic circles, for an objective and realistic appraisal of the functions and responsibilities of advertising in modern society
- To strive for increased recognition by both educators and industry professionals of the value of and need for professional education programs for advertising
- To stimulate research in advertising, especially research about professional educational programs for advertising

- To develop closer liaison with academic disciplines with which advertising is concerned, not only in primary fields such as business administration, communications, journalism, and public relations but also in the behavioral sciences, humanities, and other liberal arts areas
- To encourage closer cooperation among teachers of advertising for the development and better use of teaching materials and methods, for the expansion of recruiting programs, and for sponsorship of scholarships and internships, to attract and develop talent for the field of advertising
- To develop closer liaison with the many organizations associated with the advertising industry

The academy serves members' professional needs through its annual conference and its publications program, which includes the quarterly *Journal of Advertising,* the *AAA Newsletter,* annual conference proceedings, and a membership directory.

In addition, the academy supports scholarly research among its members by awarding several competitive faculty and doctoral dissertation research grants annually. Also, the academy makes *Outstanding Contribution to Research* awards in recognition of individuals who have made sustained and systematic contributions to advertising research. More recently, the academy has established *Teaching Excellence* and *Advertising Education* awards.

The academy encourages further professional development among its members by awarding a number of advertising industry-sponsored fellowships that assist advertising academicians in attending leading practitioner-oriented programs throughout the United States. The academy also offers its members limited placement service support.

The academy has a strong committee structure that provides a significant segment of its membership with opportunities for service. These committees include the following: Executive Committee, Awards Committee, Finance Committee, Industry Relations Committee, International Advertising Education Committee, Membership Committee, Nominating/Academy Fellows Committee, Publications Committee, Program Committee, and Research Committee.

Since its founding in 1958, the American Academy of Advertising has continued to grow in numbers and in the scope and strength of its programs in support of advertising education.

Dr. Robert L. King, Executive Secretary
The E. Claiborne Robins School of Business
University of Richmond
Richmond, VA 23173
Telephone: (804) 289-8902   Fax: (804) 289-8878
E-mail: rking@richmond.edu
Website: http://Advertising.UTexas.Edu/AAA
Journal of Advertising Website: http://www.sjmc.umn.edu/joa

The American Advertising Federation (AAF) and the Advertising Hall of Fame

The American Advertising Federation (AAF)

The American Advertising Federation is the only national association encompassing and uniting all facets of the advertising industry. Headquartered in Washington, D.C., the AAF serves 50,000 members nationwide in 207 local professional advertising federations, 115 corporations, and 248 college chapters.

Individual AAF members range from CEOs to middle managers to students and hail from advertising agencies, client companies, media organizations, online publishers, suppliers, and top universities. As a unified voice, these members cooperatively promote, protect, and shape the future of the advertising business through several objectives:

Government Relations. The AAF strives to educate legislatures and regulators on the economic and social value of advertising and self-regulation. This objective is met through lobbying on Capitol Hill, organizing grassroots campaigns, testifying at local hearings, and other communication vehicles. The AAF regularly sponsors legislative training sessions for its members.

Professional Development. The AAF holds three major conferences each year: the fall Leadership in Marketing and Communications Conference, the March Government Affairs Conference, and the June American Advertising Conference. These events feature workshops and sessions with top industry and government speakers. In addition they provide idea-sharing forums and networking opportunities. This work is also carried out via local professional advertising clubs. ·

Recognition of Excellence. The AAF recognizes the outstanding contributions of advertising and its practitioners through several award programs:

- *The Advertising Hall of Fame* (described at the end of this article) honors the lifetime accomplishments of advertising's great leaders.
- *The Advertising Hall of Achievement* recognizes trailblazers under age 40 currently making an impact in the business.
- *The National Club Achievement Competition* highlights outstanding club performance in a variety of categories.
- *The National Student Advertising Competition* each year challenges students in AAF college chapters to devise effective advertising and marketing campaigns for a corporate sponsor.
- *The National ADDY (not an acronym) Awards* is a three-tiered competition celebrating the most creative and innovative advertising in local, regional, and national markets. It is a mosaic of American advertising and the largest of all creative competitions.

Community Service and Social Responsibility. The AAF uses the power of advertising to enhance the public good by generating and implementing public service campaigns nationwide and by encouraging advertising self-regulation programs in local markets. Members also work to increase minority involvement in the advertising industry through internships, scholarships, workshops, and resource publications.

Industry Promotion. The AAF promotes and defends the role of advertising by serving as an authoritative source for the press on issues related to advertising and marketing. In 1998, the AAF also launched a multiyear campaign titled "Advertising: A New Brand of Business" to show top corporate management the importance of advertising at a time of fundamental changes in the business environment. This integrated campaign employs research, advertising, direct marketing, and public relations. In addition, the AAF works with national speakers bureaus to place top advertising executives in speaking roles that promote their professional reputation, their company, and the discipline of advertising.

Membership Benefits. The AAF makes available to its members an array of benefits, including discounts on magazine subscriptions, hotel rates, rental cars, credit cards, phone services, and more. The AAF also provides a wealth of publications to its members, including the following:

- *American Advertising:* A quarterly, four-color magazine featuring stories on business and creative trends in the industry, advertising-related policy and legislation, professional development programs, AAF activities, and more
- *Government Report:* A newsletter focusing on legal and legislative activity affecting the ad business
- *Newsline:* A camera-ready artwork of AAF news provided to newsletter editors of local clubs for use in local publications
- *The Communicator:* A bimonthly newsletter published between September and May for college chapter members providing professional development guidelines, AAF news, and more
- *The Advisor:* A bimonthly newsletter published between September and May for academic advisers to AAF college chapters

The AAF also publishes a multitude of resource guides covering topics ranging from diversity programs to club management to fund-raising.

The AAF is composed of an eclectic, informed, involved, and committed web of advertising decision makers who create, produce, buy, sell, place, broadcast, and publish the advertising that powers the American economy. It is a unifying voice for the advertising industry.

American Advertising Federation
1101 Vermont Avenue NW, Suite 500
Washington, DC 20005-6306
Telephone: (203) 898-0089   Fax: (203) 898-0159
Website: http://www.aaf.org

American Advertising Federation Hall of Fame

The Advertising Hall of Fame began in 1948 as a result of a proposal by the New York Ad Club and its president, Andrew Haire, to the Advertising Federation of America, the predecessor organization to the American Advertising Federation. Since then, 146 men and women have been elected to this illustrious group. The Council of Judges and its executive committee are appointed each year by the president of the American Advertising Federation and chairman of the Advertising Hall of Fame. These distinguished industry executives are chosen from the ranks of advertisers, agencies, media organizations, and academic institutions in the United States.

> Nominees to the Advertising Hall of Fame are judged on the following criteria: Those men and women who have completed their primary careers, who have distinguished themselves in those careers, who have contributed to the betterment of advertising and its reputation and who have significant volunteer efforts outside the workplace.

Upon induction into the Advertising Hall of Fame, each honoree receives a "Golden Ladder" trophy signifying membership in the Advertising Hall of Fame. This trophy, designed by the late Bill Bernbach, carries an inscription created by the late Tom Dillon, both of whom are members of the Hall of Fame.

The inscription reads: "If we can see further, it is because we stand on the rungs of a ladder built by those who came before us."

Members of the AAF Advertising Hall of Fame

1949
Rollin C. Ayres
Cyrus H. K. Curtis
Alfred W. Erickson
William H. Johns
Lewis B. Jones
Theodore F. MacManus
Edwin T. Meredith
John Irving Romer
Walter A. Strong
John Wanamaker

1950
F. Wayland Ayer
Stanley Clague
Benjamin Franklin
James H. MacGraw
Merle Sidener

1951
William Cheever D'Arcy
E. St. Elmo Lewis

1952
Erma Perham Proetz
J. Earle Pearson

1953
Samuel C. Dobbs
Charles Coolidge Parlin
James O'Shaughnessy

1954
Frank Presbrey
John E. Powers

1955
Henry T. Ewald
George Burton Hotchkiss

1956
None elected

1957
Herbert S. Houston
Claude Clarence Hopkins

1958
Orlando Clinton Harn
Albert D. Lasker

1959
Merlin Hall Aylesworth
Kerwin Holmes Fulton

1960
Allen Loren Billingsly
James Randolph Adams

1961
Barney Link
Harley Procter

1962
Mac Martin
Donald W. Davis

1963
Gilbert T. Hodges
Paul B. West

1964
Homer J. Buckley
Edgar Kobak
Jesse H. Neal

1965
Robert M. Feemster
Samuel C. Gale
Harrison King McCann

1966
Lee Hastings Bristol
Walter Dill Scott

1967

Ernest Elmo Calkins
Stanley B. Resor
Helen Lansdowne Resor (Mrs. Stanley B. Resor)
George P. Rowell

1968

Russell T. Gray
Charles W. Mears
Alex R. Osborn

1969

Bruce Barton
Thomas D'Arcy Brophy

1970

Don Belding
Laurence W. Lane
Graham C. Patterson

1971

None elected

1972

Leo Burnett
Ralph Starr Butler
Philip Livingstone Thomson

1973

John P. Cunningham
Bernard C. Duffy

1974

James Webb Young
Raymond Rubicam

1975

Fairfax M. Cone
G. D. Crain, Jr.
Artemas Ward

1976

William Bernbach
Victor Elting, Jr.
David Ogilvy

1977
John Caples
George Gallup

1978
John H. Crichton
Barton A. Cummings
William A. Marsteller
J. Walter Thompson

1979
Atherton Wells Hobler
Neil Hosler McElroy

1980
Tom Dillon
Roy Larsen
Shirley Polykoff

1981
Ted Bates
Charlie Brower
Bernice Fitz-Gibbon

1982
Paul Foley
Alfred Seaman

1983
Clarence Eldridge
John Elliott, Jr.
Howard J. Morgens
Owen Burtch Winters

1984
Thomas B. Adams
James S. Fish
Charles H. Sandage

1985
Donald A. Macdonald
Samuel W. Meek
Arthur Harrison Motley

1986
Carl W. Nichols
Arthur C. Nielsen, Sr.
Raymond J. Petersen
Robert W. Woodruff

1987
Eugene H. Kummel
Edward N. Ney
Vance L. Stickell

1988
Sidney R. Bernstein
Robert V. Goldstein
Ray A. Kroc

1989
James E. Burke
Raymond O. Mithun
Jean Wade Rindlaub

1990
Carl J. Ally
Sam R. Bloom
Philip H. Dougherty

1991
Neil H. Borden
Richard C. Christian
Theodore S. Repplier

1992
John S. Bowen

1993
Ralph Carson
Charles T. Coiner
Rosser Reeves

1994
Ira C. Herbert
John E. O'Toole
Michael J. Roarty

1995
Edwin L. Artzt
William M. Backer
Howard H. Bell
Thomas S. Murphy

1996
Jo Foxworth
Morris L. Hite
William E. LaMothe
Frank L. Mingo

1997
Gertrude Crain
Alex Kroll
Paul Schrage

1998
Jay Chiat
O. Milton Gossett
Joyce C. Hall
Marion Harper, Jr.
John E. Kennedy
Burt Manning
Leonard Matthews
Frank Stanton
Janet L. Wolff
Lester Wunderman

The American Association of Advertising Agencies (AAAA)

The American Association of Advertising Agencies (known as the AAAA, or Four As), is the national trade association representing the advertising agency business. It has about 530 member agencies, with 1,200 offices nationwide representing approximately 75% of all national advertising and a high proportion of all regional and local advertising placed by agencies. The Four As is important regionally as well as nationally and represents small agencies as well as large ones. The organization was founded in 1917. The Four As was set up to further the interests of advertising agencies and to maintain high professional standards.

Before an agency joins, it has to satisfy the AAAA about its professional ability, financial integrity, and business ethics. The organization is financed by dues paid by members.

The AAAA is an important source of information for its members, providing customized secondary research, which goes out as hard copy or via an online computer link. It provides management counsel and runs professional development programs and many other services. It acts as a representative of the advertising agency business in various forums, providing an extensive public relations service and regular contact with federal, state and local government and regulatory agencies. It holds several national conferences and publishes scores of booklets.

The Four As is supervised by a Board of Directors and more than 30 regional and council Boards of Governors.

There are 45-plus committees, the members of whom are employees of AAAA agencies. The strength of the organization is seen as stemming from its membership. A chairman is elected every year from the industry, and the full-time president is always an executive with significant experience in the advertising field.

The AAAA works with many other advertising-related bodies: the Partnership for a Drug-Free America, the Advertising Council, the State Advertising Coalition, the National Advertising Division/National Advertising Review Board, the Association of National Advertisers, the American Advertising Federation, the Advertising Educational Foundation, and the Advertising Research Foundation. (These are all described in this volume.)

The Four As publishes a quarterly journal, *Agency,* which contains many well-informed articles on advertising practice and on issues affecting the advertising industry. The journal goes to members of the Four As and also to many outside subscribers.

American Association of Advertising Agencies
405 Lexington Avenue
New York, NY 10174-1801
Telephone: (212) 682-2500   Fax: (212) 682-8391
Website: http://www.aaaa.org

It also has offices in Washington, DC; San Francisco, California; and Charlotte, North Carolina.

The American Marketing Association (AMA)

The American Marketing Association is the world's largest and most comprehensive professional society of marketers, consisting of more than 45,000 worldwide members in 92 countries, and 500 chapters throughout North America.

The AMA is the only organization that provides direct benefits to marketing professionals in both business and education and serves all levels of marketing practitioners, educators, and students.

Founded in 1937 as a professional nonprofit organization for marketers, the AMA's purpose is to (a) promote education, (b) assist in personal and professional career development among marketing professionals, and (c) advance the science and ethical practice of marketing disciplines.

Professional Development

Through its 500 professional and collegiate chapters, the AMA serves its members by enhancing their professional career development. AMA chapters sponsor meetings, workshops, and seminars that allow members to interface with the leading innovators and thinkers in business, research, and academia. Chapter meetings provide a forum to expand personal and professional contacts by networking with area marketing professionals from the full range of industries.

Continuing Education

Through seminars, workshops, and more than 25 national conferences held in locations across the country, the AMA continually upgrades the knowledge and skills of its members. Program topics include customer satisfaction measurement, microcomputers, research, promotion, business-to-business marketing, and more.

Magazines and Journals

The AMA Publishing Group produces eight business magazines and scholarly journals designed to enhance members' professional development and keep them in tune with the latest research and trends in various fields and industries.

- *Marketing News* is a biweekly magazine featuring new ideas and developments in marketing.
- The AMA's quarterly business magazines keep members abreast of the latest research and theory regardless of their field:
    Marketing Management
    Marketing Research
    Marketing Health Services
- The AMA's four leading-edge journals provide professionals with scholarly ideas:
    Journal of Marketing

Journal of Marketing Research
Journal of International Marketing
Journal of Public Policy & Marketing

- *AMA International Member and Marketing Services Guide* is a comprehensive guide of marketing services and AMA members.

Marketing Books

The AMA publishes some of the most important titles in marketing so members can make learning an ongoing process. AMA books address leading-edge topics in both the practical and theoretical areas of marketing, such as the following:

- *Marketing Strategies for Growth in Uncertain Times*
- *AMA Complete Guide to Strategic Planning for Small Business*
- *AMA Dictionary of Marketing Terms*

Special Interest Groups

The AMA sponsors a variety of special interest groups that address career development needs in specialized areas for marketing management, marketing research, and marketing educators.

Programs, publications, and seminars target the needs of specific industries: agribusiness marketing research, health care marketing, business marketing, consumer marketing, global marketing, marketing education, marketing research, and services marketing.

Information Center

The AMA provides a reference center with more than 5,000 books, 3,000 indexed articles, and 100 periodicals on marketing issues. Personalized services include bibliographic searches and a Software Review Center with a demonstration disc library of more than 210 titles.

International Marketing Awards/Scholarships

The AMA honors marketing professionals in business and education by recognizing contributions to the advancement of marketing.

- *Edison:* Best new products of the year
- *Charles Coolidge Parlin Award:* To honor persons who have made outstanding contributions to the field of marketing research
- *Philip Kotler Award:* For significant contribution to the field of marketing
- *Compass:* To honor the best in services innovation
- *Spire:* For superior sales promotion and achievement
- *William O'Dell and Paul E. Green awards:* For outstanding articles in the *Journal of Marketing Research*
- *Marketing Science Institute/H. Paul Root Award:* For outstanding article in the *Journal of Marketing*
- *Harold H. Maynard Award:* For best article on marketing theory in the *Journal of Marketing*
- *George Hay Brown Marketing Scholar of the Year:* To honor graduating master's degree students
- *AMA/Irwin Distinguished Marketing Educator Award:* For marketing professors

The New York Chapter of the AMA (telephone: 212-687-3280) sponsors a very important series of advertising awards. These are the EFFIEs, awarded annually. (EFFIE is not an acronym.) The trophies are given to agencies and clients responsible for advertising campaigns of proven marketplace effectiveness.

American Marketing Association
311 S. Wacker Dr., Suite 5800
Chicago, IL 60606
Telephone: 1-800-AMA-1150; (312) 542-9000
Fax: (312) 542-9001
Website: http://www.ama.org

Arcature (formerly the Coalition for Brand Equity)

Arcature is a consulting organization that advises companies on how to create, build, and manage brands for enduring profitable growth.

As the developer and chief proponent of brand loyalty management (BLM), Arcature is consultant to a wide variety of marketers worldwide. The principles of BLM have been used by marketers in packaged goods, high technology, durables, services, corporate, business-to-business, and nonprofit marketing. Arcature's principles have been applied to established brands and new brands, across developed and emerging marketplaces. Arcature has created both a thought process and an operating system to guide clients in the implementation of the principles of BLM.

More and more companies are recognizing that creating and reinforcing brand loyalty is the basis for enduring profitable growth. The objective of business is enduring profitable growth. Profit without revenue growth is false prosperity. You cannot engineer profitable growth by concentrating on cost management. Revenue growth without profit is profitless prosperity. You cannot grow share at any cost and expect to be profitable. True prosperity is based on the simultaneous growth in revenues and profit.

However, instead of being brand builders, many marketers are committing brand suicide. Instead of strengthening brand loyalty, they are exploiting their brand-loyal customers to fund marketing activities against the least loyal. Marketers need to evolve from product management to brand management to BLM.

Product management focuses on selling what businesses know how to make. They try to sell their products to the widest number of people possible. Their measure of brand strength is category share. Their business drivers are availability and market penetration. Make the product available to as many category users as possible, then maximize brand penetration, measured by the number of buyers who buy at least once.

Brand management focuses on selling what the market wants to buy. There is recognition of the importance of market segmentation; there are many different wants within a product category. Understanding segments of customers sharing common wants is the fundamental driver. Having identified a specific market, the goal is to position the brand as the superior alternative for satisfying the specific market requirements. The measure of success is brand share within a market segment.

Brand loyalty management is the next evolution. The focus shifts from a transaction mind-set to a relationship mind-set. Here the marketer's goal is not merely quantity of sales but also quality of sales. It is not enough to build a big brand; the aim is to build a strong brand. Strong brands do not just happen. We must make them happen. Building strong brands is a never-ending commitment to creating, nurturing, defending, and strengthening brand loyalty.

True market segmentation is three-dimensional. The dimensions are Who × Why × Context. What people buy (the competitive set) is a function of who buys (customer), why they buy (the motivations), and the context of use (how, when, and where). The market focus is the intersection of these three dimensions (Who × Why × Context). See Figure 1.

Brand Promise

A brand is a distinctive identity that differentiates a promise and indicates the source of the promise. How do we define the promise of a brand? We use the brand pyramid. The brand pyramid defines the relevant and differentiating

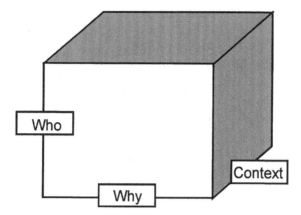

Figure 1. The Dimensions of Market Segmentation

promise of the brand. The brand pyramid consists of features, functional benefits, emotional rewards, customer values, and brand personality. See Figure 2.

Brand Power

The goal is not merely to make a promise but to be the most powerful source of
the promise. A powerful brand is a familiar identity that stands for a special

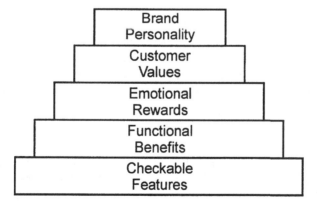

Figure 2. Brand Pyramid

Familiarity

Specialness
* Relevance
* Differentiation

Authority
* Quality
* Leadership
* Trustworthiness

Figure 3. Brand Power

promise from an authoritative source. Brand power correlates with brand value. People will pay more for powerful brands. See Figure 3.

Brand Loyalty

Brand loyalty is not the same as repeat behavior. Not all users are equally loyal. Not all heavy users are equally loyal. True brand loyalty is repeat behavior based on a genuine commitment to the brand. Users live on a brand loyalty ladder. This ladder consists of four rungs: category buyers (all brands are really the same), short-list buyers (have a small list of favored brands), preference buyers (have a favorite brand), enthusiasts (will continue to buy their favorite, even when their second choice costs less). See Figure 4.

As users move up the brand loyalty ladder, their profitability increases. An enthusiast is, on the average, 8 or 10 times more profitable than a category buyer.

Arcature has developed specific disciplines designed to implement the concepts of *market cube, brand promise, brand power,* and *brand loyalty,* as well as specific quantitative methodologies to monitor progress at each phase along the BLM chain. See Figure 5.

Arcature has also developed a five-step process to help guide the implementation of brand loyalty management. This is called the BLM operating system.

Arcature also consults on branding policy issues, such as these: What are the advantages and disadvantages of different approaches to brand architec-

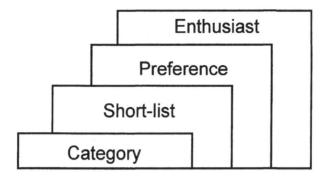

Figure 4. Brand Loyalty Ladder

ture? Which is right for a particular business situation? How do you measure brand equity, brand value, brand power, and brand loyalty? How do you organize for effective global brand management? How do you institutionalize BLM in an organization?

Arcature conducts presentations and seminars on the concepts underlying BLM and in the associated operating system. Arcature develops customized internal educational programs, including branding "universities" and the cre-

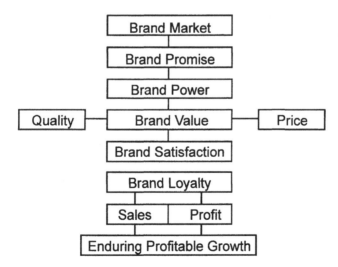

Figure 5. Brand Loyalty Management Chain

ation of customized branding handbooks and other internal learning documents. Arcature also consults on the implementation of BLM concepts.

Arcature LLC
3 Stamford Landing, Suite 300
46 Southfield Avenue
Stamford, CT 06902
Telephone: (203) 967-4900   Fax: (203) 967-3977
E-mail: ARCATURE1@aol.com

The Association of
National Advertisers (ANA)

F or nearly 90 years, two things have characterized the Association of National Advertisers' (ANA) leadership position among industry groups: (a)
its responsiveness to the interests of national and regional marketers/advertis-
ers and (b) its exclusive focus on those interests. No other association is distinguished by both these qualifications, and it has attracted a membership that includes many of the largest and most prominent marketers of goods and services
in the nation.

Today, the ANA is the premier marketing association dedicated to helping
its diverse membership build their businesses by building their brands. In the
pursuit of that mission, the ANA provides industry leadership, cutting-edge information, networking opportunities, professional training, and tools to aid
marketers in developing effective strategies and tactics to adapt to rapidly
changing marketplace dynamics.

In particular, the ANA focuses on developing best practices guidance drawn
from its unique membership base and establishing key industry benchmarks in

areas as diverse as agency compensation, Website management, and corporate and global advertising. In addition, the association is taking a leadership role in keeping its membership current on the Internet and its use and impact on marketing.

Through its Washington office, the ANA works to protect members' rights to commercial free speech; tracks key legislative and regulatory initiatives before federal, state, and local governments and regulatory agencies; and provides proactive leadership on many issues.

In sum, the ANA's needs-driven agenda is designed to help marketers on many fronts and to provide them with an effective voice with various publics.

The ANA Membership

The strength behind this enduring advertising organization is the ANA membership itself: the companies, large and small, that understand the need for shared information, collective representation, and a united front in the battle against efforts that would erode the value of advertising. Today, the association represents 260 major companies with 7,500 brands that collectively spend over $100 billion in marketing communications and advertising. Many of these major companies join the ANA to gain more direct access to programs and services.

How the ANA Works

Although only companies can be members of the ANA, individual marketing and advertising professionals participate in the association's activities and contribute expertise that benefits the membership as a whole. Employees of a member company are eligible to share in the programs and services of the association, and in fact, thousands of advertising and marketing executives annually take advantage of these opportunities. With support of the membership, the Board of Directors, working with the ANA staff, sets policy and direction for the association; the president, functioning as a chief executive officer, is responsible for executing it. Driven by the needs of its members, the association through its staff develops professional programs and publications, addresses industry issues, lobbies on advertisers' behalf, and represents their interests wherever the need arises.

The association also has organized 18 standing committees, made up of professionals from member companies. Through the efforts of ANA Marketing and Media Committees, valuable marketing information is collected and disseminated, solutions to industry problems are deliberated, and trends in media and research are tracked.

The association was formed in 1910, when a group of advertising executives from 45 companies met in Detroit to address common concerns and the state of their industry.

Association of National Advertisers
708 Third Avenue
New York, NY 10017-4270
Telephone: (212) 697-5950   Fax: (212) 661-8057
Website: http://www.ana.net

Washington, DC, office address
700 11th Street NW, Suite 650
Washington, DC 20001-4507
Telephone: (202) 626-7800   Fax: (202) 626-6161

The Audit Bureau of Circulations (ABC)

The Audit Bureau of Circulations (ABC) is an independent organization set up by the advertising industry to verify the circulation (i.e., sales) of American and Canadian newspapers and magazines. The information provided is very important because it forms the basis of all advertising rates, which represent the main economic foundation for print publications.

The ABC was set up in 1914 to provide honest standards in the vigorous and heated competition between newspaper and newspaper and magazine and magazine. Other countries have set up circulation auditing mechanisms, but the ABC is the oldest and largest such organization in the world.

The ABC has approximately 4,200 members, comprising 2,500 newspapers and magazines of all types, plus many advertisers and advertising agencies. The organization, which is supervised by a board of directors of 34 industry figures, has a permanent staff of 250 people—executives and administrators at the headquarters and a field force of 120 auditors who make their investigations in publishers' offices.

The ABC data bank provides circulation information in printed and electronic formats. Circulation figures are available as totals, broken down into geographic territories. Newspaper demographic data collected by third-party research organizations can be audited by the ABC. The main demographic data for newspapers and magazines are provided by readership surveys conducted by organizations such as Simmons Market Research Bureau, Inc. and Mediamark Research, Inc. Readership figures (i.e., numbers of readers) are invariably higher than circulation figures (i.e., numbers of copies sold). By dividing the circulation of any publication into its readership, the resultant ratio gives an estimate of the average number of readers per copy.

Audit Bureau of Circulations
900 North Meacham Road
Schaumburg, IL 60173-4968
Telephone: (847) 605-0909   Fax: (847) 605-0483
Website: http://www.accessabc.com

British Design and Art Direction (D&AD)

British Design & Art Direction (D&AD) is a professional association and an educational charity working on behalf of the design and advertising communities. Its purpose is to set creative standards, educate and inspire the next creative generation, and promote the importance of good design and advertising in the business arena.

Awards

D&AD Awards, familiarly known as the Yellow Pencils, are the largest, most internationally respected awards in the industry and have been running for close to four decades. There are now over 17,000 entries received from around the world each year. These are judged by 250 senior practitioners in the business.

Silver and gold pencils are presented each year at London's biggest creative awards night. The winning entries are then featured, with a wider body of the year's best work, in the D&AD annual showreel, CD-ROM, and DVD. Highlights from the awards are exhibited in the D&AD Touring Show that travels the world from Europe to North and South America, Australia, and the Far East.

Education

At the same time, D&AD places a high priority on education. The association invests over £1.3 million each year on running a range of innovative programs that seek to identify talented graduates, support colleges, and develop and train young creatives.

The education program has three aims. The first—to identify and promote graduates with significant talent—is, in large part, fulfilled by the student awards scheme and the Student Annual. The second aim is to support the colleges and courses involved in producing young creatives. This support is channeled through D&AD's college membership scheme, the college twinning scheme, Expo, and D&AD's program for course leaders and tutors. The third aim is to provide development opportunities for young creative professionals. Highlights include advertising and design workshops and the developing range of publications, seminars, and other events.

Events

Each year, D&AD's president invites great creative talents from around the world to share their experiences and insights. Attended by audiences of over 6,000 a year, the aim of the lectures is to inspire discussion and debate. In the last few years, speakers have included Saul Bass, Javier Mariscal, Maurice Saatchi, Sir Richard Rogers, Duane Michals, Elliott Erwitt, Malcolm Mc-Laren, Dave Stewart, Martin Sorrell, Jean-Paul Goude, David Bailey, Alan Fletcher, Jeanloup Sieff, Jeremy Sinclair, Michael Nyman, Joe Sedelmaier, Janet Street-Porter, Paul Smith, Michael Palin, Terry Gilliam, Julien Temple, Bob Gill, Rankin, Daniel Kleinman, and Jonathan Ive.

Touring Show

D&AD's Touring Show is a celebration of the best of British and international advertising. Each year, all the work that has either won or been nominated for a D&AD "Pencil" is displayed and explained in the content of current creative trends.

Publications

D&AD publishes a range of high-quality, industry-related titles in association with Laurence King Publishing and Rotovision SA. These include the following:

- The Annual
- The showreel
- The CD-ROM
- The Student Annual
- The Product Book (launch date November 1999)
- The Commercials Book
- The Art Direction Book
- The Copy Book

Membership

D&AD is run for and by its members who currently include more than 1,500 leading professionals as well as students and associates.

Full membership is an accolade reserved for those creatives whose work has appeared in the D&AD Annual. Only full members who are part of the association's constitution can vote for, or be elected as, members of the executive board. There are two other categories of membership.

Associate membership is open to those not working in a creative design or advertising function but who are recognized as encouraging and supporting D&AD's aims and ideals. International membership is open to individuals overseas who wish to keep up with the latest and best in British design and advertising.

British Design and Art Direction
9 Graphite Square
Vauxhall Walk
London SE11 5EE
United Kingdom
Telephone: +44 (0)20 7840-1111   Fax: +44 (0)20 7840-0840
Website: http://www.dandad.org

The Children's Advertising Review Unit (CARU)

Elizabeth Lascoutx

The Children's Advertising Review Unit (CARU) of the Council of Better Business Bureaus, was established in 1974 by the advertising industry to promote responsible advertising to children and to respond to public concerns. A nonprofit organization dedicated to the public interest, CARU is supported by businesses concerned with advertising to children and is the self-regulatory mechanism for evaluating children's advertising. In the early 1970s, in response to the then newly burgeoning medium of children's television, there was a great deal of discussion about whether it was appropriate for advertisers to target children at all and, if so, what sorts of messages ought to be permitted. The National Association of Broadcasters (NAB) had until then held strict sway over the kinds of advertising permitted to children, but with deregulation and the abolition of the NAB Code Authority, CARU's guidelines became the sole unified set of standards for children's advertising nationally.

CARU's Self-Regulatory Guidelines for Children's Advertising delineate those areas that need particular attention to help advertisers develop advertising to children that is truthful, accurate, and sensitive to the special nature of its audience. These guidelines, which apply to all advertising directed to children under 12 years of age, are revised periodically to reflect new insights gained from experience and research and to respond to changing market conditions. They are reviewed at least annually by CARU's Academic and Business Advisory Boards, comprising respected experts in psychology, education, communications, and media, and leaders from all aspects of the children's advertising industry. In 1996, CARU published its fifth edition to include a new section addressing the Internet. The latest revisions, in 1999, deal expressly with data collection and privacy on the Internet.

CARU's guidelines naturally deal with issues such as clear depiction of method of operation (e.g., of toys), the need for disclosure of items sold separately or assembly requirements, and the need to portray children and adults only in safe situations and using proper safety gear. But they go further and treat subjective matters such as peer pressure, appropriate pro-social behavior, and stereotyping. For instance, one guideline provides that advertisers should not imply that having or not having a specific product will make a child more or less accepted by his or her peers.

The unit's main function is the review and evaluation of child-directed advertising in all media. This is done by routinely monitoring children's magazines and comic books, commercial messages on various on-line services, data collection practices on the Internet, and children's programming on network, independent, and cable television (an average of 1,600 commercials each month). CARU also responds to competitor challenges and consumer complaints, but the majority of its inquiries stem from its own monitoring. When advertising is found to be inaccurate, misleading, or inconsistent with its guidelines, CARU works in voluntary cooperation with the advertiser to discontinue the advertising or modify it to bring it into compliance. In addition to its monitoring function, CARU regularly reviews scripts, storyboards, and Websites provided voluntarily for its review prior to production.

Children's Advertising Review Unit
845 Third Avenue
17th Floor
New York, NY 10022
Telephone: (212) 705-0123   Fax: (212) 308-4743
E-mail: elascoutx@caru.bbb.org
Website: http://www.caru.org

Competitive Media Reporting (CMR)

Competitive Media Reporting (CMR) delivers strategic advertising intelligence to advertising agencies, advertisers, broadcasters, and publishers. The company's tracking technologies collect occurrence and expenditure data, as well as the creative executions of over 750,000 brands across 15 media. To hone their competitive edge, clients use CMR data and services to perform competitive analysis, sales prospecting, strategic planning, tactical executions, and proof-of-performance.

CMR tracks more than 100 million advertising occurrences a year. It estimates expenditures and integrates ratings. It also "red-flags" creative introductions. Based on the advertising database covering more than 750,000 brands, CMR offers information in the form of timely, accurate, reliable, consistent, fully integrated intelligence packages designed to meet individual strategic and tactical needs.

Media covered include these categories:

- Network television
- Network cable television
- Spot television
- National syndicated television
- Consumer magazines
- Business magazines
- International magazines
- National newspapers
- Sunday magazines
- Local newspapers
- Network radio
- National spot radio
- Local spot radio
- Outdoor advertising
- Internet advertising

Client databases are delivered with Windows- or browser-based software with enough power to satisfy the needs of the most demanding research department yet friendly enough to put on every salesperson's laptop. Hundreds of report combinations enable clients to do the following:

- Target their best advertisers with reliable data
- Locate advertising trends in newspapers or in competing media—local, regional, or national
- Find out how much accounts and prospects are spending with the competition
- Re-create an advertiser's exact schedule in print and broadcast
- Pitch accounts with schedule recommendations
- Develop new services, products, and programs that capture advertising dollars from competing media

CMR is the preferred supplier of media intelligence nationwide, serving over 3,000 agencies, advertisers, and media companies, including 90% of the top 50 agencies and 95% of the television stations in the top 75 markets. Sophisticated computer systems watch television 20 hours a day and forward their data to CMR's multimedia database over a high-speed digital network.

There are no shortcuts to reliable local print measurement, and CMR remains the only company that accurately collects and measures zoned newspaper editions and preprinted inserts. Most publishers send their zoned editions, preprints, and special sections directly to CMR for measurement. This method is supplemented by a network of over 200 in-market households that serve as collection centers for newspapers, direct mail, and other local print products.

CMR sets the standard for newspaper data processing with an exclusive zone implosion technique that re-creates the measured newspaper from its individual editions and reports ad lineage and expenditure in complete agreement with the rate card. Special sections are uniquely identified and titled to preserve their value. Every ad, regardless of size, is measured every day with a level of accuracy warranted in client agreements.

CMR data collection methodologies are refined through client relationships and years of continuous media measurement. Every data collection center is company owned, enforcing high quality standards. CMR data are sourced by reporters and professional organizations worldwide and are universally accepted as the standard in competitive measurement.

CMR has an office in three cities:

Competitive Media Reporting
11 West 42nd Street
New York, NY 10036
Telephone: (212) 789-1400   Fax: (212) 789-1450

Competitive Media Reporting
5055 Wilshire Blvd., Seventh Floor
Los Angeles, CA 90036
Telephone: 1-800-562-3282; (213) 954-3244
Fax: (213) 954-3235

Competitive Media Reporting
180 N. Michigan Avenue, Suite 1600
Chicago, IL 60601
Telephone: (312) 782-6898   Fax: (312) 782-1807
Website: http://www.cmr.com

The Council for Marketing and Opinion Research (CMOR)

The marketing and opinion research industry operates in an environment that is often hostile to its interests:

- Despite the best efforts of industry associations, abuses of the research process continue by those who use the guise of research to sell products or to raise funds.
- Recent media coverage of the research industry has been more negative than positive, as writers have questioned the validity of research and suggested that the public should refuse to cooperate in marketing or public opinion research.
- The identity of the research industry is vague, and therefore it is of little wonder that the public and their legislators are confused as to the differences between research and telemarketing.

As a result of this hostile environment, two significant threats have arisen in recent years to challenge the research industry: (a) restrictive legislation and

(b) declining respondent cooperation. In each case, the industry has had to move quickly and decisively to protect its ability to conduct reliable and valid research.

Problem 1: Restrictive Legislation

In the past 7 years, the number of bills the research industry has monitored has *at least doubled* every year. In 1998, for example, thousands of bills were proposed that could potentially affect marketing research and public opinion polling. Areas of proposed legislation included the following:

- Auto dialer bills
- Junk phone bills
- Asterisk—or do-not-call bills
- Telephone-monitoring bills
- Caller ID/call-blocking bills
- Time-of-day bills
- Data/personal privacy bills
- Political telemarketing or so-called push-polling bills

In addition, some legislative moves have had a powerful, albeit indirect, effect on the market research industry. In Canada, proposed legislation would have empowered the government to protect privacy interests by regulating unsolicited telephone calls. (Research calls were included in the definition of telemarketing.) The California Supreme Court has interpreted the state's "eavesdropping law" to include extension telephones as "eavesdropping devices." This means that the monitoring of research calls could be subject to criminal eavesdropping penalties if the issue were to be litigated before the courts of that state.

If all the legislation introduced in the last dozen years affecting marketing and opinion research had become law, the environment for research would be bleak:

- In many states, researchers would be required to get *permission* before asking a potential respondent to participate in a telephone survey research call.
- California would restrict media and advertising research.
- New York would require registration for consumer product research.

- Random digit dialing would be prohibited in many states.
- Research data would be transmitted *only* with respondent permission.
- No research calls could be made on Sundays.
- No research calls could be made after 5 (or 7) p.m.
- Audible beeps would be required for monitoring telephone interviews.
- Political polling would be prohibited unless the candidate or party name was revealed.

Problem 2: Declining Respondent Cooperation

Industry studies have documented a steady decline in respondent cooperation. When defined in terms of refusals, phone refusal rates have gone up from 40% in a 1988 "Your Opinion Counts" project, to 46% in a 1997 CMOR "Respondent Cooperation" audit.

The reasons for declining cooperation rates are many:

- Increased telephone contacts of all kinds
- Consumers have less time, are at home less
- Fraudulent/abusive activities by nonresearchers
- Increasing concerns about personal privacy
- Research-related problems
- Increased use of answering machines, caller ID, and call blocking, which may exacerbate refusal problem

The Research Industry's Response

The Council for Marketing and Opinion Research (CMOR) was established in 1992. Its members consist of research companies, research users, and industry associations. Together in the CMOR they strive to further the acceptance of marketing and opinion research by the public and the government. It was imperative that the research industry move quickly and decisively on issues of restrictive legislation and respondent cooperation to ensure that marketing and opinion research would not be restricted or prohibited.

The CMOR Mission

The CMOR was established to protect and increase the value that marketing and opinion research represents to the public and industry. This will be accomplished by (a) influencing legislation and regulations for the protection and enhancement of the marketing and opinion research process, (b) preventing passage of restrictive legislation while working to balance the need for information against the right of individual privacy, and (c) promoting internal research practices to encourage respondent cooperation and self-regulation.

CMOR Objectives

- To establish a unified industry voice
- To monitor and lobby state and federal legislation
- To work proactively with government to protect the research industry from abuses
- To promote internal research practices that will encourage respondent cooperation
- To establish a discrete identity for and enhance the value of research
- To strengthen research alliances
- To support efforts of other industry associations

The CMOR represents 120 corporate members. These include many of the leading advertisers and market research organizations in the United States.

Council for Marketing and Opinion Research, Inc.
170 N. Country Road, Suite 4
Port Jefferson, NY 11777
Telephone: 1-800-887-CMOR; (516) 928-6206
Fax: (516) 928-6041
E-mail: info@cmor.org
Website: http://www.cmor.org

The Council of American Survey Research Organizations (CASRO)

The Council of American Survey Research Organizations (CASRO) is the national trade association of commercial survey research companies located in the United States, representing nearly 180 firms. Its mission is as follows:

- To provide the environment and leadership that will promote the profitable growth and best interests of those firms and other entities engaged in the survey research industry
- To promote the establishment, maintenance, and improvement of the highest possible professional and ethical standards
- To communicate the standards, contributions, achievements, and value of the survey research industry to clients, the public, and other key groups

CASRO's Code of Standards and Ethics for Survey Research are mandatory for all CASRO members. The code sets forth the agreed-upon rules of ethical conduct for survey research organizations. It has been organized into sections describing the responsibilities of a survey research organization to respondents, clients and outside contractors, as well as its responsibilities in reporting survey results.

CASRO works to serve its members, the industry, and the public. For most of its history, it has served as the watchdog for any proposed changes in government regulations or legislation that could affect the research industry. And importantly, it works with other industry associations to coordinate industry-supported initiatives in the areas of government affairs, respondent cooperation, assessing client needs from research, education and training, and professional and industry identity. There are sets of guidelines that address business practices, as well as specific aspects of the survey research process. These include guidelines regarding the following:

- Business practices
- Data collection
- Data processing
- General health and safety
- Forensic research
- Interview design
- Problem definition
- Sample design
- Survey reporting
- Telemarketing

Council of American Survey Research Organizations
3 Upper Devon
Port Jefferson, NY 11777
Telephone: (516) 928-6954   Fax: (516) 928-6041
Website: http://www.casro.org

Cox Direct— Annual Surveys of Promotional Practices

C ox Direct, one of the largest direct-mail companies in the United States, is responsible for an annual survey of promotional practices that has set the industry standard. The surveys have been published continuously for more than two decades; the first year reported was 1976. Cox publishes data from three separate sources.

Packaged Goods Manufacturers

Information is provided on the share of dollars allocated to the three main promotional categories: trade promotions, consumer promotions, and media advertising, as well as a range of special topics—product couponing, product sampling, Internet/World Wide Web marketing, and retail account-specific marketing.

Data are aggregated from companies covering the following product categories: foods, household products, health and beauty care, soft drinks and candy, drugs and remedies. The respondents are split approximately equally between organizations with annual sales of $1 billion or more and less than $1 billion.

Consumers

An annual survey focuses on consumers' use of coupons, samples, Internet/World Wide Web marketing, purchase of store-prepared meals/foods, and the outlets where the consumers purchase grocery and health and beauty care products. Replies to the questionnaire come from female and male respondents, in the approximate proportions of 3:1.

Grocery Retailers

This section of the report details the sources of grocery retailers' promotional dollars and their allocation among major promotional categories. Special topics covered include product sampling, product couponing, store-prepared meals, account-specific marketing, and Internet/World Wide Web marketing.

National, regional, and local stores are aggregated, and a wide range of store sizes is covered.

Cox Direct—National Headquarters
8605 Largo Lakes Drive
Largo, FL 33773
Telephone: 1-800-678-2743; (727) 393-1270
Fax: (727) 399-3061
Website: http://www.coxdirect.com

Cox Direct—Eastern Region
70 Seaview Ave., 5th Floor
Stamford, CT 06902
Telephone: 1-888-261-7784; (203) 328-8940
Fax: (203) 328-8950

Cox Direct—Western Region
The Chancellory
One Pierce Place, Suite 295W
Itasca, IL 60143
Telephone: 1-800-657-7220; (630) 467-0130
Fax: (630) 467-0140

The Direct Marketing
Association (DMA)

The Direct Marketing Association (DMA) is the largest trade association for businesses interested in interactive and database marketing, with nearly 4,500 member companies from the United States and 53 other nations.

Founded in 1917, its members include direct marketers from every business segment as well as the nonprofit and electronic marketing sectors. Included are catalogers, Internet retailers and service providers, financial services providers, book and magazine publishers, book and music clubs, retail stores, industrial manufacturers, and a host of other vertical segments, including the service industries that support them. According to a DMA-commissioned study conducted by The WEFA Group, direct marketing sales in the United States exceeded $1.37 trillion in 1998. Approximately $759 billion in direct marketing purchases were made by consumers, and $612 billion were made by businesses.

The DMA publishes numerous consumer pamphlets that assist in the process of buying directly by mail, telephone, or computer, including the following: *The Great Catalog Guide; Opening the Door to Opportunity: A Simple*

Guide to Understanding How Direct Marketers Use Information; Make Knowledge Your Partner in Mail or Telephone Order Shopping; Sweepstakes Advertising: A Consumer's Guide; and *Shopping by Phone—A One-Stop Guide to Consumer Protection.*

The DMA sponsors three important consumer programs:

- The DMA's Mail Preference Service (MPS), established in 1971, enables people to reduce the volume of advertising mail they receive at home by having their names removed from any national mailing lists, including commercial and nonprofit solicitations.
- The Telephone Preference Service (TPS), launched in 1985, offers consumers the same kind of name removal program for national telephone solicitation lists.
- The Mail Order Action Line (MOAL), also established in 1971, helps consumers who have unresolved problems with mail order transactions.

The DMA sponsors an extensive ethics program. The DMA Committee on Ethical Business Practice, a peer review committee, measures mailings and offerings against DMA-established ethics guidelines. The DMA Ethics Policy Committee analyzes consumer concerns about current marketing practices as new issues arise. It then translates the responses to these concerns into recommended operational guidelines, which it disseminates through its guidelines booklets: *DMA Guidelines for Ethical Business Practice; DMA Guidelines for Personal Information Protection; DMA Guidelines for Mailing List Practices; DMA Guidelines for Acceptance of Print Mail Order Advertising; DMA Guidelines for Acceptance of Direct Response Broadcast Advertising; DMA Guidelines for Marketing by Telephone;* and *Online Privacy Principles and Guidance.*

The DMA also sponsors a twice-yearly forum for industry leaders to meet with regional regulatory and consumer officials at the DMA's Dialogue series. The meetings are cosponsored by the DMA, the National Association of Consumer Agency Administrators, and the Council of Better Business Bureaus. The DMA works to maintain consumer protection with agencies such as the Federal Trade Commission, the U.S. Postal Inspection Service, the National Association of Consumer Agency Administrators, the National Consumers League, the National Coalition for Consumer Education, the Food and Drug Administration, the National Association of Attorneys General, and the Council of Better Business Bureaus.

Direct Marketing Association
1120 Avenue of the Americas
New York, NY 10036-6700
Telephone: (212) 768-7277   Fax: (212) 302-6714
Website: http://www.the-dma.org

The Direct Marketing Educational Foundation (DMEF)

Laurie J. Spar

Separately incorporated from the Direct Marketing Association (DMA), the Direct Marketing Educational Foundation (DMEF) was established in the mid-1960s with the goal of improving the quality and increasing the scope of direct marketing education at the college and university level. Its ultimate objective is to encourage the teaching of direct and interactive marketing and direct response advertising so that college graduates will be encouraged to choose direct marketing careers and can be well prepared for jobs in related businesses where "direct" is playing an increasing role.

Direct Marketing Collegiate Institutes and Graduate Seminars (intensive seminars in direct marketing taught by leading practitioners for college juniors, seniors, and graduate students) are conducted annually in various parts of the country. A 2-day campaign workshop for seniors is held at direct response agencies. "College Days," semiannual programs at DMA Conferences and Trade Shows and on college campuses, introduce students and professors to the field and facilitate networking with practitioners. A direct response advertising competition (Collegiate ECHO), sponsored by leading corporations, gives student teams the opportunity to work as advertising agencies and create direct or integrated campaigns for leading corporations. Significant prizes are awarded with the purpose of furthering direct marketing education. Student membership in the DMA is now available through the DMEF.

The DMEF serves as a clearinghouse and publishes a directory of summer internships in direct marketing. It also publishes direct marketing career information and, although not a placement service, offers career guidance.

To encourage and help professors teach this method of marketing and advertising, 3-day "Professors' Institutes" are conducted annually on a national and regional basis. Taught by leading practitioners, the program communicates the basics and provides a forum for the exchange of ideas and materials that can be used in teaching.

The annual Direct Marketing Educators' Conference is a 1-day conference held in conjunction with the DMA's Annual Conference and Exhibition. The agenda includes original research papers, abstracts, and other special topic sessions. Proceedings are published in *Frontiers in Direct Marketing Research.* There is no registration fee, and the first 100 registrants are offered complementary DMA registration. Cash prizes are awarded for the two best papers and to the "Outstanding Educator" and other "Distinguished Teachers."

A complete series of direct marketing courses, developed by the DMEF in collaboration with Western Connecticut State University's Ancell School of Business, is now available through the foundation. These courses were developed as a model direct marketing curriculum for other colleges and universities to adopt.

In addition to these services, the DMEF offers DMA and Special Segment Council memberships, discounts on DMA publications, and fellowships to DMA seminars. It also offers teaching materials, including a 15-minute video (*Direct/Interactive Marketing: What's in It for Me?*), cases and sample course outlines, a data set library, resources of the Direct Marketing Association, newsletters to educators, and information about various direct marketing courses. The DMEF publishes the *Journal of Interactive Marketing.*

Presently, with over 15 annual programs, the DMEF can track hundreds of professors who now teach the subject and students who, after attendance at DMEF programs, quickly rise up the direct marketing success ladder. Complete direct marketing courses have grown from 6 in 1975 to at least one course in over 200 colleges and universities, with scores of professors including the subject in related courses.

Direct Marketing Educational Foundation
1120 Avenue of the Americas
New York, NY 10036-6700
Telephone: (212) 768-7277   Fax: (212) 790-1561
Website: http://www.the-dma.org/dmef

The European Association of Advertising Agencies (EAAA)

The mission statement of the European Association of Advertising Agencies (EAAA; sometimes known as the E Three-As), is *to secure an optimal legal and professional working environment for advertising agencies in Europe.* Europe is defined by the Council of Europe—that is, the theoretical maximum number of member states is 44.

The EAAA, which was founded in 1959 in Norway, today consists of the 18 leading ad agencies, national agency associations in 28 countries, and (since 1998) the 14 leading international media specialist agencies in Europe.

The association is a limited Belgian company, predominantly owned by its agency members. The highest governing body is the Annual General Assembly, which elects the president, agrees on the annual objectives and strategies, sets the budgets, and ratifies the members of the Executive Board. These Executive Board members are elected (2, 3, or 4 for each membership group), by the three member categories—that is, the International Agencies Council, the National Associations' Council, and the Media Agencies' Council. These three councils elect their own council chairmen and also set their own council-specific objectives. At the 40th Anniversary Annual General Meeting in 1999, it was decided that the association should be developed further, into new areas of commercial communication. The purpose was to reflect in a better way the membership structure of the majority of the national associations, which are broadening their scope of operation from advertising to most, or all, aspects of commercial communication.

The EAAA's national associations enlist about 3,000 agencies in Europe, and the association covers over 80% of the total advertising volume. The total European advertising business, measured in media value alone (excluding fees and production), amounted to some EURO 60,000,000,000 in 1998.

The EAAA is the sole agency industry representative in Europe that both deals with the European Commission, in the capacity of a hearing body, and acts as a nongovernmental organization (NGO) with a consultative status within the Council of Europe. The EAAA's preferred mode of operation within the advertising industry is to be an active part of the European Advertising Tripartite (EAT), of which the EAAA is a founding member.

To fulfill the demands set out in the mission statement, the EAAA focuses on three main objectives:

1. To promote fair freedom of commercial speech
2. To continuously upgrade the education of present and future advertising agency professionals
3. To secure a social acceptability for advertising

As a prerequisite for promoting fair advertising rights as well as social acceptability, the EAAA is involved as a founding member of the European Advertising Standards Alliance (EASA), in the self-regulation of advertising.

The principle of the EAAA organization is embedded in the slogan "Commitment Through Involvement." Its board, committees, and working groups are made up of, and in most cases also chaired by, member experts. The key board committees are the Education & Training Committee, the Legal & EU Policy Committee, and the New Media Committee. Among the working groups, key roles are played by the CFO (Chief Finance Officers') Group, the TV Production Group, and the Media Research and Print Production Groups. Hosted by the EAT, special task forces involving the EAAA deal with specific challenges, such as children and advertising, car advertising, alcohol advertising, and food advertising. The EAAA also works as a partner to the Council of Europe on research projects—for example, a recent "AdFora" project for European Community/DGXIII, analyzing the roles of advertising in new interactive media.

The association hosts two home pages on the World Wide Web, one for public information purposes and one for members only, replacing old systems with monthly bulletins, or "facts files." Since 1999, the EAAA has issued a quarterly bulletin, *The Ad Business,* distributed widely outside the membership group.

The annual conferences of the EAAA are among the largest of their kind, the most recent ones having been held in Rome in 1996, Dublin in 1997, Budapest in 1998, and Bergen, Norway, in 1999. The 2000 conference is scheduled to take place in South Africa. The EAAA acts as a patron for various advertising events—the Golden Drum creative awards in Portoroz, Slovenia, and the International Advertising Festivals in Helsinki, Finland.

In 1999, the EAAA signed a deal with the world's leading advertising effectiveness award scheme, the EFFIEs. Together with the New York Chapter of the American Marketing Association, the EAAA will, through member associations, host annual Euro-Effie awards, for successful cross-border campaigns in Europe.

European Association of Advertising Agencies
Rue St. Quentin 3
1000 Brussels
Belgium
Telephone: +32 (2) 280-1603   Fax: +32 (2) 230-0966
E-mail: info@eaaa.be
Website: http://www.eaaa.be

The European Society for Opinion and Marketing Research (ESOMAR)

F ounded in 1948, the European Society for Opinion and Marketing Research (ESOMAR) is today the World Association of Opinion and Market Research Professions (WAPOR), uniting 4,000 members in 100 countries, both users and providers of opinion and marketing research.

Members can be found in all industry sectors, from advertising and media agencies to universities and business schools, as well as in public institutions and government authorities.

ESOMAR's mission is to promote the use of opinion and marketing research for improving decision making in business worldwide.

ESOMAR fulfills its mission through the following:

- Conferences held throughout the world
- Professional publications on all aspects of opinion and marketing research

- Training and education, through workshops and distance learning
- Promotion of codes of professional and ethical conduct and guidelines of best practice
- Representation of the research industry to international bodies

Management

ESOMAR is managed by an international council of eight members, including a president and a vice president, who are elected by the members of the society. The council determines strategy and oversees the finances. ESOMAR is a not-for-profit organization, but it applies good business practice to all its operations.

The activities are managed by the director general, appointed by the council, and an international, multilingual team of specialists, located in Amsterdam, dedicated to the society's objectives and aspirations.

Congress and Conferences

ESOMAR events offer an update on the latest developments from experts, and an international networking opportunity to meet people who share the same interests both at business sector and competence level. ESOMAR organizes an annual Congress and Exhibition, attracting over 1,500 professionals from around the world. Due to fast-growing membership from outside Europe, conferences are also organized in Latin America and Asia Pacific, usually on a bi-annual basis. In organizing some events, ESOMAR cooperates with other international organizations that share the same objectives, such as the Advertising Research Foundation (ARF), the World Federation of Advertisers (WFA), and the International Advertising Association (IAA). See the separate articles on these organizations.

Publications

The annual ESOMAR directory contains a concise listing of ESOMAR members by country and by company/organization, plus full details of the research institutes with an ESOMAR member and a description of the services they offer. The directory is also available on ESOMAR's Website.

ESOMAR's congress and conference books contain a wealth of seminar papers. An electronic database provides full-text access to the publications. Other publications include an annual industry report, studies on research prices around the world, and standardized demographic classifications that can be used in international surveys. The ESOMAR monograph series of books features original state-of-the-art papers about specific subjects. ESOMAR also publishes a monthly newsletter, *NewsBrief,* and a quarterly journal, *Marketing and Research Today.*

Education

Education is an important mission for ESOMAR as it is one of the main elements through which it can influence the research industry system. The workshop program covers international/global research and market intelligence themes that ESOMAR is uniquely suited to develop. ESOMAR workshops provide an overview of techniques and are organized in an interactive way to help participants learn how to apply and use the techniques under discussion.

ESOMAR also runs 1-day preconference/congress workshops. These are targeted at junior, first-time participants or clients who require an introduction to the main event through learning about related tools, techniques, and technologies.

In addition, ESOMAR has formed a worldwide education alliance with the Market Research Association Institute, USA (MRAI) and the University of Georgia Center for Continuing Education to provide a distance learning course on the "Principles of Marketing Research." Through 10 study modules, this comprehensive program gives researchers working in marketing research institutes and client companies easy access to a course with the "core body of knowledge" of marketing research.

Codes and Guidelines

One of ESOMAR's most important roles is to encourage the highest levels of professional standards through codes of conduct complemented by guidelines to best practice. Together with the International Chamber of Commerce (ICC), ESOMAR has developed an International Code of Marketing and Social Research Practice. All ESOMAR members as well as the management of their companies undersign this code and undertake to comply with the technical and ethical principles of the code, which has also been adopted by members of the ICC and by over 68 marketing research associations in 41 countries around the world. The code is complemented by guidelines for good research practice on subjects ranging from tape and video recording of interviews and group discussions to conducting marketing and opinion research using the Internet.

The ESOMAR/WAPOR Guide to Opinion Polls incorporates ESOMAR's Code for the Publication of Public Opinion Poll Results and Guidelines to Their Interpretation (recommended by the Council of Europe to member governments for national self-regulation), and the Guideline on the Conduct of Pre-Electoral Polls. ESOMAR encourages effective self-regulation through these codes and guidelines, and compliance is implemented by national associations and by ESOMAR's Professional Standards Committee.

Representation of the Industry

The market research sector is being affected by the increasing volume of national and international laws on data privacy, consumer protection, and the Internet. Although not aimed at market research, these laws can affect the right and freedom to conduct research.

ESOMAR holds an annual meeting of leaders of national marketing research associations from all over the world to discuss issues of common concern. Advised by public affairs consultants and specialist lawyers, ESOMAR together with the European Federation of Associations of Market Research Organizations (EFAMRO) monitors and reviews proposed legislation in Europe that can restrict the freedom to conduct research.

ESOMAR has liaisons with international bodies such as the EU Commission to ensure that legislators take into account the legitimate interests of the research industry and to gain recognition of internationally accepted professional standards being practiced by the research community.

ESOMAR advocates free access to opinion and marketing research information without restrictions from national or international governments.

Contact ESOMAR

ESOMAR has representation in over 70 countries worldwide (contact details available on the ESOMAR Website).

European Society for Opinion and Marketing Research
Vondelstraat 172
1054 GV Amsterdam
The Netherlands
Telephone: +31 (20) 664-2141   Fax: +31 (20) 664-2922
E-mail: email@esomar.nl
Website: http://www.esomar.nl

The Federal Trade Commission (FTC) and How It Regulates Advertising

Jan Slater

A dvertising, by far, is the most visible part of any business. In general, the public doesn't know how a product is manufactured, distributed, or priced, but people can sing along when the advertising jingle for a product is played on the radio, or they can remember a slogan or discuss an advertisement with friends.

The basis of advertising is truth. Advertising industry associations the American Advertising Federation (AAF) and the American Association of Advertising Agencies (AAAA) both provide strict guidelines and codes for "truth in advertising" among their members. And advertisers and advertising agencies alike should realize that the smart consuming public knows the truth. But advertising is under constant criticism for presenting half-truths and making statements that are more often misleading than informing. Because of this, the advertising industry is heavily scrutinized and regulated.

Several entities are in place to ensure truthful and responsible advertising. The industry promotes itself as being self-regulated by the aforementioned associations and the Better Business Bureaus' National Advertising Division (NAD) and National Advertising Review Board (NARB; both described in this volume). The Food and Drug Administration (FDA) of the federal government enforces laws on labeling and nutritional content information on food products, and the Federal Communications Commission (FCC) allows television and radio stations to review and reject advertising they regard as objectionable.

However, the primary regulator of advertising is the federal government through the Federal Trade Commission (FTC). It is helpful to examine the FTC from a broad perspective relating to its history and structure. As is evident in the discussion that follows, the FTC's strengths or weaknesses are often determined by the administration in power at the time.

History of the FTC

Regulating business was the focus of the presidential election of 1912. The topic had been much debated in the early 20th century. The Sherman Antitrust Act, passed in 1890, had little power or even much definition of its power, and under the Department of Justice, it was slow to act. Politicians and businessmen alike called for an agency to monitor business practices and restraints of trade. All three candidates, William Taft, Woodrow Wilson, and Theodore Roosevelt, campaigned on a platform of governmental regulation.

Wilson won the election of 1912 and proceeded to call for a commission that would provide advice, guidance, and information to companies. He also proposed that specific practices be declared illegal and suggested the penalties for those practices. After much discussion, debate, and compromise, Wilson signed the Federal Trade Commission Act in 1914, which deemed "unfair methods of competition" unlawful. This act formed the government agency to be known as the Federal Trade Commission, which would be responsible for regulating and protecting business—primarily, antitrust concerns. The wording, however, was purposely left vague and undefined, not only to include the business practices of the day but not to exclude those that might be invented in the future.[1] This lack of explicitness has plagued the FTC ever since.

The FTC borrowed the model set by the Interstate Commerce Commission in 1887 and established a five-person agency. Commissioners appointed by the president and confirmed by the Senate served staggered terms of 7 years each, and no more than three commissioners could be of the same political party. This structure of appointment is still in place today.

In its infancy, the development of the FTC was slow. It stumbled regularly, and many of its battles were lost by judicial review in the courts. In general, it was thought to be a rather ineffective force. The commission investigated a variety of practices it considered to be unfair methods of competition, such as price discrimination, selling below cost, misbranding, trade name copying, and deceptive advertising. The courts failed to support the FTC's actions in many cases, testing the commission's authority to define "unfair methods of competition."[2] But just prior to the Great Depression of the 1930s, the FTC found success in the courts with cases against companies for false advertising. It was to be the FTC's greatest achievement since its inception, and because of the success rate (the courts upheld 22 of 29 FTC orders on deceptive advertising through 1931), the commission gradually focused much of its attention on this practice.[3] The most famous ruling of the time was against the American Tobacco Company.

George Washington Hill was head of the American Tobacco Company. Hill was a powerful man, both in ego and advertising clout. In 1929, he was spending $12.3 million a year advertising Lucky Strike cigarettes.[4] He restricted his advertising agency to the exclusive use of hard-sell advertising techniques to market Lucky Strikes and insisted on the testimonial approach, which eventually got him into trouble with the FTC. At the time, 1929-1930, testimonials were not only overused in the advertising industry, but they were making outrageous and unbelievable claims. The Lucky Strike advertising jumped into the fire and featured opera stars testifying to the benefit the cigarettes had on their singing. The most prominent advertisement, however, featured actress Helen Hayes, who endorsed smoking as an alternative to eating candy. The headline was "Reach for a Lucky instead of a sweet." That prompted the FTC into action, and in 1930, it ruled that the American Tobacco Company must halt all testimonials by endorsers who had not actually used the product. In addition, the ads were required to indicate a paid testimonial as such and could no longer use the claim that smoking cigarettes would help people control their weight.[5]

This FTC ruling, the depressed economic conditions of the 1930s, and rampant criticism of advertising during that period coincided with a powerful consumerist movement. Money was scarce, and advertising was attacked for promoting waste and making exaggerated claims. Consumers believed that advertising attempted to make them feel guilty for not buying what they could not afford. The public also believed that the depression was caused by artificially high prices brought about by monopolies. The consumer movement looked to the government for protection.

President Franklin Roosevelt's "New Deal" had an antitrust element. He called on the FTC to restore competition through antitrust prosecution, and he believed that the FTC should have a role in consumer protection. The Wheeler-Lea Act of 1938 was legislation of FDR's New Deal; by amending Section 5 of the Federal Trade Commission Act, it provided the commission with extended powers. Wheeler-Lea deemed false advertising unlawful as an "unfair or deceptive practice if the public was being deceived."[6] Most important, the amendment gave the FTC the power to enforce cease-and-desist orders by fining those who did not comply, and it allowed the agency to investigate false advertising even without a complaint.

The consumer movement was gaining momentum and found much to support in the Wheeler-Lea Act. In the 2 years following passage of the act, the FTC ruled on 18 deceptive advertising cases, sending a profound message to advertisers and advertising agencies. But World War II subdued the angry consumer and provided some relief for the advertising industry. Advertising practices were minor concerns during wartime, and the FTC left Madison Avenue alone. For the moment, consumerism was dead, but the same concerns would be revisited some 30 years later.

During the late 1940s and early 1950s, the commission primarily focused on cigarette advertising claims and disclosure. Many cigarette advertisements used endorsements from physicians claiming medicinal benefits. These ads were carefully scrutinized, and Kools and Camels were both forced to stop listing false benefits of cigarette smoking. In 1955, the FTC issued Cigarette Advertising Guides, with which many companies voluntarily complied.

By the 1960s, the commission seemed to be gaining strength. President John F. Kennedy wanted to strengthen the FTC and made influential appointments—people who vowed to enforce the laws against false advertising. To enhance this stand on consumer protection, Kennedy established the President's Committee on Consumer Interests. But in fact, the FTC did not do much except to mandate cigarette warning labels on packages and in ads. Politically and socially, the country was in a state of unrest from the Civil Rights Movement and the war in Vietnam. The American people were skeptical of everything—government, big business, and certainly, advertising. Consumerism was on its way back with a vengeance, and the consumer's champion was Ralph Nader.

Nader came on the scene in 1966 with *Unsafe at Any Speed,* a book calling for safer cars and stricter safety requirements for the domestic automotive industry. But it really wasn't until 1969 that he publicly criticized the FTC for its failure to protect consumers. On his own, Ralph Nader asked the sponsors of 58 national advertisments to substantiate their advertising claims. Of the 40 replies he received, one advertisments retracted the claim, and Nader found the claims of the other 39 ads inadequately supported. He petitioned the FTC to require substantiation, and the commission agreed. The FTC now began requiring companies to submit information on safety, performance, quality, and comparative pricing.[7] Furthermore, the commission began to study the implied intent of the advertising claims, more than just the surface meaning.

In the meantime, President Richard Nixon had requested a special commission of the American Bar Association (ABA) to study the performance of the FTC and provide recommendations for improvement. The ABA report was just as critical of the commission as Nader had been. Fueled by Nader and the ABA report, Nixon appointed strong leaders to reorganize the FTC, and a more consumer-oriented approach came about in the 1970s.

During the 1970s, the commission was at the height of its power and influence. It had strong leadership, solid budgets, adequate staffing, and a supportive Congress. Advertising received unprecedented scrutiny. In 1971, the FTC made the first request for substantiation of advertising claims from automobile manufacturers. Advertisers were required to obtain substantiation of claims prior to the placement of ads. Corrective advertising became a remedy for deceptive advertising. The commission could order the advertiser to run corrective advertising to overcome the deception caused by claims that the FTC ruled misleading. From 1970 to 1978, the FTC's annual budget had grown from $14 million to $65 million.[8]

But the powerful and well-supported FTC would not continue into the 1980s. President Jimmy Carter was pro-regulation and appointed aggressive pro-regulation commissioners to lead the strengthened FTC. But by 1978, Congress was revolting against regulation in general, and the FTC got caught in the revolution. Congress had been supportive of the FTC through the 1970s, and in some ways Congress empowered the commission to make it more influential. But Congress members were not prepared to deal with the backlash from their own constituents who had become the targets of the FTC's power. Immediately, Congress proposed restrictions on the FTC and tried to impose a legislative veto measure, which was eventually found unconstitutional. Problems worsened by late 1979 as Congress restricted the agency from engaging in "any new activities" for 30 days. And just 6 months later, funding completely ran out for the Commission, which literally closed down the agency until Congress reappropriated funds.[9]

Ronald Reagan took office in 1981 and made good his promise to reduce the agency's profile and reduce its budget, and he asked Congress to place restrictions on its legal authority. The much scaled-back commission was most affected in its consumer protection activities.

Until this time, deception in advertising did not require proof. That is, the commission did not have to prove that indeed the advertisement deceived consumers; it only had to prove that the advertisement had the "capacity or tendency to deceive" the public. James C. Miller III, Reagan's appointed FTC chairman, changed all that. He substituted the wording "likely" for "capacity or tendency" and required proof that a proportion of consumers were "likely" to be deceived by the advertising claim.

At the same time, the advertising industry began pushing for a definition of the term *unfairness* in the FTC's doctrine. The industry believed that without a legal definition for both the advertisers and the FTC to work within, unfairness could be defined at the whim of a commissioner and would not be consistent across all cases. But Congress would not budge.

The Reagan years made the rather benign years of the 1950s look active. Because of the lack government intervention and protection, the state attorneys general moved to fill the void. This was not the first time that individual states had undertaken the task of protecting consumers from false advertising. In 1913, the American Advertising Federation and *Printer's Ink,* the industry's trade magazine, lobbied state legislatures to adopt the *Printer's Ink* statute enforcing truth in advertising. The statute penalized false and misleading advertising, stating that any company or person using an untrue, deceptive, or misleading advertisement would be guilty of a misdemeanor. By 1913, the statute was introduced and passed in 15 states, and after only a few years, 37 states had enacted the statute or variations of it.[10]

In the 1980s, the states took action to protect consumers and functioned as 50 individual agencies enforcing the law against false and deceptive advertising. In many instances, however, the individual states joined forces with other state attorneys general to file suit against national advertisers whose advertising practices were deceptive.

By 1988 when President George Bush took office, the FTC was under constant criticism from consumers, consumer interest groups, and the state attorneys general. In 1989, the ABA undertook another study of the FTC. The report was meant to help the Bush administration strengthen and reorganize the commission, just as it had assisted Richard Nixon 20 years earlier.

The ABA report emphasized that the FTC was the proper regulator of national advertising and suggested that state attorneys general should limit their regulatory jurisdiction to practices "that harm consumers within a single state."[11] According to the ABA, the FTC's mission should be to attack those practices that harm in many states, but the report urged the states and the FTC to work together. The ABA expressed concerns about the budget cuts the commission had sustained and suggested that lack of money had affected the agency's effectiveness in terms of resources and the number of cases it could investigate. But the ABA was very specific in its charge that the FTC "can and should do more to articulate its advertising law-enforcement agenda," and that uniform national standards should be vigorously enforced and consistently interpreted.[12]

The FTC under the Bush administration was more active than during the Reagan years, but that wasn't too difficult. Its mission was primarily to mend fences with consumers and the states. Much of the commission's attention was focused on the investigation of unsubstantiated advertising claims within the weight loss industry. The commission worked more closely with the state attorneys general and used the 1990 Nutritional and Education Act of the Food and Drug Administration as a guideline for claims made in food product advertising.

When President Bill Clinton took office in 1993, there was speculation that his FTC would be more active than in the past 12 years, but it would not be as active as in Jimmy Carter's time. Clinton's transition team reported on the FTC but recommended no major overhaul of the agency. The primary suggestion was directed at reallocating resources, but the report made no mention of advertising specifically.

Nevertheless, an FTC debate between Congress and the advertising industry was finally resolved in 1994. The debate began in 1976 when an FTC inquiry wanted to deem all children's television advertising unfair. For 14 years, advertising industry associations had lobbied Congress to eliminate the FTC's "unfairness" authority, arguing that the lack of definition caused varying interpretations for each case. Finally, Congress, with the help of the industry, provided a legal definition of unfair advertising and signed it into law late in 1994. The bill defines unfairness as "acts or practices that cause or are likely to cause substantial injury to consumers which is not reasonably avoidable by consumers themselves and not outweighed by countervailing benefits to consumers or competition."[13] Although the industry wanted the unfairness authority stripped from the FTC, this new definition seemed a victory for advertisers and their agencies. Wally Snyder, AAF president and an FTC advertising regulator for 16 years, said that the definition of fairness was necessary to prevent an activist FTC from initiating "fishing expeditions" against advertisers. Basically the ruling requires the FTC to have "reason to believe" that the unfair or deceptive acts or practices are prevalent.[14]

Structure of the FTC

As discussed earlier, the president appoints FTC commissioners; these serve staggered 7-year terms. The president appoints the chairman from one of the five commissioners and can do so immediately after taking office. However, he cannot appoint new commissioners until any current commissioner's 7-year term expires. The executive branch of government is responsible for making those appointments in the best interest of the commission, although many appointments are well-known to be political favors. Although both the White House and Congress approve the budget for the FTC, the budget is actually developed and monitored by the Office of Management and Budget.

The FTC organization (shown in Figure 6) is the basic structure imposed by Caspar Weinberger's reorganization in the early 1970s.[15] Several divisions and 10 regional offices are under the authority of the commissioners. Advertising practices fall under the Bureau of Consumer Protection, together with credit practices, energy and product information, product reliability, and professional services.

The commission's authority and power are influenced by the three external governmental branches: legislative, judicial, and executive. Not only does Congress approve the budgets and the appointments to the commission, it can also enact legislation that can be used to reduce, eliminate, or empower the authority of the FTC. Instances of this have been previously discussed in the historical section. Two levels of the federal court system regularly review FTC decisions: the Court of Appeals and the Supreme Court. This ensures the FTC is within its limits under Section 5 of the FTC Act and that what the FTC has deemed as illegal, is indeed illegal.

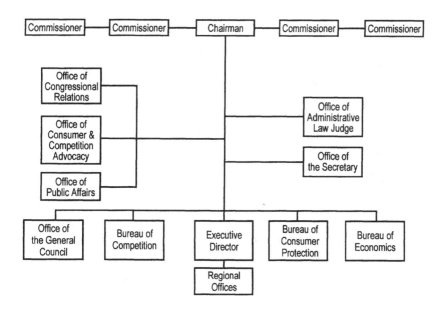

Figure 6. FTC Organizational Structure

How the FTC Works

Two terms give the FTC authority: *deception* and *unfairness*. The unfairness issue was discussed in an earlier section; this section will focus primarily on deception.

Recall that before 1983 the FTC had only to prove that an advertisement had the tendency to deceive or mislead. The policy wording was changed to "likely to mislead," which put the burden on the FTC to show that the ad actually had influenced or misled the consumer. Criteria for deception are considered on a case-by-case basis. However, as a general rule, for deception to occur, the claim in the ad must cause the consumer to take some action, influence his or her decision process, or both. The deception is determined after the ad has been exposed to the consumer. Typically, the commission studies three areas of information regarding deception: substantiation of claim, endorsements, and product demonstrations.

Substantiation

Within an advertisement, any claim of superiority or difference, based on survey results, taste tests, exaggerated demonstrations of the product in use (known as "torture tests"), or scientific studies—requires supporting documentation prior to the broadcast or publication of the advertisement. In the circumstances when the FTC requires it for investigation purposes, the advertiser must have documented proof that the claim was substantiated prior to the placement of the ad.

Endorsements

In the past, the FTC has focused on testimonials and products endorsed by celebrities because consumers rely on these endorsements in their purchase decisions. The FTC requires proof that indeed the endorser—a celebrity or actual user—does use the product. If product comparisons are made, the endorser must have tried the compared brand as well. In cases in which the endorsement is found to be deceptive, the endorser as well as the advertiser can be held responsible.

Product Demonstrations

Any claim that is demonstrated must be accurately shown. This can be very vague and difficult to interpret. In certain cases, for instance in food photography, it is often impossible for the product to withstand the hot lights and long hours required of a production session. Therefore, agencies often substitute a substance that looks attractive in place of the product itself. This is one of the devices used to enhance product appearance (a procedure given the general name of "propping"). For example, it is well-known that a mixture of glue and water is sometimes substituted for milk, and mashed potatoes are substituted for ice cream. The vagueness occurs when the substitution enhances the product with qualities it does not inherently possess. Basically, the FTC is concerned if the ad misrepresents the *performance* of the product. According to Lee Peeler, associate director for advertising practices of the FTC, "If you need to use mashed potatoes for ice cream for lighting or shooting purposes, that's not deceptive. If you focus in and say 'look at the creamy texture,' it is." [16]

Complaints Structure and
Methods of FTC Enforcement[17]

Complaints to the FTC can be filed by competitors, consumers, consumer interest groups, or by the FTC itself. Once a complaint is filed, the commission begins its investigation, which usually requires substantiation from the advertiser. The responsibility for the investigation falls within the Bureau of Consumer Protection and is headed by a staff attorney. Depending on the outcome of the investigation, the FTC can choose to close the case, use informal enforcement methods, or issue a complaint against the advertiser.

If the advertisement is found to be deceptive, the commission issues a complaint against the advertiser and issues a consent decree. Basically, the decree is a formal document requesting the advertiser to stop the deceptive ad or ads. By signing this agreement, the advertiser admits no guilt but says only that the advertisement in its current form will be discontinued. Many cases are concluded in this manner. It saves publicity and litigation expense, and the advertiser is given the opportunity to work with the commission in determining claims that could be used in future advertisements. If the deceptive ad is continued after the consent decree is signed, the advertiser can be fined $10,000 per day until the ad is stopped.

If the advertiser refuses to sign the consent decree, the commission will issue a cease-and-desist order, legally prohibiting further use of the ad. Before this order is finalized, a hearing is conducted before an administrative law judge (ALJ). The ALJ uses all the evidence acquired during the investigation and listens to the advertiser's defense. Following the hearing, the judge has 90 days either to dismiss the case or enforce the cease-and-desist order. Most advertisers sign a consent decree following the hearing, but the company can appeal the decision to the full commission and to the Court of Appeals and to the Supreme Court if it desires, as seen in Figure 7. However, seldom do the cases get this far. Remember that the FTC investigates the advertisements after they have been placed in the media. By the time the investigation and hearings are completed, the advertisement has probably been replaced, and the expense of time and financial resources seems hardly efficient.

The cease-and-desist order may require the advertiser to submit to affirmative disclosures or corrective advertising. Affirmative disclosures may be used

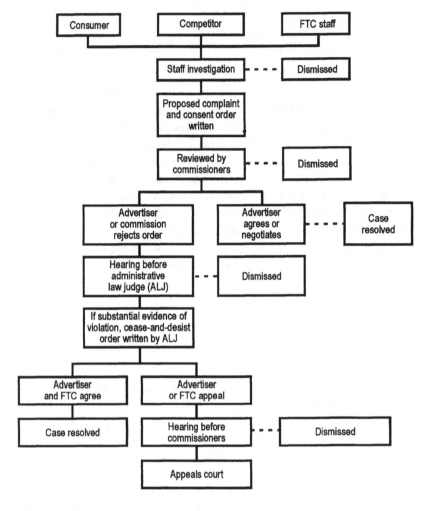

Figure 7. FTC Complaint Structure

as a disclaimer, if the advertiser were to make similar claims in future advertisements. The best known examples of affirmative disclosure requirements
are in automotive advertisements regarding rebates or lease rates and in cigarette advertising where the surgeon general's warning is required.[18]

The FTC may require the advertiser to run corrective advertising when it is determined, via research, that just discontinuing the ad will not remedy the problem of deceiving consumers. In fact, the FTC believes that deceiving ads have had some residual effects on consumers' beliefs. Corrective advertising is only a remedy in the most severe cases and has been used as such only since the 1970s.

Federal Trade Commission
600 Pennsylvania Ave NW
Washington, DC 20580
For general information telephone: (202) 326-2222
The Consumer Response Center can be used for complaints: 1-877-FTC-
HELP (382-4357)—toll-free number
Website: http://www.ftc.gov

Notes

1. Mary Ellen Zuckerman, "The Federal Trade Commission in Historical Perspective: The First Fifty Years," in Patrick Murphy and William Wilke (eds.), *Marketing and Advertising Regulation: The FTC in the 1990s* (Notre Dame, IN: University of Notre Dame, 1990), 169-199.

2. Ibid.

3. Ibid.

4. Stephen Fox, *The Mirror Makers: A History of American Advertising and Its Creators* (New York: Vintage, 1984).

5. Ibid.

6. Zuckerman, "The Federal Trade Commission in Historical Perspective."

7. Fox, *The Mirror Makers: A History of American Advertising and Its Creators.*

8. Kenneth L. Bernhardt, "The FTC in 1978: Some Observations From a Marketing Academic," in Patrick Murphy and William Wilke (eds.), *Marketing and Advertising Regulations: The FTC in the 1990s* (Notre Dame, IN: University of Notre Dame, 1990), 114.

9. William J. Baer, "At the Turning Point: The Commission in 1978," in Patrick Murphy and William Wilke (eds.), *Marketing and Advertising Regulations: The FTC in the 1990s* (Notre Dame, IN: University of Notre Dame, 1990), 94-106.

10. James Playsted Wood, *The Story of Advertising* (New York: Ronald Press, 1958).

11. Steven W. Colford, "ABA Panel Backs FTC Over States," *Advertising Age*, April 10, 1989, 1.

12. Patrick Murphy and William Wilke (eds.), *Marketing and Advertising Regulation: The FTC in the 1990s* (Notre Dame, IN: University of Notre Dame, 1990).

13. Steven W. Colford, "AAF Support Pact for Fencing with FTC," *Advertising Age*, March 14, 1994, 32.

14. Ibid.

15. William F. Arens and Courtland L. Bovée, *Contemporary Advertising* (Burr Ridge, IL: Irwin, 1994).

16. Julia Miller, "Shoot Fast, 'Cut Back on Trickery,'" *Advertising Age,* October 17, 1994, 29.

17. William Wells, John Burnett, and Sandra Moriarty, *Advertising Principles and Practice* (Englewood Cliffs, NJ: Prentice Hall, 1992), 50-53.

18. Thomas R. Hillhouse, "Government Controls of Advertising," in Felix H. Kent and Elhanan C. Stone (eds.), *Legal and Business Aspects of the Advertising Industry* (New York: Practicing Law Institute, 1982), 235-262.

The Free-Standing
Insert (FSI) Council

The Free-Standing Insert (FSI) Council of North America was founded in 1997 to educate marketers, retailers, and consumers about the continued value of FSI coupons and to spearhead an effort to increase industry efficiency and effectiveness. To help achieve the council's objectives, several initiatives have been implemented and others are underway:

- A comprehensive market research program was developed to understand better the results and the potential of FSI usage. Topics explored to date include the effect of FSI coupons on consumer brand loyalty and on trial and repeat behavior, as well as the impact of full-page FSIs versus half-page FSIs.
- The Brand-Loyal Index is a new attitudinal measurement tool developed by KRC Research of New York and underwritten by the FSI Council. It is designed to gauge consumer attitudes on brand usage, preference, and loyalty, as well as the relationship of these elements to coupon use and brand FSI participation.

- The Brand-Building Hall of Fame was created as a forum to recognize and learn from brands that were built and sustained with the use of FSIs. The first-ever members of the Hall of Fame were inducted at PROMO Expo '98 at Navy Pier in Chicago.

Coupons: An Indispensable Tool for the Shopping Public

Coupons help Americans save $2.9 billion a year (the 1998 Coupon Fact Book, CMS, Inc). For many wise shoppers, coupon use is a way of life and an essential factor in helping them meet their household budgets. As a matter of fact, a recent study showed that 78% of consumers named "acceptance of coupons" as one of the key reasons they shop at a store—helping to increase retailer profitability and promote store loyalty. (Promotion Decision, Inc., March 1997.)

FSIs: A Proven Value

Given the importance of coupons to America's shoppers, it is no surprise that FSI coupons—which account for more than 90% of all coupons distributed—bring considerable value to marketers and retailers alike. FSIs are not only the most popular but also the most effective type of coupons, offering advertising and recall value in addition to the monetary promotional incentive. According to recent research, FSIs provide marketers the most rapid return on investment—between 71% and 79% of their cost within 12 weeks. Research also shows that FSI coupons help build brand loyalty not only by encouraging product trial but also by driving repeat purchase.

In addition, FSI coupon redeemers tend to be high-consumption shoppers.

FSI Council Founders

The FSI Council was formed by Lyndon E. Goodridge, professor of business and economics at the University of New Hampshire, and representatives from CMS, Inc.; Wallace Marx & Associates; NCH/NuWorld Marketing, Ltd; Promotion Decisions, Inc; News America Marketing; and Valassis Communications, Inc.

Free-Standing Insert (FSI) Council
4700 W. Lake Avenue
Glenview, IL 60025-1485
Telephone: (888) FSI-0881   Fax: (847) 375-4777
E-mail: fsi@amctec.com
Website: http://www.fsicouncil.org

Genootschap Voor Reclame (GVR) (Netherlands)

Genootschap Voor Reclame (GVR; Advertising Society) is the parent of virtually all of the associations in the communications industry in the Netherlands. The first articles of association date back to 1927. Over the decades, GVR has grown to become a strongly identified association under whose patronage well-known organizations have risen, such as Stichting Reclame Code (Advertising Code Foundation), the Direct Marketing Institute (now DMSA), Stichting Reclame en Marketing Onderwijs (SRM; Advertising and Marketing Education Foundation), the GVR Professor's Chair in Commercial Communications at the University of Amsterdam, Stichting Arbitrage Instituut Sponsoring (Sponsoring Arbitration Foundation), and Stichting Stuurgroep Reclame (Advertising Steering Group Foundation).

The GVR works in association with the British advertising journal *Admap* to produce GVR monographs. Through the GVR, members can subscribe at a considerable discount to a unique new advertising database from the World Advertising Research Centre (WARC) in England. (See the article on *Admap* in this volume.) The GVR is the only provider of WARC in the Netherlands. In addition, the GVR is actively working on the new Dutch Advertising Museum.

Full Coverage of the Field

GVR is not only an interest group that represents the rights of one specific body; it is more of an eclectic club where people from different fields are welcomed—where they can meet, pick up pointers from each other, help each other out, and entertain each other. The multidisciplinary character gives GVR its own appeal and significance. Among the nearly 900 members are both marketing representatives and company heads, the audiovisual producer as well as the media guru, both the publisher and the creative director, the exhibit builder and the researcher.

Professional Debate

The mission of GVR is to be a source of inspiration to everyone who works in the marketing communications industry in the Netherlands, to make a contribution toward the development of this professional field and of its individual members. GVR promotes expertise and ability and brings different fields together in one active network. In addition, GVR stands up for the general interests of the marketing communications industry as an independent, objective association. GVR does this with this stated attitude: "open, (inter)active, high quality, multidisciplinary and, most importantly, fun."

The cohesion between all those different fields continues to present members with new perspectives. People never stop learning in the communications field. That is what makes a career in this industry so appealing.

Headquarters

GVR acts as an endorser and support for numerous specific sections: ACMC (Association of Cultural Marketing & Communications), AV (Audio-Visual Communications), ESAH (Exhibition Services Association, Holland), OCC

(Order of Communications Consultants), POPAI (Point-of-Purchase Advertising Institute, Benelux Office), and SPONSORING (joint venture of Sports Sponsoring Platform and Sponsors for Art).

GVR International

GVR is a member of the IAA (International Advertising Association) in the Netherlands. It keeps abreast of developments in Europe through the Advertising Steering Group. The monthly newsletter, *GVR Info,* contains interesting articles from international sources.

GVR Professor's Chair

Professor Giep Franzen has held the GVR Chair in Commercial Communications at the University of Amsterdam since January 1, 1994. Every year, more than 200 students attend his lectures on brand policy and communications. With a background in the field (Franzen was cofounder of FHV, currently FHV/ BBDO [Franzen, Heye and Veltman/Batten, Barton, Durstine and Osborn]), he is an ideal person to bring science and practical application together. In this capacity, Giep Franzen is also involved in two other GVR educational projects: the *GVR Monographs* (on topics in the field of marketing communications) and *GVR Presents* . . . Professionals and researchers who have been guests at GVR include Neil Swan (The Research Business), Phil Dusenberry (BBDO), Susan Ashley (research systems corporation, or rsc), Garth Hallberg (O & M Direct), Professor Andrew Ehrenberg (South Bank Business School), Winston Fletcher (Bozell), and Andrew Roberts (Taylor Nelson Sofres).

Other GVR Activities

- GVR Seminars
- GVR Café
- *GVR Info*
- GVR Slogans

- Back to the University Desks
- GVR Book Presentations

Genootschap Voor Reclame
Vliegtuigstraat 26
1059 CL Amsterdam
The Netherlands
Telephone: +31 (20) 669-9777   Fax: +31 (20) 669-3738
E-mail: gvr@euronet.nl

Gesamtverband Werbeagenturen (GWA)

Henning von Vieregge

Gesamtverband Werbeagenturen was founded in 1952 as the Society of Advertising Agencies—Gesellschaft Werbeagenturen (GWA). It amalgamated with the Trade Association of German Advertising Agencies—Wirtschaftsverband Deutscher Werbeagenturen (WDW)—in 1986 to become the German Association of Advertising Agencies. The WDW was successor association to the Verband Deutscher Werbeagenturen und Werbemittlungen (ADW)— the Consortium of German Advertising Agencies.

GWA stands for prestige and substance. Its member agencies represent almost 13,000 employees and equivalent billings of DM 19.3 billion (circa 70% of the total volume of advertising placed with agencies). The GWA in Frankfurt acts for 151 advertising agencies with 250 offices located all over Germany, focusing on the cities of Hamburg, Düsseldorf, Frankfurt, Munich, and Stuttgart.

GWA stands for efficient advertising quality. The GWA "Effie" Awards in gold, silver, and bronze, for advertisements of excellence in terms of effectiveness and creativity, highlight the significance of advertising as a decisive marketing instrument. The Effie Award categories are consumer goods, durables, services, corporate presentations, trade, and public benefit corporations. Advertising quality is documented in GWA's Members Yearbook, Television Yearbook, and Yearbook on CD-ROM.

GWA denotes professional ethics. Members follow the principles set down in GWA's standards of practice: to benefit clients, convince the public, and bring success to GWA members. Agencies wishing to join the association are carefully scrutinized to ensure they adhere to these principles.

Three features characterize GWA's services:

- GWA represents the interests of its member agencies vis-à-vis its partners on the market—that is, clients, the media, and their representatives. Backed by GWA's prestige, agencies can negotiate clear and beneficial operating arrangements with clients and subcontractors.
- GWA is the advocate for advertising agencies and the advertising profession as a whole—with the general public, politicians, and the business community. GWA explains the economics of advertising to the lay public; articulates the needs of the advertising business, particularly of its members; and thereby contributes to how quality advertising is perceived in a context of free trade and democracy.
- GWA supports its members, keeping them informed of issues relevant to successful advertising. It organizes and facilitates an interchange of experience at management and expert levels. GWA backs up the competitive capability of its members by providing management studies, operational comparisons, cost accounting, and specimen contracts. Services also include legal consultancy, TV-spot services, and seminars that can be provided direct by GWA's own service company.

GWA does not stand alone. It is a member of the German Advertising Federation, Zentralverband der Deutschen Werbewirtschaft (ZAW), Bonn, and of the European Association of Advertising Agencies (EAAA), Brussels; and it actively participates in other organizations such as the German Advertising Standards Authority, Deutscher Werberat.

Close contacts and exchange of information are maintained with non-European advertising agency associations, particularly the American Association of Advertising Agencies (AAAA), New York.

Gesamtverband Werbeagenturen GWA
Friedenstrasse 11
D-60311 Frankfurt am Main
Germany
Telephone: +49 (69) 25 60 8-0   Fax: +49 (69) 23 68 83
E-mail: info@gwa.de
Website: http://www.gwa.de

The History of Advertising Trust Archive (HAT) (United Kingdom)

The History of Advertising Trust Archive was formed in 1976 to encourage the study of all aspects of the growth and development of advertising. It subsequently broadened its remit to include the related fields of marketing, media, and public relations. The HAT Archive contains over 2 million items and is one of the largest collections of its kind in the world, with U.K. material dating from 1800 onward. Although the HAT Archive specializes in U.K. material, it also holds some European and North American material. It is an educational charity.

HAT has built up one of the largest archives, consisting of paper, film, tape, fiche, and photography. The HAT Archive holds print, television, cinema, and radio advertisements; proofs, Cromalins (color separations), and artists' work;

storyboards; artifacts; campaign and client memoranda; and research. Every new U.K. TV commercial comes to HAT.

The HAT Archive consists mainly of rescued and donated material, but it also has some 25 client archives. HAT is happy to take client material, providing that it may be made available for study and is judged to have sufficient historical value or potential.

HAT is archivist to the Advertising Association (United Kingdom) and numerous other media-related bodies. It holds corporate archives, large and small, of agencies, institutions, and advertisers, some long gone. Its historic library and periodicals collection is unrivaled in its field within the United Kingdom.

HAT is currently putting its catalogue on-line via the library of the University of East Anglia (United Kingdom). This is expected to take some years to complete, but it may be accessed now via http://www.lib.uea.ac.uk/HAT/hatwelc.htm.

HAT offers subsidized research facilities for academics, for postgraduate and other university and college students, and also for school teachers and senior individual school students. In association with the Institute of Practitioners in Advertising (United Kingdom), it also offers one bursary per academic year, normally for a postgraduate student who wishes to use the HAT Archive for a considerable period.

HAT's financial policy is to be self-supporting as far as possible, with income derived from client archiving, research and information services, and the sale of its publications. To complete its educational, rescue, and preservation work and to finance its free exhibitions and the free availability of its catalogue via the Internet, HAT depends on donations, legacies, and private grants. As an independent archive, it receives no government support beyond that accorded to all U.K.-registered charities.

A valuable source of financial support for HAT is its circa 260 Corporate Friends. These represent the main British advertising agencies; media independents; production houses; professional and trade organizations; media, marketing, and related companies; regulatory bodies and trade associations; significant advertisers; and charitable trusts and academic institutions.

HAT publishes a monthly newsletter, *HATNEWS*. Its *Journal of Advertising History* is not currently published.

History of Advertising Trust Archive
HAT House
12 Raveningham Centre
Raveningham
Norwich NR14 6NU
United Kingdom
Telephone: +44 (150) 854-8623   Fax: +44 (150) 854-8478
E-mail: hat@uea.ac.uk
Website: http://www.hatads.org.uk

The Incorporated Society of British Advertisers (ISBA)

The Incorporated Society of British Advertisers (ISBA) represents £6.5 billion of marketing communications expenditure and is the single body, within the United Kingdom, to represent advertisers' interests across all marketing communication disciplines.

Founded almost 100 years ago, the ISBA's fundamental remit is to vigorously promote and protect the interests of British advertisers. By acting as their "voice," ISBA influences government, the media, agencies, consultants, suppliers, and other bodies in the marketing communications industry to help create and sustain an environment that maximizes the effectiveness of its members' marketing activities.

The ISBA is unique in the fact that membership is available only to advertisers. The ISBA also offers its members practical advice on all forms of marketing communications activities and information on industry developments. Training workshops and seminars keep members up to speed on developments in best practice, as do ISBA publications. The ISBA aims to take a lead within the industry by drawing together and publishing best-practice guidelines on a variety of issues within the marketing communications mix.

The ISBA publication list to date includes documents on everything from direct marketing, sales promotion, sponsorship and sponsorship evaluation, to producing TV commercials and art-buying guidelines. The ISBA has also carried out the most authoritative and comprehensive report of U.K. agency remuneration, *Paying for Advertising,* which has already sold over 165 copies. *Evaluating Agency Performance,* which looked at what advertisers think of their agencies, gave the industry insight into how agencies were performing. The sequel to this publication was launched in 1999 and looks set to lead the agenda within the industry once more.

The ISBA's role can be seen on two levels. Already outlined is the work carried out for individual members to make their jobs easier and make the flow of information within the industry more controlled. On a wider level, ISBA plays a key role within the industry in influencing decision makers in the legislative process. This role is key to members as increased regulation within the commercial communication arena has a direct impact on their ability to market their products and services effectively.

The success of self-regulation within the advertising industry in the United Kingdom is second to none. The ISBA focuses much of its public affairs agenda on the rights of advertisers to communicate commercially and their ability to do this responsibly in a self-regulatory environment.

The issue of children and advertising is, at present, of vital concern to the ISBA because Sweden, which will take on the EU presidency in 2002, does not allow advertising to children on its terrestrial television channels. Sweden has expressed a wish for a Europe-wide ban on advertising to children to be considered, and the ISBA is working with the U.K. Advertising Association and the World Federation of Advertisers to fight such proposals.

The ISBA must maintain a high profile within the media to be seen by decision makers, the public, and its members as actively having a "voice." The trade press has traditionally gone to the ISBA for comment on news stories and reported the work the ISBA is currently undertaking. Since early 1998, the ISBA has become more vocal with both the national press and broadcast media. Directors have appeared on everything from Radio 4's *Today* program to ITN's *Lunchtime News*—all of which endorse the ISBA's position as the only true representative of U.K. advertisers.

At the ISBA's 1999 annual conference, President Peter Blackburn called on delegates to unite and work together for the good of the industry. Since then, the ISBA has welcomed into membership eight blue-chip companies who represent over £136 million of ad expenditure. But the ISBA intends to go further over the coming years and increase its membership base. As its Director General John Hooper, CBE, explains,

> ISBA's growth has a direct effect on its lobbying power within the industry. The more advertisers we represent, the louder our collective voice becomes. Advertisers recognize that progress can best be made through collective action and we are the vehicle which enables them to achieve this.

Incorporated Society of British Advertisers
44 Hertford Street
London W1Y 8AE
United Kingdom
Telephone: +44 (0)20 7499-7502   Fax: +44 (0)20 7629-5355
Website: http://www.isba.org.uk

Institut de Recherches et d'Etudes Publicitaires (IREP)

I REP—the Institute for the study and research of publicity activities—is a major French professional association, founded in 1958. It is a nonprofit organization.

IREP's mission is to provide

— a window for displaying new research,
— a laboratory for new research methodologies, and
— an observations post for locating research innovations in France and abroad.

IREP combines the forces of advertisers, agencies, media, media consultants, and professional institutes. Membership comprises organizations in these fields.

The activities of IREP include the following:

• Seminars on a range of research-focused topics

- Cooperative project teams at which various types of organizations meet together to examine
    media strategy,
    pretesting procedures,
    measurement of advertising effects,
    control of communication activities,
    research systems, and
    studies of audiences and the strategic employment of such studies.
- Exchange of views on the larger topics confronting the business
- Continuous review of the advertising marketplace in France
- Publication of articles and reference works
- An archive open to professionals in the various fields and to universities and journalists

The most recent publications of IREP are these:

- *Le Marché Publicitaire Français* (The French Advertising Market)
- Four reference works covering the field:
    Volume One—The Brand
    Volume Two—Advertising Effectiveness
    Volume Three—The Logic of the Consumer and the Logic of Advertising Language
    Volume Four—The Media

Institut de Recherches et d'Etudes Publicitaires
62 rue La Boétie
75008 Paris
France
Telephone: +33 (14) 563-7173   Fax: +33 (14) 225-9228
E-mail: irep@easynet.frst

The Institute of Canadian Advertising (ICA)

John G. Sinclair

The Institute of Canadian Advertising (ICA) was founded in 1907 as Canada's national association for advertising agencies. The institute operates from its head office in mid-Toronto and has a permanent staff of eight persons. It is administered by a 20-person Board of Directors, all of whom are CEOs of member agencies.

Members include all major Canadian advertising agencies, multinational and domestic, with head office and branch offices located from Halifax to Vancouver. Current membership is 66 companies, representing approximately three-quarters of national advertising billings placed in Canadian media. Capitalized billings of ICA agencies amounted to about $CAN6½ billion in the 1998 year.

The ICA was originally founded in 1907 with the name of Canadian Association of Advertising Agencies. Its purpose was to represent agencies in any areas of mutual interest, particularly with regard to maintaining the commission discount system offered by placing advertisements in Canadian newspapers.

These actions led to strong and friendly relationships with the newspaper industry, a situation that has continued to the present day. The association maintained a set of entrance and financial standards "to ensure stability of its member companies and to minimize any threat of non-payment of obligations to media and production organizations."

The name of the association was changed in 1965 to Institute of Canadian Advertising and L'Institut de la Publicité Canadienne.

Educational courses have long been an important activity of the ICA. Industry instructors provide training in basic advertising skills, including marketing, creative work, media, research, and promotion. Many of these courses are conducted in classrooms on the ICA premises in Toronto. Others are offered in major cities across Canada. In a typical season, about 1,000 students are enrolled in ICA classes.

In 1960, ICA launched a major, multiyear course designed to imbue the fundamental business knowledge and skills needed for working in or with an advertising agency. The course was called CAAP—Certified Advertising Agency Practitioner—and successful completion permitted graduates to use the designation CAAP after their name. Each year, this prime educational vehicle is offered in Toronto; it has also been conducted in Montreal, Vancouver, and Alberta. The CAAP course has been hailed as an extremely valuable part of an advertising career, and there is no comparable offering in agency training anywhere else in North America.

The ICA provides a wide range of benefits to its agency members. Among the more important are relations with federal and provincial governments, relations with advertiser and media associations, and relations with other agency associations around the world. Member surveys are done each year to provide information on industry salary levels and agency profitability.

In recent years, ICA has given considerable attention to the study of the effectiveness of advertising. In early 1994, the association published a hardcover text on this subject, *Advertising Works,* written by two ex-agency executives, John Dalla Costa and Alan Middleton. The book is regarded as a superior, current work on the advertising process. It contains a very complete and up-to-date bibliography on the subject of advertising and was updated and enlarged in 1997.

The ICA was a Founding Partner of the 1993 Canadian Congress of Advertising, which sponsors the publication of collections of Canadian advertising case studies based on the measurement of effects. The first volume, titled *Canadian Advertising Success Stories, CASSIES 1* (edited by James Dingwall,

George Clements, and Alan Middleton), was published in 1993. By the end of 1999, four volumes had been published.

ICA is deeply involved with Canadian talent performers and negotiates, in collaboration with the Association of Canadian Advertisers, the union contracts with ACTRA (Alliance of Canadian Cinema, Television and Radio Artists) and other organizations representing acting, voice, and musical talent. The ICA operates a counseling service to assist in interpreting and applying the collective agreements to the production of television and radio commercials.

Institute of Canadian Advertising
Yonge-Eglinton Centre
2300 Yonge Street, Suite 500
Box 2350
Toronto, Ontario, M4P 1E4
Canada
Telephone: 1-800-567-7422; (416) 482-1396
Fax: (416) 482-1856
E-mail: ica@ica-ad.com
Website: http://www.ica-ad.com

The Institute of Practitioners in Advertising (IPA)

Tessa Gooding

The professional body in the United Kingdom for advertising agencies, or any company that produces or places advertisements, is the Institute of Practitioners in Advertising (IPA).

The IPA was originally the Association of British Advertising Agents (ABAA), an association formally recognized by the Board of Trade in November 1917.

The association's records date from 1917 and reveal the part that the ABAA played for the government during World War I. It was the responsibility of an ABAA committee to handle the recruitment campaign through the National Service Department: a historic initiative for the ABAA that was recognized in a letter of thanks written by Neville Chamberlain, the government minister responsible.

The ABAA became the IPA in 1927. Since that time, the IPA has grown in size and stature. Today, it represents 201 corporate members who between them handle over 80% of all advertising placed by U.K. agencies. In addition to corporate members, there are also around 1,000 personal members among the total agency staff of some 13,000.

The mission statement of today's organization is to "anticipate, serve and promote the common professional interests of advertising agencies."

The IPA has always been a member's organization with its own code of conduct. To become a member, a company has to satisfy the IPA Council as to its professional competence and meet a number of financial requirements.

The IPA is governed by 48 council members who are senior advertising agency executives drawn from IPA corporate membership and elected by IPA members. Heading the IPA Council is the IPA president, a 2-year elected term of office.

On a day-to-day basis, the IPA is run by a full-time secretariat of experienced professionals in law, training, commercial production, research, media, trade union negotiations, agency finance, marketing, information, and public relations. The IPA secretariat is headed by the director general.

The IPA has a dual role within the agency business. First, it acts as spokesman for its members, representing them on issues of common concern and speaking on their behalf in negotiations with media bodies, government departments, and unions. In this way, the IPA is often successful in modifying draft legislation. It also works in close cooperation with other advertising bodies, such as the European Association of Advertising Agencies and the U.K. Advertising Association, where appropriate. (See the articles on these two organizations.)

Second, the IPA contributes to the effective operation of its members through its legal, advisory, training, and information services on matters of central importance to their businesses (e.g., TV and print production, media, advertising controls, and legislation). It plays a major role in the training of agency personnel both through residential management courses and in shorter skills-based courses.

Part of the work of the IPA is driven by a number of committees made up of senior agency personnel. In this way, the IPA is able to draw on a wide range of expertise and is able to reflect and represent the day-to-day practitioners of the industry.

Membership in the IPA also brings a number of financial benefits. Each year, IPA members collectively place about £7,000 million with the media. As a result, the IPA has considerable influence with the main media bodies in relation to terms of business, recognition, and credit registration. In media research, there are also special subscriber rates through the Broadcasters Audience Research Board (BARB) and the National Readership Surveys (NRS).

The IPA also produces a number of indicator surveys: on agency staff levels, salaries, costs, profitability, TV viewing trends, and so on. From time to time, it will take on special studies—for example, looking at the careers of women in advertising—and special projects—for example, making the case for advertising during a recession. It has a continuing publication program, with the objective of contributing to the quality of agency management.

The IPA also runs a number of award schemes for the industry—for example, for media planning, recruitment, and business-to-business advertising. The most prestigious is the biennial IPA Advertising Effectiveness Awards scheme, set up in 1980. For this scheme, agencies have to submit detailed evidence, presented in a 4,000-word case history, that isolates advertising's effect from the rest of the marketing mix, to prove it has met its objectives.

Institute of Practitioners in Advertising
44 Belgrave Square
London SW1X 8QS
United Kingdom
Telephone: +44 (0)20 7235-7020   Fax: +44 (0)20 7245-9904
Website: http://www.ipa.co.uk

The International Advertising Association (IAA)

The International Advertising Association (IAA) is the only global partnership of marketing communications professionals. Established in 1938 as the Export Advertising Association, it took its present name in 1954. The IAA is a nonprofit organization, funded by membership dues and member contributions. The World Secretariat is in New York City.

Mission

The main priorities are as follows:

- *Value of Advertising:* Promote the critical role and benefits of advertising as the vital force driving all healthy economies and the foundation of diverse, independent, affordable media in an open society

- *Advocacy:* Protect and advance freedom of commercial speech and consumer choice
- *Advertising Self-Regulation:* Encourage greater practice and acceptance of voluntary self-regulation of advertising by the industry
- *Professional Development:* Take the lead in state-of-the-art professional development through education, training, and internship programs for the marketing communications industry of tomorrow
- *Industry Forum:* Provide a forum to debate emerging professional marketing communications issues and their consequences in the fast-changing world environment

Membership

The IAA offers its members a *worldwide network* of marketing communications professionals, readily available for referrals, networking, and contacts:

- Over 5,300 members in 95 countries
- 97 corporate members
- 59 organizational members
- 61 chapters
- 1,680 associate members
- 23 associates chapters
- 42% of the membership is in Europe, 20% in Asia and the Pacific region, 17% in the Mid-East and Africa, 11% in the United States and Canada, and 10% in Latin America and the Caribbean.

Promoting the Value of Advertising

One of the IAA's most important achievements in explaining and promoting the value of advertising is its *Campaign for Advertising,* popularly referred to as the *Right to Choose* Campaign. Launched in 1992, it continues to be the first-ever and only global, all-media, pro bono campaign that explains the value of advertising to consumers (individuals and governments) and the benefits in their daily lives.

Against a background of continuing threats to the free flow of information on products and services, less than favorable consumer attitudes toward advertising, and the lack of understanding of its real value and benefits, the objective of the campaign has been to arrest and convert that thinking and develop real support for advertising's role in free market economies. Attitude research carried out has shown that the IAA campaign has been "remarkably effective" in achieving that.

Over US$500 million in pro bono time and space has been donated to date, and the campaign is running in 220 countries and territories. There is continuing strong demand for the supporting *Case for Advertising* booklet that has gone through a number of printings and is available in several languages.

Stemming from the research work associated with the campaign, the IAA has undertaken consumer attitude studies, to continue researching consumers' attitudes to advertising. So far, research has been carried out among 91,000 consumers in 58 countries, and more studies are planned.

As another new and very effective way of explaining the value of advertising, the IAA has commissioned a series of economic impact studies. These quantify the economic contribution advertising makes to the economy of a country, and the findings are presented to government ministers and politicians, bureaucrats, the media, and key figures in the business. Covered so far are Argentina, Colombia, Costa Rica, Dominican Republic, Estonia, Mexico, Paraguay, Poland, Romania, Turkey, Venezuela, and Spain (with the World Federation of Advertisers). Studies in other markets are planned.

Because the Campaign for Advertising had proved extremely successful in demonstrating the key role of marketing communications in today's world, the IAA decided to mark its 60th anniversary year of 1998 by doing something to benefit the world's children. So the *Give a Kid a Hand* Campaign was created. The objective is to highlight the needs of children and what each individual can do to help. This is done without duplicating what is already being done very effectively by many others, by calling on people to give their time, not money, by volunteering to those efforts. The TV spots and print ads have been taken up by the major international media. All IAA chapters in over 60 countries around the world received the materials with instructions about how to adapt the program to local markets. The Website for the campaign is http://www.giveakidahand.org.

Advocacy

To protect and advance freedom of commercial speech and consumer choice, the IAA operates at a number of levels. It undertakes direct advocacy efforts as and when invited by its chapters or members in the country concerned. It is strongly involved in information monitoring, lobbying, and coordination activities in Europe and European institutions through support for the Brussels-based European Advertising Tripartite (EAT).

The IAA responds regularly to requests for information (RFIs) to help resource advocacy efforts by its members and allied organizations. It encourages the production and distribution of supportive advocacy resource materials, including those authored by independent academics and professionals. It continues to cultivate and expand its many contacts and working relationships with its organizational members and with other major associations in the marketing communications field.

As a means of developing and building the bank of bedrock argumentation to be used in advocacy, the IAA initiated an international symposium, *Advertising and the Media in an Open Society.* Distinguished independent experts, political philosophers, sociologists, editors, journalists, and others are invited to speak out from their chosen disciplines on the symposium's platform, to articulate the broader arguments in favor of freedom of commercial speech and advertising, without which vibrant, pluralistic, affordable media could not exist.

The symposium has so far been presented in Ankara, Bucharest, London, Warsaw, Budapest, Buenos Aires, Caracas, Hong Kong, Johannesburg, New York, and Saudi Arabia (the latter under the title, *Advertising and the Media in a Free-Market Economy*).

Advertising Self-Regulation

Self-regulation by the industry of marketing communications, within an overall legal framework, is widely acknowledged as the most cost-effective method of keeping advertising "legal, decent, honest and truthful." Promoting self-regulation is a major IAA priority. It directly supports the work of two regional coordinating bodies, the Brussels-based European Advertising Standards Alliance (EASA) and the Latin American Sociedad Interamericana para la Libertad de Expresion Comercial (SILEC), based in Caracas, Venezuela.

The IAA assists its chapters and other bodies involved in setting up appropriate codes and systems in their countries, as well as systems for dealing with transborder complaints within regional trading blocs. Much use is made of the IAA booklet *The Case for Advertising Self-Regulation,* authored by Jean

Boddewyn, Ph.D., professor of international business at Baruch College, City University of New York and an acknowledged expert in this field.

As a backdrop to the principle of self-regulation, the IAA has published a monograph titled *Advertising & Constitutional Protections*. As a work in progress, this shows the extent to which freedom of commercial speech is constitutionally protected in world markets.

Professional Development

In line with its mission to take the lead in state-of-the-art professional development, the IAA continuously seeks to advance the level of marketing communications education in international markets and maintains an ongoing global advertising education network.

Accreditation

The network incorporates nearly 40 accredited institutes worldwide—leading universities, colleges, and professional schools, where marketing communications courses are taught. Accredited institute faculty members often work collaboratively with IAA chapter professionals and World Secretariat staff members and also network with one another. Institute performance standards are consistently monitored through annual quality assurance reports. Each institute awards the IAA Diploma in Marketing Communications to graduates who complete a program of studies in accordance with IAA's global curricular standards.

Universities, colleges, and professional schools offering quality marketing communications courses that meet IAA's requirements can apply directly for accreditation or be nominated by a local IAA chapter. Full details of accreditation procedures and fees for institutes are available from the IAA World Secretariat in New York and on the IAA Website.

Syllabi

The IAA has four approved curricular models:

- Standard
- Creative/production
- Media/merchandising/public relations
- Liberal arts

The models have a common core and allow for further study in functional areas of specialization. Several of the institutes additionally offer advanced courses for young professionals.

InterAd

InterAd, the IAA's annual international student advertising competition, provides hands-on experience, requiring students to form "ad agency" teams and prepare a comprehensive marketing communications strategy, with creative support, for an "in vivo" client. Each school may enter three teams. There is no limit to the number of students who can serve on a team. However, no student may be a member of more than one team.

Since 1994, thousands of students from dozens of countries have participated. The most recent competition, InterAd IV, drew 70 eligible entries from 111 teams in 37 countries.

Education Conferences

The IAA Worldwide Education Conference, held biennially, attracts leading marketing communications educators and professionals. Regional education conferences, focusing on specific topics designed for enhancing the quality of marketing communications education are convened in accord with market dynamics.

The IAA Internship Program

This program provides hands-on, state-of-the-art training for promising talent in the international marketing communications industry. It has been designed to serve IAA's corporate members, IAA accredited institutes, IAA chapters, young IAA professionals, and students. The program works in tandem with the IAA Professional Development Program.

Among its many features, the Internship Program does the following:

- Incorporates in-depth exposure, via a marketing communications experience and educational seminars
- Provides for mentoring
- Offers hands-on work experience, with opportunities from among all sectors of the marketing communications industry (advertisers, agencies, media, and the related services), at locations in the United States and around the world, depending on availability
- Allows credit toward degree requirements or a certification of completion
- Is flexible and adaptive to the specific needs of individual IAA chapters and corporate members
- Enables students and young professionals to gain a competitive edge in the job market and their careers

The program is open to students who are currently enrolled in an accredited college or university, majoring in marketing/communications/advertising. Foreign students, who are interested in coming to the United States, should be undergraduates, enrolled in an accredited college or university, with no previous U.S. study or internship. The endorsement of the program by the U.S. State Department with a USIA (U.S. Information Agency) designation, enables the IAA to provide visas for a number of foreign student participants.

The internship assignments range from 4 to 8 weeks. Internships often run parallel to university schedules: In the Northern Hemisphere, June to September; others January to March.

Depending on local laws, customs, company policies, and university policies, financial compensation (including wages and certain local expenses) and/or university credit is provided.

The IAA provides this service free of charge to both students and corporate sponsors. Housing and travel are the applicant's responsibility. The IAA provides only information sources.

Students interested in an internship assignment are invited to complete and submit an application form, a typed one-page résumé, a one-page statement about career goals and why the applicant should be considered for an IAA internship, and an official transcript from the university. Applications are due by February 1. The IAA World Secretariat maintains a database of available positions and interested candidates. Strengths and interests are evaluated and matched to company needs. Finalist candidates are then contacted by the IAA for placement.

Congresses, Conferences, and Events

The IAA World Advertising Congress is a biennial highlight for the association and has earned a reputation as an important gathering for marketing communications executives from around the world. Regional conferences are held regularly in Europe, Latin America, the Middle East, Africa, and the United States. IAA chapters themselves put on conferences, seminars, and events for their members, as well as business lunches with key speakers. (See Website for information.)

Information Technology

The IAA Website offers over 200 pages of association information, including publications, chapter events, and more. Developed as a member service, the site provides introductory information on the association's mission and programs. It receives thousands of visitors each week. In 1999, the site added its IAA En Español section with selected articles in Spanish.

Communications

The Annual Report highlights the association's activities and programs. The *Membership Directory*, the "Who's Who" of international marketing communications professionals, lists individual members by country and provides current and historical data on the IAA. It is available both as a printed publication and a CD-ROM.

The IAA produces a number of communications pieces on a regular basis.

- *IAA World News*
- *Perspectives*
- *Hotline*
- *IAA Campaign for Advertising Update*
- News Releases
- Express Clips
- *Professional Development Newsletter*

International Advertising Association
World Secretariat of the IAA
521 Fifth Avenue, Suite 1807
New York, NY 10175
Telephone: (212) 557-1133   Fax: (212) 983-0455
E-mail: iaa@iaaglobal.org
Website: http://www.iaaglobal.org

The International
Advertising Festival, Cannes

In 1954, inspired by the International Film Festival, which had been staged in Cannes since the late 1940s, a group of European cinema screen advertising contractors felt that the makers of advertising films should receive similar recognition from their colleagues in the feature film industry. As a result, they established the International Advertising Film Festival, originally held alternately in Cannes and Venice, until the French city became its permanent home in 1984.

As the industry changed and television became more prominent than cinema, films from both media were presented irrespective of whether they were TV or cinema commercials, and they were judged according to technical criteria. There were, for example, categories for commercials of different lengths, live action, animation, and so on. By 1967, however, it seemed more appropriate to split films into categories by product or service. This structure has been constantly updated to accommodate new products, services, and marketing trends.

169

In 1992, the festival organizers broadened the event to reflect the multimedia approach of advertising campaigns that incorporated both audiovisual and printed media and launched the Press & Poster section. From 1994, the Young Creatives competition allowed the new generation of creatives to participate in their own contest. In 1998, interactive marketing and advertising—Websites and on-line advertising—were added to the event, and the Cyber Lions were born. And finally, in 1999, Media Lions were launched, allowing the media companies to join the festival with their own competition celebrating creative use of media. This continual improvement has transformed the festival into the world's major platform for exhibiting the best creative work from the international advertising community.

To complement the showcase of the Press & Poster entries and the screening of the 5,000 commercials submitted, the festival has developed a program of high-profile seminars organized by some of the biggest names in the industry, making Cannes a great learning experience.

Traditionally held at the end of June, the festival is a unique opportunity for professionals to study the best of the world's advertising and recharge their batteries. As competitors, they have the chance of seeing their work singled out for the highest form of praise—winning one of the industry's most respected prizes in the world.

International Advertising Festival
27 Mortimer Street
London W1N 7RJ
United Kingdom
Telephone: +44 (0)20 7291-8444   Fax: +44 (0)20 7291-8400
E-mail: pr@canneslions.com
Website: http://www.canneslions.com

The International Federation of Periodical Publishers (FIPP)

The International Federation of Periodical Publishers (FIPP) is a trade association with membership from national associations and magazine publishing companies and associate members worldwide.

History

FIPP was founded in Paris, France, in 1925 as the Fédération Internationale de la Presse Périodique. The administration has operated from London since 1939.

FIPP works through national associations and their memberships to establish, promote, and advance on a worldwide basis optimum conditions for the development of periodical publishing. The principal role of FIPP is to foster formal and informal alliances between publishers of magazines to exploit successful publishing ideas, marketing initiatives, and technological opportunities.

Main Membership Organizations

Today, the membership of FIPP consists of more than 34 national magazine associations and almost 100 publishing and associate companies in direct membership. FIPP serves a global market with a total annual advertising expenditure revenue in the region of US$40 billion and approximately 100,000 titles, based on figures from *FIPP/Zenith World Magazine Trends 1999/2000*.

FIPP Mission

The FIPP mission is to promote nationally and internationally the common editorial, cultural, and economic interests of magazine publishers, both in print and electronic media. FIPP focuses its activities on freedom of the press, intellectual property, information provision, freedom to advertise, freedom of distribution, and environmental protection as follows:

- *Information:* FIPP provides the platform to strengthen links between magazine publishers worldwide to exchange knowledge, experience, and ideas.
- *Freedom of the press:* FIPP supports and defends freedom of a pluralistic press.
- *Freedom of advertising:* FIPP upholds the freedom to advertise and the right to free commercial speech and promotes the use of advertising in magazines worldwide.
- *Freedom of distribution:* FIPP supports and defends the freedom to distribute press products and encourages equal opportunities for all publishers to access all markets and all consumers.
- *Intellectual property:* FIPP defends the ownership of the intellectual property rights of publishers, in any form.
- *Environmental protection:* FIPP supports the development of ecological standards and promotes good practices in all parts of the magazine production chain.

Categories of Work and Main Topics of Current Concern

Other priorities and activities in addition to the main activities involve implementing the FIPP mission:

Alliances—to maintain links with other relevant bodies. FIPP is recognized by and involved with the following: the International Advertising Association, the World Federation of Advertisers, the European Association of Advertising Agencies, the European Advertising Tripartite, Distripress, Intergraf, the International Chamber of Commerce, the Index on Censorship, Universal Postal Union, the World Health Organization, and the World Press Freedom Coordinating Committee. Close cooperation is kept with the European Federation of the Periodical Press (FAEP), the World Association of Newspapers (WAN, formerly FIEJ), and the International Publishers Association (IPA—representing book publishers) to deal with current issues affecting publishing throughout the world.

Advertising Promotion—to help boost advertising expenditure in magazines by the exchange of relevant research and other information and by encouraging the conduct of forward-looking research programs. A major undertaking in 1999 was the publication of a report *Take a Fresh Look at Print: New Insights into the Effectiveness of Print in the Media Mix,* which brings together and interprets a large volume of research data demonstrating the contribution that print advertising in general (magazines and newspapers) makes toward an improved return on the investment made by companies in media advertising.

Database—to seek cost-effective ways to develop a database of magazine trends in main markets as well as titles in FIPP membership. *The FIPP/Zenith World Magazine Trends Handbook* is published annually. This is a primary data source of worldwide magazine publishing trends, of practical use to publishers, advertising agencies, consultants, merchant banks, and other press observers. The 1998/99 volume covers 42 countries with information for each country on the number of titles published, readership levels, advertising and copy sales revenue, and title-by-title data for the main titles. The leading publishing groups, main advertisers, and top advertising categories in each country are also identified.

Information. To keep members in touch with each other and allow them to benefit from the knowledge gained by different countries, the international FIPP review of changing markets and marketplaces, *Magazine World,* is sent out five times a year to more than 2,000 key contacts. *Magazine World Update* is a bimonthly fast-fax/e-mail information service available exclusively to members. *PASIG (Publishers Ad Sales Information Group)* is an abstracting service that summarizes a wide range of research material likely to be of interest to publishers. It is currently circulated to members on request, in both hard copy and computerized form, and will shortly be available on the Internet site through the World Advertising Research Centre. (See the article on *Admap.*)

Networking. In addition, there are opportunities for strengthening links between magazine publishers and publishers' associations from all over the world: through meetings of special interest groups, special presentations featured at group/committee meetings, and specially tailored seminars, as well as through the biennial FIPP World Magazine Congress. FIPP has its own Website providing full information about the magazine industry worldwide, including a diary of associated events, publications, and services.

FIPP Secretariat

The present Secretariat is as follows:

- President and COO—Per R. Mortensen
- General Manager—Helen Bland
- Information Executive—Greg Stevenson

International Federation of Periodical Publishers
Queens House
55/56 Lincoln's Inn Fields
London WC2A 3LJ
United Kingdom
Telephone: +44 (0)20 7404-4469   Fax: +44 (0)20 7404-4170
E-mail: info@fipp.com
Website: http://www.fipp.com

The International Radio & Television Society Foundation (IRTS)

The goal of the International Radio & Television Society Foundation (IRTS) is to bring together the wisdom of yesterday's founders, the power of today's leaders, and the promise of tomorrow's young industry professionals.

The foundation evolved from an organization founded in 1939 to provide education and dialogue about important communication issues. As the industry confronts change at every level, the need for a forum capable of helping to create a shared body of knowledge and information continues to grow.

The foundation staff organizes approximately 45 sessions each year. Perhaps the most visible of these are the monthly Newsmaker Luncheons that have long been a tradition on executive calendars. In addition to popular, regularly scheduled seminars, the IRTS's fund-raising supports a four-pronged effort to improve electronic media education:

- The Faculty/Industry seminar, where 75 professors from across the nation come to New York for 5 days of intense meetings and seminars with key industry leaders.
- Annual case studies accessible on the foundation's Website (http://www.irts. org) to assist communications and business school professors in bringing timely, reality-based exercises into the classroom.
- The Minority Career Workshop committed to increasing minority representation in the business. Of those attending the 1998 workshop, 20% were hired as a direct result of the event.
- The Summer Fellowship Program, which has proven to be an instrumental career stepping-stone for some of the industry's most motivated young executives. Graduates of this annual 9-week communications "boot camp" have contributed to every segment of the business.

The IRTS believes that education is a lifelong process that is best achieved through firsthand knowledge. The programs of the organization are planned with this end in view.

International Radio & Television Society Foundation
420 Lexington Avenue, Suite 1714
New York, NY 10170
Telephone: (212) 867-6650   Fax: (212) 867-6653
Website: http://www.irts.org

The Internet Advertising Bureau (IAB)

Founded in 1996, the IAB is the leading on-line advertising association, with more than 300 active member companies in the United States. Its activities include evaluating and recommending standards and practices, undertaking research to document the effectiveness of the on-line medium, and educating the advertising industry about the use of on-line advertising. Current membership includes companies actively engaged in the sales of Internet advertising, with associate membership for companies that support advertising: interactive advertising agencies, measurement companies, research suppliers, technology suppliers, traffic companies, and other organizations from related industries.

A global organization, IAB member countries include Belgium, Canada, France, Germany, the Netherlands, Italy, Switzerland, and the United Kingdom, and it is currently developing membership in Hong Kong, Australia, and Brazil, as well as other countries in Europe. The IAB and the Internet Local Advertising & Commerce Association (ILAC) agreed to combine their organizations in July 1998.

The organization is run by a board and a number of officers. It arranges regular meetings for members. It has set up local committees within the United States and a number of national working committees. The general membership can vote and participate in the committees.

The IAB, which offers a number of specific resources, provides the following benefits to its members:

- A collective voice representing the interests of companies engaged in selling Internet advertising
- A forum for evaluating and shaping the direction of the industry
- An industry-wide view of key developments in on-line advertising
- An educational resource to further professional development
- A platform for communication to diverse audiences, including advertisers, advertising agencies, and other industry groups
- A network of pioneering professionals
- Free job postings in the Job Hotline section of the IAB Website
- Company listing and hot link on IAB Website

Internet Advertising Bureau
Barbara Sweetman, Administrative Director
38 Tyler Circle
Rye, NY 10580
Telephone: (914) 921-6988   Fax: (914) 967-2538
E-mail: barbara@iab.net
Website: http://www.iab.net

The Magazine Publishers of America (MPA)

The Magazine Publishers of America (MPA) is the industry association for consumer magazines. Established in 1919, the MPA represents more than 200 U.S.-based publishing companies with more than 1,200 titles, more than 75 international companies, and more than 90 associate members providing services to the industry.

Objectives

The MPA continues to aggressively pursue the five major objectives defined by its Board of Directors:

1. Building confidence in the future of magazines
2. Increasing our share of advertising dollars

3. Protecting our interests in the government arena
4. Promoting magazine readership and sales
5. Developing new revenues from magazine franchises

Departments

Government Affairs. The MPA promotes and protects the industry's interests at all levels of government. To receive the *Washington Newsletter* or for information about MPA Government Affairs activities, call Government Affairs at (202) 296-7277 or send e-mail to government_affairs@magazine.org

Advertising, Marketing, and Research. The MPA works to increase magazines' share of the overall advertising market. To find out more about magazine effectiveness presentations and research and how to integrate industry information into sales efforts, call Advertising Marketing at (212) 872-3724 or send e-mail to ad_mktg@magazine.org

Consumer Marketing. The MPA works to increase magazine sales through both single-copy and subscription distribution channels. To receive the *Consumer Marketing Newsletter* or for information on the Retail Conference, call Consumer Marketing at (212) 872-3772 or send e-mail to consumer_marketing@magazine.org

International Affairs. The MPA serves as a liaison and information source for domestic and international members regarding publishing outside the United States. In recent years, the magazine business has become truly global. Today's magazines move from country to country and language to language with ever-increasing ease. Hand in hand with this surge, the MPA has become a nexus for publishers throughout the world. For more information or to receive *The Newsletter of International Publishing,* call International Affairs at (212) 872-3771 or send e-mail to international@magazine.org

Professional Development. The continuing vigor of the MPA, and the strength of the industry as a whole, depends greatly on forums for exchanging information. The MPA conducts nearly 100 practical seminars and workshops covering all areas of magazine publishing. For more information, call Professional Development at (212) 872-3767 or send e-mail to prof_dev@magazine.org

Media Credit Association (MCA). The MCA monitors the payment habits of advertising agencies and clients to assist publishers in making sound credit decisions. For more information, call MCA at (212) 872-3777 or send e-mail to mca@magazine.org

Information Center. The MPA compiles industry-specific information from a wide variety of sources for its members and their clients. The Information Center is a storehouse of information both historical and current concerning magazines. Thousands of inquiries are answered each year from members, the advertising community, and the press on virtually all aspects of magazine publishing. For more information, call the Information Center at (212) 872-3745 or (212) 872-3746 or send e-mail to infocenter@magazine.org

Membership. The MPA is the trade association for the consumer magazine industry representing more than 200 domestic publishing companies. Companies that issue magazines at least four times per year are eligible to join. MPA also accepts international publishing members as well as associate members, which are service providers to the industry. MPA members benefit from government representation, promotion of the medium to the ad community and to retail outlets, industry-specific information and research, access to professional development programs, and networking among peers. For more information on Membership call (212) 872-3751 or send e-mail to membership@magazine.org

Publishers Information Bureau (PIB). The Publishers Information Bureau is a membership organization that measures magazine advertising spending and advertising pages by category and title. With a membership representing roughly 85% of consumer magazine advertising in the United States, PIB is recognized as the primary source for consumer magazine advertising data. For access to this information, call the MPA Information Center at (212) 872-3746 or send e-mail to pib@magazine.org

Research

AC Nielsen Sales Scan. The Sales Scan compares the purchase behavior of consumer households that were exposed to specific campaigns in magazines with a matched group of households that were not exposed to magazine advertising. The impact of 10 magazine campaigns running in the second quarter of 1998 was analyzed, as well as the relative sales impact of the advertising over time.

1999 Magazine Handbook. This is a comprehensive guide for advertisers, advertising agencies, and magazine marketers.

Advertising Effectiveness Survey (Millward Brown). This is a study documenting the role magazines play in a media mix.

PIB Ad Revenue and Page Totals. This is the Publishers Information Bureau magazine advertising revenue report.

Foote, Cone & Belding (FCB) Media Research Report: Questioning the Magazine Niche Myth. This edition of FCB's *Media Research Report* gives assurance that magazines, far from being relics living on borrowed time, are a vibrant medium. They have kept pace with the changing media landscape and are very much part of the contemporary scene, commenting and advising on all facets of the frenetic lives of today.

The Mercer Study. In light of numerous changes in the single-copy magazine channel in recent years, the MPA determined in mid-1998 that the time was right to take a fresh, independent look at how the magazine industry as a whole could take positive, concerted action to improve performance.

Multi-Media Research Study: The Advertising Impact of Magazines in Conjunction with Television. This research study, conducted in two waves by the PreTesting Company and funded by the MPA, is a landmark study that evolved out of a need by advertisers, ad agencies, and publishers to learn more about the synergy of television and magazine advertising.

Magazine Publishers of America
New York
919 Third Avenue
New York, NY 10022
Telephone: (212) 872-3700   Fax: (212) 888-4217
Washington, DC
1211 Connecticut Avenue, NW
Washington, DC 20036
Telephone: (202) 296-7277   Fax: (202) 296-0343
Website: http://www.magazine.org

The Marketing Science Institute (MSI)

The Marketing Science Institute (MSI) is a not-for-profit institute established in 1961 as a bridge between business and academia. Its mission is to bring together executives and academics in marketing and related fields to create knowledge that will improve business thought and practice. Today, MSI's worldwide network includes executives from approximately 70 sponsoring corporations and leading researchers from more than 100 universities.

At the core of MSI's activities is the institute's research-priority-setting process. Every 2 years, the MSI board of trustees—representing member companies and the academic community—identify issues of key importance on which they want to encourage academic research. MSI then solicits research proposals on these priority topics and funds research projects conducted by university scholars. At any given time, there are 100 to 125 MSI-sponsored projects in progress.

Research findings are presented at members-only conferences and workshops. At these meetings, new ideas about implementation and future research are stimulated by discussion among MSI-company executives and marketing scholars.

Completed research projects are also reported and distributed in the MSI working paper series, which now includes well over 200 current titles (as well as a backlist of about 300 titles). These address a broad spectrum of management issues related to marketing, including a number on advertising and promotion. The working papers present significant new knowledge in the field, emphasizing whenever possible how this knowledge will affect both business practice and theory. Most subsequently appear in scholarly journals.

In addition, *Insights from MSI,* a newsletter targeted specifically toward the managerial audience, highlights new ideas and insights from current research that will assist managers in improving business performance.

Marketing Science Institute
1000 Massachusetts Avenue
Cambridge, MA 02138-5396
Telephone: (617) 491-2060   Fax: (617) 491-2065
Website: http://www.msi.org

The Marketing Society (United Kingdom)

The Marketing Society was formed 40 years ago and has grown to become the most influential and respected professional body for senior marketers and general managers in marketing-oriented companies in the United Kingdom. Membership is open only to individuals; there are no corporate members. The society's mission statement is that the society should be

> the one professional body to which membership is essential for all senior marketers. The Marketing Society aims to be universally accepted as the champion of marketing excellence, influencing its successful evolution, inspiring and supporting Society members, and encouraging debate and contacts between them.

The society has approximately 3,500 members. One third are at the chairman/managing director/CEO level. One third are marketing directors, and one third are senior marketing managers.

The society offers a wide range of relevant member benefits. Principal among these are the following:

- A nation-wide series of conferences, events, and seminars addressed by top business leaders on the key topical issues of the day. Attendance at most of these events is free of cost to members.
- *Market Leader.* A prestigious journal free to members. Available on subscription to nonmembers. (See separate article.)
- A special Careers Advisory Service in the members' section of the society's Website.

Marketing Society
St. George's House
3—5 Pepys Road
London SW20 8NJ
United Kingdom
Telephone: +44 (0)20 8879-3464   Fax: +44 (0)20 8879-0362
E-mail: info@marketing-society.org.uk
Website: http://www.marketing-society.org.uk

The Market Research Council

The Market Research Council was organized and held its first official meeting (with 13 members present) on January 14, 1927, at the Harvard Club in New York City. The purpose of its organization was to promote marketing research.

The major objectives of the Market Research Council are these:

- To stimulate scientific study and sound thinking in marketing research theory and practical application
- To strive constantly for advancement in the techniques of fact finding, analysis, and presentations
- To broaden the field for marketing research by stimulating a wider acceptance and use of its services
- To encourage the study of marketing research as a profession in schools and colleges
- To provide the focal point around which marketing research men and women can gather for the development and advancement of their mutual interests
- To invite speakers to the monthly meetings to discuss studies, techniques, and problems pertaining to marketing research related subjects

The Market Research Council, with approximately 188 members, has four categories of membership and meets the third Friday of each month (September—June) at the Yale Club of New York.

Market Research Council
234 Fifth Avenue, Suite 403
New York, NY 10001
Telephone: (212) 481-3038   Fax: (212) 481-3071
E-mail: mgmtoffice@aol.com

The Market Research Society (MRS) (United Kingdom)

David Barr

With more than 8,000 members worldwide, the Market Research Society (MRS), based in the United Kingdom, is the largest international membership organization for professional research practitioners and others with an interest in market, social, and opinion research. As such, it is the leading provider of professional codes and qualifications, as well as the training and career development resources to support these. MRS is a substantial supplier of publications and information services, conferences and seminars, and many other networking opportunities. It is also "the voice of the profession" in its media relations and public affairs activities.

Membership in the society is available within various grades offering a range of associated benefits. Qualification-based entry was introduced at the beginning of 1997. All members are required to abide by the MRS Code of Conduct when carrying out research, and a Professional Standards Committee meets regularly to review and enforce the code, which reflects not only the ethical rules but also legislation that may impose on the conduct of bona fide market research.

Membership of the MRS reflects a wide spectrum of interests, and these are represented by various Special Interest Groups—for example, Independent Consultants, Census, Human Resource, General Insurance, Business and Industrial, Online Research, and International Research. Events and meetings are held on a regular basis.

The MRS runs a full program of residential and single-day training courses—ranging from "Introductory and Essentials" courses providing a basic grounding in the principles of research to "Refining Skills" and "Specialist" courses for the advanced researcher. All courses are open to nonmembers and are fully integrated into the Continuing Professional Development programs. Business and management skills are included in the program, in addition to the "craft" skills of research.

The MRS produces a wide range of publications: *Research,* a news-based magazine aimed at keeping members up to date with industry news and events; *ResearchPlus,* a quarterly themed publication, each issue covering a different aspect or topic (recent coverage has included Business to Business, International Research, and Customer Care); *MRScene,* the house magazine of the MRS, providing a regular forum of communication on professional matters and society activities; *Journal of the Market Research Society,* a quarterly academic journal; and the *Research Buyer's Guide,* a directory of bona fide market research agencies.

The MRS flagship event is the annual conference, held in March each year. The conference attracts attendance of over 1,000, including many international delegates. As well as being an invaluable opportunity to meet colleagues and make new contacts, the conference provides a forum for discussion of current issues and developments in market research. Several more specialist seminars are also held throughout the year on topics such as advertising and media research.

Several projects aim to encourage, recognize, and reward the accomplishment of excellence. Distinguished individuals can be awarded Fellowship of the Market Research Society (FMRS). The best papers at the annual conference, and from those published in the *Journal of the Market Research Society,* are also acclaimed at an annual awards ceremony.

On a broader level, the Market Research Society is funding an initiative to improve perceptions of market research among the media, business community, and the general public with special emphasis on differentiating between professional market research and other forms of data collecting. In addition, a public affairs program is directed at informing and influencing government, regulators, and policymakers.

Market Research Society
15 Northburgh Street
London EC1V 0JR
United Kingdom
Telephone: +44 (0)20 7490-4911   Fax: +44 (0)20 7490-0608
Website: http://www.marketresearch.org.uk

The Market Research Society of Australia (MRSA)

Mission

The mission that describes the essence of the Market Research Society of Australia (MRSA) and its ambitions in a way that provides a rationale for it to exist, is to develop and implement market research in Australia by providing standards, ongoing education, and member services, and by informing the wider community.

Vision

A vision statement that provides a clear picture of what the members of the MRSA are trying to create together becomes a compass when other indicators of direction seem to be gone. The MRSA's vision statement is for market research to be understood, valued, and widely used by business, government, and the community, and for the MRSA qualifications and standards to be the guarantee of quality.

Objectives

- To promote market research courses within tertiary institutions and to continually enhance the professional skills of members
- To establish and maintain high technical and ethical standards
- To promote the value and benefits of market research by communicating with the government, clients, and the public
- To meet the varied needs of members by providing the range of service consistent with the efficient use of resources
- To provide and demonstrate positive leadership to members and others on all matters of concern to the profession
- To build the membership by securing the participation of all members of the profession
- To develop an efficient organization structure and administration to ensure that the most effective use is made of time and funds contributed by members

Brief History

A burgeoning of interest in market research led to the formation of the Market Research Society of Victoria in August 1955. When New South Wales formed a division in 1959, the name of the total society was changed to the Market Research Society of Australia and a National Council was formed to coordinate the activities of the two divisions. Further divisions of the society were formed in South Australia (1960), Western Australia (1969), and Queensland (1975). The society today has over 1,500 members nationally. In 1960, the MRSA became a member of the International Marketing Federation. In 1968, the MRSA played host to the third Asian and Pacific Marketing Conference of the International Marketing Federation. Australian market researchers and the MRSA itself are both now accepted in high standing in the league of international market researchers.

The first code of Marketing and Social Research Practice was published by the European Society for Opinion and Market Research (ESOMAR) in 1948. This was followed by a number of codes prepared by national market research societies and by other bodies such as the International Chamber of Commerce (ICC), which represents the international marketing community. In 1976, ESOMAR and the ICC decided that it would be preferable to have a single International Code instead of the differing ones, and a joint ICC/ESOMAR Code was therefore published in the following year (with revisions in 1986).

Subsequent changes in the marketing and social environment, new developments in market research methods, and a great increase in international activities of all kinds, including legislation, led ESOMAR to prepare a new version of the International Code in 1994. This new version sets out as concisely as possible the basic ethical and business principles that govern the practice of market and social research. It specifies the rules that are to be followed in dealing with the general public and with the business community, including clients and other members of the profession.

After a review of the code, the MRSA adopted the ICC/ESOMAR Code in 1995, as the MRSA Code of Professional Behavior.

Membership

Members include economic analysts, psychologists, social researchers, market researchers, marketing analysts, people in marketing and advertising management, fieldwork suppliers, interviewers, statisticians, users of market research, academics, and students.

Main Activities

- Diploma of market research through a number of accredited universities
- Planning and implementation of 1- and 2-day training courses
- Annual national conference
- Seminars
- Monthly members newsletter
- *National Directory and Year Book*
- *Bi-Annual Directory of Syndicated Research*
- *Australasian Journal of Market Research*
- 1300 Survey Line—for respondents to check the bona fide of interviewers
- Comprehensive, informative Website

Market Research Society of Australia
Level 2
345 Pacific Highway
Crows Nest, NSW 2065
Mailing address:
PO Box 697
North Sydney, NSW 2059
Australia
Telephone: +61 (2) 9955-4830   Fax: +61 (2) 9955-5746
E-mail: sydney@bigpond.com.au
Website: http://www.mrsa.com.au

The Media Research Club of Chicago (MRCC)

The Media Research Club of Chicago is the most vigorous organization of its type in the United States. It was founded in 1953, when three good friends met for lunch at a restaurant named L'Aglon on the southeast corner of Rush and Ontario. They were Gene Blackwell (then research director of *American Weekly*), Ira Bix (research director of *Farm Journal*), and Jean Fletcher of the Newspaper Advertising Bureau. They formed the nucleus of what was first an informal association of research directors from various Chicago print media companies.

The club's membership was initially limited to researchers from the print media: magazines and the Chicago newspapers. They were Myra Fox of Million Market Newspapers, Tom Patrick and Don Parise of the *Chicago Tribune*, Barbara Johnson of CBS Publications, Martin Tarpey and Angelo Juarez of the *Chicago Sun-Times*, Larry Tootikian of *Woman's Day*, and Paul Gillete of *Pulse*.

The first president of the club was Jean Fletcher. She was responsible for inviting speakers to every club luncheon. It is not known who succeeded her as president, but we do know that Angelo Juarez, Hugh Martin, and Larry Tootikian served as presidents in the 1960s. Hugh Martin, then research director at WIND (a Chicago radio station), had the distinction of being the first club president from the broadcast community. Through the early 1970s, the following people served as president: Tom Patrick of the *Chicago Tribune,* Barbara Johnson of CBS Publications, Andy Donchak and Linda Fischer of WIND, and Sue Hodgson of IMS (Interactive Marketing Systems). The latter was the first president from the media research supplier's side.

Luncheon meetings from the 1950s to the late 1970s were quite informal, with 4 to 15 people attending. Luncheon speakers were usually from advertising agencies or research suppliers. Occasionally, the members would present some of the work they themselves had done.

Some of the first people who came to speak at club luncheons were Jim Yergin, who developed radio's NuMath; Seymour Banks and Joe Plummer of Leo Burnett; Ron Kaatz of J. Walter Thompson; Gale Metzger of Statistical Research, Inc.; Leo Bogart of the Newspaper Advertising Bureau; and Joan Baer of Post/Keyes/Gardner.

During the presidency of Ray Sheehy (WGN Radio)—1979 to 1981—there was greater participation from advertising agencies and media research suppliers. Sheehy's desire to expand the membership led to increased attendance at MRCC luncheons. Indeed, Kevin Killion, then with Leo Burnett's Media Research staff, was the next president, thus becoming the first club president from the agency side.

Alice Sylvester (J. Walter Thompson), in her first year as president, organized the club's first biennial research symposium. The topic that year was TV commercial zapping. The symposium drew a surprisingly large number of people from New York as well as Chicago, since it was the first event of its kind that dealt with the issue of commercial avoidance. The club also formalized its Academic Exchange Program, which provided college students with their first exposure to media research as a profession.

Under the presidency of Roger Baron (Foote, Cone & Belding), the MRCC established a scholarship fund for college students majoring in the field of advertising. That same year, 1989, the MRCC also established and promoted design standards for media research software development. The following year, the club held its first computer applications exposition and also began to publish its monthly newsletter, *The MRCC Review,* with Bernadette Cognac, vice president and senior account manager of Simmons Market Research Bureau, as editor.

In 1991, the MRCC decided to change its academic grants from funding scholarship to funding original media research studies. Two doctoral students were the first recipients of the MRCC research awards: Rose Johnson of Georgia State University looked at how television commercial clutter affects older viewers; Lauren Tucker of the University of Wisconsin—Madison examined African American values and how they may affect product and media usage.

The presidency of Beth Uyenco (DDB Needham) filled the club's coffers and brought in a wide range of speakers. The 1992 symposium on micromarketing was a big success, and a concerted effort to attract more interest in the academic community resulted in educators joining from universities in Illinois and Wisconsin.

During his 1993-94 presidency, Bill Ross (Nielsen Media Research) resurrected the MRCC Media Research and Computer Expo, originally started in 1990. It has become one of the best attended industry expositions outside New York. In 1994, Ross spearheaded Media Research in an Interactive World, the first symposium of its kind that concentrated on the issue of measurement in the interactive arena.

In 1995, the club newsletter, *The MRCC Review,* was redesigned and expanded. And for the first time, the MRCC began to cosponsor events, including Guerrilla Media, in conjunction with the American Marketing Association, and How Media Work, with *Inside Media* and Katz Television Group. In 1996, the club expanded its educational activities, supporting two $1,000 research awards to doctoral students and establishing the $1,000 Ronald Kaatz Student Internship in media research.

The programs in 1997 brought in record numbers of attendees to the monthly meetings. The Expo was expanded not only to include both marketing and media research but also to offer international software suppliers the opportunity to exhibit their wares. In 1998, the club continued to support media research education, offering two $1,000 research awards as well as two $1,000 student internships.

The MRCC continues to have many speakers from media research suppliers, but the scope has expanded to include speakers from advertisers, agencies, and the media as well. Attendance at monthly meetings is open to members and nonmembers. Monthly meetings draw an average of 70 people, about half of whom are members.

The MRCC has gained national stature through its biennial symposia, research supplier workshops, research grants, and luncheon programs that include speakers from across the country. It has evolved into a genuine national forum for the exchange of ideas among media research professionals.

The newsletter of the organization, *MRCC Review,* contains many articles of interest to media professionals. It is published nine times per year.

The president until 2001 is Scott Turner, who can be reached at the following:

Mediamark Research Inc.
444 N. Michigan Avenue
Chicago, IL 60611
Telephone: 1-800-245-1551   4Fax: (312) 329-0443
E-mail: sturner@chi.mediamark.com
Website: www.mrcconline.com

The National Advertising Division, National Advertising Review Board, and the Self-Regulation of Advertising

Rana Said

A dvertising is not a highly trusted industry. Consumers, in general, view advertising as far more misleading and deceptive than it is allowed to be by law. This was not always the case. Early studies of consumers' attitudes indicated that advertising did not rank highly among the important issues in Americans' lives, and their specific attitude to the subject was, on the whole, one of indifference.[1] Not until the late 1960s was this attitude replaced with a growing skepticism of business in general and advertising in particular, coinciding with the rise of consumerism and consumer advocates. During this time, consumer protection agencies created new departments to handle consumer information, and legal services were made increasingly available to the public. All these factors created a climate in the late 1960s and early 1970s of high demand for more regulatory action.

The Federal Trade Commission (FTC) and state legislation represent two methods of controlling advertising through legislation. The FTC, described elsewhere in this volume, performs a policing function by being the primary federal mechanism for taking action against deceptive or unfair advertising, and by its existence, it has the added function of deterring untruthful advertising through threat of action. With such a powerful legislative body in place, why is it necessary for the industry to have its own self-regulatory mechanism? An answer to this will be outlined in this chapter by studying the current system for self-regulation and other methods of regulation not embodied in the law.

The primary mechanism of industry self-regulation is an industry body: the National Advertising Division and the National Advertising Review Board (hereafter referred to as NAD/NARB); its main objective is to advocate the highest standards of truth and accuracy in national advertising. The NAD/NARB is primarily in place to regulate advertising for the benefit of both the consumers and other advertisers, ensuring that they, too, play by the rules. A secondary role of the NAD/NARB is a self-interested one: to maintain the perception that the advertising industry is taking the initiative to control its own. Advertising is not free from puffery or the use of tasteless tactics; indeed, many advertisements rely solely on these techniques for lack of a better idea. While consumers have a certain degree of tolerance for use of such techniques in advertising, they have virtually none for advertising that does not present a truthful or accurate picture of the product. Everyone—the consumer, the advertiser and the advertising agency—stands to lose from deceptive advertising. The majority of advertising is for consumer goods that are purchased *repeatedly,* and there is no stronger punishment than the consumer's not buying the product again.

In answering the question posed earlier—Why are self-regulatory methods in place?—it is worthwhile to examine the history, structure, and current mechanism of the NAD/NARB. In addition, other methods of self-regulation, such as media prescreening and preclearance methods, that are not embodied in the law but which contribute to keeping deceptive advertising away from the consumer, will be described briefly. Self-regulation methods differ substantially from federal and state legislation on several levels, the most important of which is their degree of effectiveness in accomplishing what they are in place to do.

Background

Founded as a centralized regulation mechanism, the NAD/NARB system was a reaction to increased public criticism of advertisers and the advertising industry. Encouraged by advocates such as Ralph Nader, consumers aimed their anger at the FTC, which was perceived as being ineffective in controlling the advertising industry. This sentiment coincided with Nader's writings and an American Bar Association (ABA) report in 1969, both of which concluded that the FTC was not effectively carrying out its job of protecting the consumer. The general view was that *more* control was needed. The FTC's control of the advertising industry depends on the administration in place, and like many branches of the federal government, the power of the FTC varies in level of control and regulation depending on the particular presidency. This was evident during the 1980s when deregulation under the Reagan administration weakened the FTC's overall control. Furthermore, the level of advertising self-regulation itself depends on other social and economic factors and varies according to government regulation.

The formation of the NAD/NARB signified the attempt on the part of the industry (a) to take a proactive role in response to the criticism cast toward advertising, (b) to protect consumers and advertisers from deceptive advertising, and (c) to pre-empt an increase in government intervention and legislation. The latter is, arguably, the main *raison d'être* of the NAD/NARB mechanism.

History of the NAD/NARB

In 1971, the National Advertising Review Council (NARC), a nonprofit corporation, was founded as a governing body for the NARB. The four supporting organizations were (a) the Council of Better Business Bureaus (CBBB) (the local Better Business Bureaus operate advertising review boards), (b) the American Association of Advertising Agencies (AAAA), (c) the Association of National Advertisers (ANA), and (d) the American Advertising Federation (AAF). The NAD—the National Advertising Division of the CBBB—was subsequently assigned to be the NARB's investigative unit. The NAD's procedures state that "The NAD shall be responsible for receiving or initiating, evaluating, investigating, analyzing, and holding initial negotiations with an advertiser on complaints or questions from any source involving the truth or accuracy of national advertising." The NAD handles this in one of two ways: It may either solve a dispute or direct it to the NARB for review.

The establishment of the NAD/NARB can be attributed to the efforts of three men: Howard Bell, then president of the AAF; Victor Elting Jr., then vice president of advertising for Quaker Oats Company; and Fred Baker, a past AAF chairman.[2] These men symbolized the cooperative efforts of the advertisers and the advertising industry associations. Elting was the prime mover in sketching the early outline for the NARB, which loosely resembled the British self-regulatory mechanism—the Advertising Standards Authority (ASA). Elting presented his idea to the Chicago Advertising Club on September 17, 1970. His original draft saw the NARB as a review council of seven members. His earliest proposal was simple enough and involved having a code director and a staff to receive complaints, investigate them, and negotiate solutions with advertisers in private; a case would be closed when the advertiser modified the advertisement. The pressure felt by the advertising industry was reflected in Elting's concluding remarks to the Chicago Advertising Club: "There are ticking sounds that we hear in all the pressure groups, congressional hearings, and other forums that are meeting to decide our fate. Let's defuse them by having the strength and courage to determine our fate for ourselves."[3]

In the summer of 1971, the NAD was finally staffed and headed by Roger Purdon, a former creative director of Leo Burnett in Great Britain. The NARB's first chairman was Charles Yost, a past U.S. ambassador to the United Nations. The first members were a mix of agency executives, academics, and executives from among the large advertisers.

The absence of a specific code for the NARB is a remnant of its earliest days when complaints were evaluated under other existing codes, such as the Advertising Code of American Businesses and the Creative Code of the AAAA. By the time the final proposal for the NARB was ready to be presented, it had undergone several changes; the primary one was the removal of a media sanction because it would have violated antitrust laws, and this weakened the threatening power that the NARB would have possessed.

The NARC board of directors is charged with providing counsel and advice regarding the self-regulatory mechanism of the NARB. The NARB acts as the appellate branch of the NAD in cases in which advertisers refuse to accept the NAD decision. Even though the NAD/NARB is an industry mechanism and some have referred to it as a "form of private government,"[4] it coexists and is interdependent with the FTC. Much of the criticism toward the NAD/NARB is characteristic of criticism of all industry self-regulatory mechanisms—doubt that a trade-supported regulatory body would provide an objective scrutiny of deceptive advertising. Nonetheless, the FTC and the NAD/NARB work in conjunction with each other; if a case is presented that is legal in nature, the NAD forwards it to the appropriate legal agency, and having the NAD/NARB in place provides an added scrutiny for cases that are deceptive in nature.

Early Cases

The NARB's earliest days were difficult. Consumer groups and public members eager to test this new mechanism submitted large numbers of complaints that were often not within the realm of the NAD. An early example involved a complaint against Mattel's *Shoppin' Cheryl Doll.* It was claimed that it encouraged a vast consumption of goods. Clearly, this was not within the NARB's definition of deceptive advertising and was therefore dismissed.[5]

Barely 3 years old, the NAD/NARB's existence was threatened as a result of what was later called "the Denver Case." A complaint was brought to the local Better Business Bureau advertising review board in Denver, Colorado, against a weight reduction company, Pat Walker's, relating to false testimonials and promises claimed in the advertising. However, instead of responding to the review board, Walker's filed suit against the local advertising review board and the local Better Business Bureau citing infringement of civil rights laws, the Fourteenth Amendment, and antitrust laws. Although the case was against the local advertising review board, it was still considered a threat to the NARB at large because the local mechanism functions in the same way as the NAD/NARB. After a legal and financial battle that lasted 9 months, the decision was announced in favor of the local advertising review board: The suit was dismissed.

Some of the criticism of the system at that time was well-founded. As with any new mechanism, things moved slowly, and the internal devices that formed the basis of the mechanism sometimes failed. Complaints were lost, and records were not always in order. On the whole, the first couple of years were turbulent, and the general opinion was that the system was not doing much in regulating the industry. This opinion was later modified as the NAD/NARB made some positive procedural and operational adjustments in response to a lot of the criticism.

Advertising to Children

In areas such as advertising to children, the overlap between the FTC and the NAD/NARB makes sense. In 1974, 3 years after the formation of the NAD and following more distrust and criticism of children's advertising (as well as advertising posing as children's programming), the Children's Review Unit (CRU), now the Children's Advertising Review Unit (CARU), was established as a division of the NAD to promote responsible advertising to children. (See the article describing the Children's Advertising Review Unit.) This formation resulted in three main actions:

1. Adoption of a set of standards based on the Association of National Advertisers' Children's Television Advertising Guidelines
2. The beginning of systematic monitoring of children's TV commercials, together with continual review of commercials submitted to the unit before being granted clearance for broadcast
3. The seeking of counsel from professionals knowledgeable about children's perception and behavior

Regarding children's TV advertising, two major concerns were (a) the role of host-selling or -sponsored programs that may be disguised as programming and (b) the overlapping areas between sponsored programs as entertainment and regular programming as entertainment.

Purpose of the NAD/NARB

The main purpose of the NARB as written in its Statement of Organization and Procedures is to "sustain high standards of truth and accuracy in national advertising." It should be noted that the NAD/NARB body was formed to handle "national advertising." This is defined in the CBBB procedures as "paid commercial advertising disseminated in all of the United States, or in a substantial section thereof, or test-market advertising prepared for national campaigns." Issues pertaining to local advertising are dealt with through a different review mechanism under the Better Business Bureaus (BBBs) and will be discussed in a later section. In addition, the NAD/NARB is concerned solely with matters of truth or accuracy in advertising or with advertising's capacity to mislead. These two issues are actually not as precisely defined as they sound: Many advertisements are "borderline." The decision is at times reliant on subjective judgment. "Capacity to mislead," in this case, is different from the FTC's stringent definition of that phrase. In simplest terms, an advertisement is considered misleading if the claim made is not justifiable. The NAD standard for "deception" is far wider than the literal and legal one. The NAD/NARB uses these as general guidelines, although no formal code exists. Complaints that relate to issues of taste or decency are not heard by the NAD, with limited special exceptions. In such a case, the items are referred to the NARB for study, completely bypassing the NAD in the process. Furthermore, if the complaint relates to issues of unlawful business practices, it will be referred to a suitable government agency.

To date, the NAD/NARB has dealt with a good deal more than 3,000 cases. While this is a substantial number, it is insignificant in relation to the number of national advertisements aired or printed each year. On average, the NAD/NARB reviews approximately 200 advertisements per year.

The primary aim of the NAD/NARB when it was established was to improve advertising as a whole. The specific guidelines were these:

- To deal with matters of fact, truth, and accuracy
- To deal with substantiation
- To ensure that advertising provides relevant and adequate disclosure
- To ensure that advertising contains no false disparagement
- To ensure that advertising contains no deception, intended or otherwise
- To ensure that advertising is in accordance with FTC precedents

While these guidelines are helpful in deciding on cases in the postmortem analysis of advertisements that are brought to the NAD/NARB, they are less helpful as overall guidance to monitoring advertisements, because they are fairly general. Researchers have made recommendations for making the system more effective, primarily by the adoption of a formalized code for the NAD/NARB.

Local Advertising

The NAD/NARB does not oversee cases pertaining to local advertising. Such complaints and issues are handled by the local BBB units or local advertising review boards (LARBs). The BBB provides local businesses with "advice" regarding the legal aspects of advertising, specifically in issues of truth and accuracy, but unlike other regulatory agencies, the BBB screens advertisements before the fact. The LARBs are patterned after the NAD/NARB and are directed at businesses advertising locally.

Structure of the NAD/NARB

The NARB is the top tier of the multitiered NAD/NARB system. The NARB consists of a chairman and 70 members (and as many alternate members as the chairman specifies). Of these, 40 members must be affiliated with an advertiser; 20 with an advertising agency; and to ensure representation, 10 are public members. The chairman is elected by the NARC Board of Directors and holds office for 1 year; all other members, also selected by the NARC, hold office for 2 years. The responsibility for appointing an NARB hearing panel is borne by the chairman. Each of these hearing panels is composed of 5 NARB members. The role of the NAD as the investigative arm of the NARB is twofold:

1. It serves as a hearing body to which consumers or competitive advertisers may bring their complaints.
2. Through routine monitoring of broadcast, cable, and print advertising, it may initiate cases itself.

The length of time it takes a case to be completed is variable. However, unlike government legal processes, it is not unusual for a case to be resolved in a matter of months.

How the NAD/NARB Works:
The Resolution Process

The process by which the complaint is handled is best illustrated graphically (see Figure 8). The complainant first contacts the NAD with the issue. After checking the advertisement, the NAD can take one of three actions. If the advertisement does not fall within the definition of "national" and is judged not to fall into the "truth and accuracy" function of the NAD, the complaint is de-

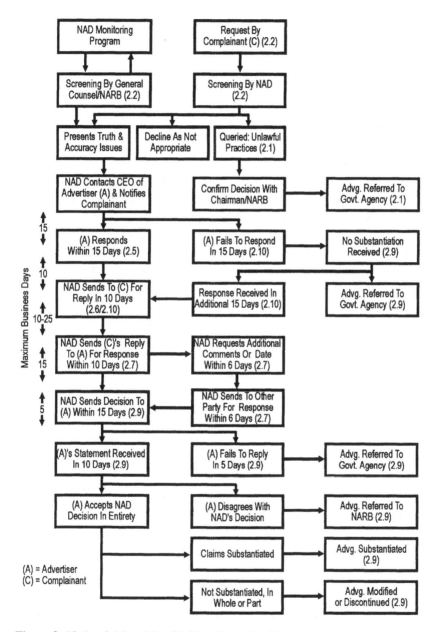

Figure 8. National Advertising Division Resolution Process

NOTE: The numbers in parentheses refer to sections in NAD/NARB/CARU Procedures, as amended September 29, 1993.

clined as "not appropriate." If the initial review by the NAD indicates that the advertising promotes an unlawful product or service or is false, deceptive, or misleading, and the advertiser will not participate in the self-regulatory process, NAD prepares a review of the facts with relevant exhibits and after consulting with the NARB chairman, forwards this to the appropriate federal or state law enforcement agency.

National Advertising Division Resolution Process

If, after the preliminary checking process, the NAD finds that the complaint relates to issues of "truth and accuracy" and is "national," then it contacts the CEO of the "offending" advertiser and notifies the complainant. If the advertiser fails to respond within the allocated 15 days and no substantiation is received, the advertising is referred to a government agency. If the advertiser does respond, the NAD sends it to the complainant for reply and forwards the complainant's reply to the advertiser for response. The NAD then prepares its decision on the truth and accuracy of the claims at issue and provides a copy of the "final case decision" to the advertiser who in 10 days must provide an "Advertiser's Statement." In cases in which the NAD decides that some claims are still not substantiated, this statement makes clear whether or not the advertiser agrees to modify or discontinue the advertising. If the advertiser fails to reply, the advertising is referred to a government agency. If, however, the advertiser accepts the NAD decision in its entirety and substantiates the claims, the case is considered closed. If the advertiser accepts the decision but the claims are not substantiated, the advertising is modified or discontinued.

If the advertiser disagrees with the NAD's decision, the advertising is referred to the NARB for an appeal of the decision. If the advertiser still disagrees with the NARB's decision, the case is forwarded to the FTC or the appropriate government agency. This seldom occurs. In fact, it was more than 20 years before a case was referred to the FTC by the NARB for the first time after an advertiser refused to modify a commercial.

Publication of Results of Complaints

The issue of publicity plagued the system in its early years. Details about cases, including names of the defendants, "leaked" to the press, and refusal by the

NARB to discuss active cases was translated by the trade press as shielding nonperformance. In 1972, the NARC ruled that outcomes of cases would be released only when the advertiser and complainant agreed.

Today, the results of the cases are published in the *NAD Case Reports* produced at least 10 times each year. This "newsletter" is divided into three sections: advertising referred to NARB, advertising substantiated, and advertising modified or discontinued. Each case report includes a summary of the cases concluded during the previous month. In these case reports, the advertiser's name is listed, followed by the basis of inquiry and the decision and, where applicable, an advertiser's statement or a resolution statement. Some case summaries are also reported in the CBBB's *Advertising Topics* newsletter, and copies of panel reports are available from the NARB. The trade press frequently reports on the outcome of cases after they have been resolved or closed. When substantiation is required by the advertiser, this is printed under the section of "advertising substantiated," followed by a brief description of the basis of inquiry and the decision.

Other Regulatory Mechanisms

Other forms of regulation exist that are not embedded in the law but which also serve to keep advertisers in line. The primary method, preclearance by the media, relates more to issues of taste and decency.

Television Networks and Magazines

Most of the major television networks and other traditional broadcast and print media have followed their own codes for accepting advertisements. For example, until 1982, the National Association of Broadcasters (NAB) had a number of stringent rules and regulations under its NAB "Code of Good Practice" which was set up in 1929. Part of this code related to advertising, and ironically, the dissolution of the NAB code was because of a court ruling that it placed unjustified restrictions on advertising. Following that, the code was eliminated in its entirety. Although the code no longer exists, broadcasters still have the final say in accepting advertising.

Examples of prescreening also exist in the print media. *Reader's Digest* has stringent codes governing the acceptance of advertisements. As is clearly stated in its media kit, "Advertising for cigarette, tobacco and alcoholic beverage products is not accepted." The editors of the magazine are cautious about issues of taste and decency and scrutinize advertisements involving nudity and suggestive advertisements on a case-by-case basis. Political advertisements that are too partisan in tone are also handled cautiously and often rejected. The Magazine Publishers of America (MPA) has set down guidelines for acceptance of advertisements that include labeling an advertisement that resembles an editorial piece. *Reader's Digest* is not alone in abiding by this last guideline. In terms of acceptance of advertising and content, few magazines actually set stringent standards for acceptance of advertisements, but other magazines that do, include the *New Yorker, Ladies Home Journal, Good Housekeeping,* and the *National Enquirer.* All these magazines employ departments to screen advertisements, and depending on whether or not the advertisement is considered tasteful, a suggestion is made to the advertiser. *Good Housekeeping* goes a step further in "endorsing" certain products through its Seal of Approval, which lends credibility to products advertised in its pages.

The clearance methods for advertising acceptance rarely seem to rely on strict standards of ethics and honesty but, rather, are guided by the motivation of deterring further regulation and often are based on media professionals' judgments.

The specific method employed by the print and broadcast media may differ slightly with each medium, but the existence of such codes for acceptance of advertisements in almost all the media plays a role in the deterrence of advertisements that would be labeled deceptive or deemed unacceptable according to some part of a network's or other medium's code. The networks hold the ultimate power in rejecting or accepting advertisements. Similarly, magazines hold the right to refuse any advertisement based on content.

Interestingly, such codes currently stand as the only method of "before-the-fact" screening of advertisements—the only form of *preventive* control. "Case-by-case enforcement actions by the Federal Trade Commission, the self-regulation cases of the NAD/NARB, and many trade association codes only take action after the public has been exposed to the messages."[6]

The broadcast media codes for acceptance of advertisements have been studied in some detail. The broadcast industry, in the implementation of these codes, retains staff members to review incoming advertisements. The logistics of this review invariably depend on the structure of the particular station, thus affecting the number of reviewers or the nature of the review (i.e., by committee or individual) that the advertisement is exposed to before clearance is granted. Again, each specific station may handle this in a somewhat different method, but the fact remains that the advertising must undergo some form of clearance before it is considered acceptable for airing. If the advertising is not deemed acceptable for exposure, the broadcasting body can take one of three actions:

1. It can require the advertiser to amend or alter a commercial on the grounds of "taste."
2. It can ask the advertiser to substantiate a claim that is made.
3. The most obvious and powerful action: It can simply reject the commercial/advertisement.

While methods of clearance still exist in the major networks, clearance departments in the industry as a whole are being cut out.[7]

Individual Advertisers and Agencies

Self-regulation by individual advertisers and agencies, through an administration of a standards and ethics code, is an additional self-regulation system employed by advertisers. Two of the largest advertisers, Procter & Gamble and Unilever, are examples of companies subscribing to this system. The reason for this is quite simple; most advertisers benefit from engaging in honest and truthful discourse. Several advertising agencies maintain their own codes, ensuring that they abide by these codes through internal legal departments or independent counsel. Furthermore, certain industry groups or associations have set up their own industry codes or some other sort of advertising review procedure. As early as 1980, 22 such groups existed.[8] In addition to these, advertising agency associations, advertisers' associations, and media associations have also devised their own forms of self-regulation. An example of this is the American Association of Advertising Agencies (AAAA) which provides its members with the "AAAA Standards of Practice." In taking the initiative to set up these various codes and regulations, the burden is shifted partly back to the advertisers and the agencies themselves.

National Advertising Division
Council of Better Business Bureaus Inc.
845 Third Avenue
New York, NY 10022
Telephone: (212) 705-0114   Fax: (212) 308-4743
Website: http: www.bbb.org

Notes

1. S. A. Greyser, *Cases in Advertising and Communications Management* (Englewood Cliffs, NJ: Prentice Hall, 1972).

2. E. J. Zanot, "The National Advertising Review Board, 1971-1976," *Journalism Monographs,* 1979, 59.

3. Ibid.

4. J. J. Boddewyn, "Advertising Self-Regulation: True Purpose and Limits," *Journal of Advertising,* vol. 18, no. 2, 1989, 19-27.

5. Zanot, "The National Advertising Review Board."

6. H. J. Rotfeld, "Power and Limitations of Media Clearance Practices and Advertising Self-Regulations," *Journal of Public Policy & Marketing,* vol. 11, no. 1, 1992, 87.

7. H. J. Rotfeld, A. M. Abernethy, and P. R. Parsons, "Self-Regulation and Television Advertising," *Journal of Advertising,* vol. 19, no. 4, 1990, 18.

8. P. A. LaBarbera, "Analyzing and Advancing the State of the Art of Advertising Self-Regulation," *Journal of Advertising,* vol. 9, no. 4, 1980, 27-38.

The National Association
of Broadcasters (NAB)

For 75 years, the National Association of Broadcasters (NAB) has provided the resources and leadership necessary to advance the interests of radio and television broadcasters everywhere. The NAB is their voice in Washington—before Congress, federal agencies, the courts and on the expanding international front. As we enter the exhilarating era of digital radio and television, the telecommunications landscape is rapidly changing. The goal of the NAB is to keep broadcasters on the leading edge of that change.

The NAB is a full-service trade association. Beyond its work on Capitol Hill and at the Federal Communications Commission, it provides a wide range of practical member services, including internationally renowned conventions and expositions. Through industry research, legal expertise, timely publications, and a wide array of communications vehicles, the NAB keeps broadcasters out front on policy issues, technology trends, and management techniques.

The NAB's legislative and regulatory success is the direct result of grass-roots political involvement by local broadcasters who work tirelessly to educate and inform policymakers about the broadcasting industry's needs and priorities. They actively participate through the NAB Radio and Television boards, more than 20 working committees, direct lobbying efforts, and TARPAC (Television and Radio Political Action Committee), the NAB's political action committee.

The NAB's partnership with thousands of radio and TV members has helped to secure an optimistic future for the industry. The NAB's priority is to work as hard to serve its member stations as they work to serve their communities.

The NAB offers the following specific services to its members:

- *Advertising services*—including advertising opportunities, event sponsorship, and promotional items
- *Conventions and expositions*
- *Corporate communications*—including media relations, member communications, and graphic design
- *Government relations*—including legislative representation, grassroots involvement, and political action
- *Human resource development*—including employment opportunities and career assistance
- *International and associate group*—including international liaison, membership services, international conferences, and recognition
- *Legal and regulatory affairs*—including regulatory representation, legal advice, and law and regulation conferences
- *Meetings and conference services*—including conference coordination, convention housing, and travel discounts
- *National campaigns*—including public service, community outreach, and coalition building
- *Radio*—including member services, radio conferences, and radio awards
- *Research and information group*—including industry research, financial and trend analysis, and computer support
- *Science and technology*—including spectrum management, standard setting, and new technology development
- *Television*—including member services, conferences and training, and video magazine
- *NAB Education Foundation*—to advance professional education in the field

National Association of Broadcasters
1771 N Street NW
Washington, DC 20036-2891
Telephone: (202) 429-5300   Fax: (202) 775-3520
Website: http://www.nab.org

———

The National Newspaper Association (NNA)

Established in 1885, the National Newspaper Association (NNA) is the national voice of America's community newspapers. The NNA represents the owners, publishers, and editors of America's community newspapers and is today the largest newspaper association in the United States. Originally called the National Editorial Association, the organization's name was changed in 1965. The mission of the National Newspaper Association is to "protect, promote and enhance America's community newspapers."

The NNA protects community newspapers through an active and effective government relations program that addresses the issues affecting community newspapers. These issues include postal costs and service delivery; copyright, First Amendment, and access issues; taxation; public notice; and employment laws and regulations. The association has a national grassroots program composed of newspapers in almost every congressional district. Its annual Government Affairs Conference is the premier national meeting on public policy issues affecting newspapers. NNA members are kept abreast of key policy issues and developments through member-only publications such as *Capital Star,* the *NNA Policy Handbook,* and issue alerts.

The NNA promotes community newspapers by educating readers, advertisers, and policy officials on the benefits and value of community newspapers. In addition to industry statistics, the association provides information about community newspapers through publications such as its membership directory. NNA members with an Internet Website also receive a free listing and link on NNA's Website. The NNA also recognizes the best in community journalism through its annual Better Newspaper Contest, Best of the States Contest, and Community Development and Promotion Awards program.

The NNA enhances community newspapers by providing information, solutions, and strategies on current and emerging issues affecting the business interests of community newspapers. Its flagship publication, *Publishers' Auxiliary,* is the oldest newspaper serving the newspaper industry. Other valuable sources of information include the Annual Convention and Trade Show, the NNA Resource Center, and various educational programs and seminars. The association provides a valuable forum through which community newspaper executives share concerns and ideas with their peers across the country. It also provides a number of valuable business benefits, such as libel insurance, for its members.

The NNA is committed to working in close partnership with state and other newspaper associations on issues of mutual interest. It is also partnered with other organizations outside the newspaper industry. Through membership in the NNA, community newspaper executives have access to a wide range of information and allies.

The NNA is governed by a Board of Directors elected by the membership. With the exception of the officers, board members are elected to represent specific geographic regions. The NNA has established 11 regions through the United States. The NNA Board of Directors also includes representatives from the American Court and Commercial Newspaper Association, Suburban Newspaper Association, and Newspaper Association Managers. NNA members are eligible to serve on the Board of Directors and on committees established to address significant issues, such as new technologies.

Membership in the NNA is open to nondaily and daily newspapers with at least 20% editorial content. Free and paid circulation publications are eligible for membership. Electronic and on-line publications may also join the NNA.

Additional membership categories are available to students and academics, college newspapers, and retired community newspaper executives. Companies who sell to the newspaper industry or do business with newspapers are also eligible for membership.

National Newspaper Association
1010 North Glebe Road, Suite 450
Arlington, VA 22201
Telephone: 1-800-829-4NNA; (703) 907-7900
Fax: (703) 907-7901
E-mail: susan@nna.org
Website: http://www.oweb.com/nna

The New Products Showcase and Learning Center (NPSLC)

The New Products Showcase & Learning Center (NPSLC) in Ithaca, New York, is a collection of over 65,000 once-new grocery products. Robert McMath, founder and president, uses this ever-growing resource library as a basis for his consulting business. With his associates, he runs new product ideation workshops for clients, offers "reality checks" for those interested in launching new products, and provides historical documentation and expert testimony on intellectual property and product liability issues.

Having spent 30 years collecting and monitoring products entering the market, Mr. McMath is one of the country's foremost experts on why new products fail. *Fortune* 500s, start-up manufacturers, entrepreneurs, package designers, and academics—both international and domestic—use his services to beat the odds (over 80% of new products fail).

In 1998, he released a highly acclaimed book titled *What **Were** They Thinking? Marketing Lessons I've Learned From Over 80,000 New-Product Innovations and Idiocies.*

New Products Showcase and Learning Center
742 Cascadilla Street
Ithaca, NY 14850
Telephone: (607) 277-4053   Fax: (607) 277-9719
E-mail: mraymond@showlearn.com
Website: http://www.showlearn.com

The Newspaper Association of America (NAA)

The Newspaper Association of America (NAA) is a nonprofit corporation serving more than 1,700 member newspapers in the United States and Canada. NAA members account for more than 87% of U.S. daily circulation. Membership also includes many nondaily U.S. newspapers and other newspapers in the Western Hemisphere, Europe, and the Pacific Rim. Several hundred individuals, organizations, and businesses allied with the newspaper industry are associate members of the NAA.

The NAA was formed on June 1, 1992, by the merger of the American Newspaper Publishers Association (founded in 1887), the Newspaper Advertising Bureau, and five other marketing associations: the Association of Newspaper Classified Advertising Managers, the International Circulation Managers Association, the International Newspaper Advertising and Marketing Executives, the Newspaper Advertising Co-op Network, and the Newspaper Research Council.

The NAA serves the newspaper industry and its individual members in these strategic efforts:

- Retaining or building advertising share in all categories and improving newspapers' sales and marketing capabilities
- Advocating and communicating the views and interests of newspapers to all levels of government and supporting newspapers' interest in First Amendment issues
- Encouraging a diverse workforce and reflecting that diversity in newspaper products
- Providing research analysis and practical guidance on long-term competitive developments to ensure continued revenue growth through new product and business development
- Providing technical guidance to enable newspapers to serve effectively their readers and advertisers

NAA is a member of the International Federation of Newspaper Publishers, the World Press Freedom Committee, and the International Press Telecommunications Council. The NAA also maintains close, cooperative relations with other newspaper and journalism organizations. It sponsors several major meetings, including its annual convention and NEXPO.

NAA publications include the following:

- *Facts about Newspapers,* a statistical analysis of the newspaper industry
- *Presstime,* the NAA's flagship publication covering the newspaper industry and its trends
- *TechNews,* a bimonthly publication that explores the industry's changing technology

Newspaper Association of America
1921 Gallows Road, Suite 600
Vienna, VA 22182-3900
Telephone: (703) 902-1600   Fax: (703) 917-0636
Website: http://www.naa.org

The One Club
for Art and Copy

The One Club for Art and Copy is a nonprofit organization dedicated to promoting creativity in the craft of advertising. Founded in 1975, The One Club has approximately 1,000 members, including copywriters and art directors. As part of its mission to promote high standards of creative excellence, The One Club produces the advertising industry's most prestigious awards program, *The One Show*. Judged by a panel of the advertising industry's elite creative directors, this annual event acknowledges excellence in art direction and copywriting in a variety of categories, including television, radio, newspapers, magazines, billboards, and public service announcements. The coveted One Show "Gold Pencils" are regarded as the zenith of achievement in the advertising world.

1998 marked the inauguration of One Show Interactive®, a live awards program designed exclusively for the new media community.

The One Club regularly produces a variety of events and materials that encourage aspiring advertising people to hone their craft. These programs include the following:

- "Gold on Gold" lectures (award-winning industry professionals discuss the creative process)
- Portfolio reviews
- The One Show College Competition
- Creative workshops
- *One*—a quarterly magazine by and for advertising creatives
- Gallery exhibitions
- The One Show Annual, showcasing the best advertising worldwide

In 1995, the One Club established an education department, dedicated to fostering the creative talents of advertising students nationwide. This department administers scholarships to outstanding students in advertising programs at a variety of advertising schools across the country.

The One Club preserves the advertising industry's heritage by honoring creative legends by installing them in the Creative Hall of Fame.

The One Club publishes regularly the following:

- The One Show Annual Volume of award-winning advertisements
- Reels of the best television advertisements every year
- The One Show Interactive Annual Volume, showcasing new media advertising
- *One,* a magazine of creativity, with a selective circulation of 7,000 copies, which mainly go to creative people in the advertising agency world

The One Club for Art and Copy
32 East 21st Street
New York, NY 10010
Telephone: (212) 979-1900   Fax: (212) 979-5006
E-mail: oneclub@inch.com
Website: http://www.oneclub.com

The Outdoor Advertising Association of America (OAAA)

F ounded in 1891, the Outdoor Advertising Association of America (OAAA), Inc., is the trade association for outdoor advertising, representing over 90% of industry revenues. Through advocacy of reasonable legislation, support of sales and marketing efforts, and commitment to quality operations on all levels of business, the OAAA is the united voice of outdoor advertising.

The OAAA's 700 members consist of domestic and international outdoor and out-of-home operators, suppliers, and advertisers.

Government Affairs

The OAAA represents the industry on Capitol Hill and before the U.S. Department of Transportation. It is actively involved in working with congressional members and their staffs on legislative issues affecting the industry and with officials at the Federal Highway Administration on issues relating to implementation of the Highway Beautification Act and related rule making.

The OAAA builds and maintains a grassroots network of industry activists and provides legislative and regulatory updates on a regular basis. OAAA staff members provide technical assistance, training, and materials on legislative, political, and regulatory issues to OAAA members and to a national network of state associations.

Marketing and Industry Promotion

Located in New York City, the OAAA's marketing office works with advertisers, agencies, investors, and educators to increase awareness and understanding of out-of-home advertising. The association provides valuable information, including creative and research assistance, sales and marketing materials, and educational seminars.

The OAAA sponsors the annual OBIE awards (named after the prize, an Egyptian Obelisk), which recognize creative excellence in out-of-home advertising, and holds an annual Out-of-Home Media Seminar for buyers and planners.

Communications

The OAAA provides press alerts and guidance to its members, serves as an industry press resource, and coordinates national public service campaigns. It develops and houses an extensive publications library of newsletters, brochures, videos, economic data, ongoing research, surveys, and issue portfolios. Many items are available to the public through a publications catalogue and on the OAAA Website.

Membership Services

The OAAA provides useful training and education opportunities, including a National Convention, Operations School, Legislative Fly-In, and Legal Forum.

Product Quality and New Technologies

The OAAA works with its members to enhance billboard quality, improve safety, set standards, conduct research and development, and encourage new technologies. Involvement with major federal regulatory agencies ensures that safety is paramount in all outdoor operations.

Outdoor Advertising Association of America
Headquarters:
1850 M Street, NW Suite 1040
Washington, DC 20036
Telephone: (202) 833-5566   Fax: (202) 833-1522
Marketing Office:
12 East 49th Street, 22nd Floor
New York, NY 10017
Telephone: (212) 688-3664   Fax: (212) 752-1687
E-mail: info@oaaa.org
Website: http://www.oaaa.org

The Partnership for a Drug-Free America (PDFA)

The Partnership for a Drug-Free America (PDFA) is one of the most prominent and effective organizations that mobilizes advertising for the public
good.

The Early Years

Thanks to a small group of founding members and the support of the American
Association of Advertising Agencies (AAAA), the partnership has grown
from a four-person team into a national office with a staff of 30, backed by
thousands of volunteers from the advertising, media, and creative communities, all working together to reduce drug use in America. In the early 1980s,
Phillip Joanou, former chairman and chief executive of Dailey & Associates,
Los Angeles, and a former member of the AAAA's Board of Directors, became convinced that mass media—television, radio, film—were glamorizing
drugs. As an experienced advertising executive, Joanou came to believe that

the decision to use drugs could be viewed as a traditional consumer product choice and so could be influenced by changing people's attitudes. The advertising industry, with its roots in persuasive communication, could play a crucial role in the national drug crisis by "unselling" drugs in much the same way that the industry helps its clients sell their products and services.

Joanou envisioned a massive antidrug campaign that, unlike traditional public service advertising, would be run in optimal media availabilities nationwide, all donated by broadcasters and publishers.

In 1985, Joanou presented his idea to the Executive Board of the AAAA. The following year, the AAAA provided $300,000 to fund research and to start what was then called the Media-Advertising Partnership for a Drug-Free America. The AAAA also brought in the late Richard O'Reilly, formerly with Wells, Rich, Greene and NW Ayer, as the partnership's first executive director.

The advertising and media industries responded to the partnership's mission with vigor. In the first 9 months of operation, the media donated approximately $115 million in time and space. Advertising executives, including Allen Rosenshine (chairman of BBDO), Lou Hagopian (then chairman of NW Ayer and the AAAA), Dan Burke (retired president of Capital Cities/ABC), and Richard McLaughlin (publisher of *Reader's Digest*) joined in to help.

The partnership hit full stride quickly with the addition of Jim Burke as its chairman in May 1989. Burke, in just 2 years, took the partnership's annual media support from $115 million to $365 million. Since 1986, more that $3 billion in broadcast time and print space and 600 antidrug ads have been donated to the partnership's national campaign.

The partnership has been honored with many of the most prestigious awards in the advertising and marketing fields, including the only Grand Effie ever awarded for a public service campaign. That honor went to Goodby, Silverstein & Partners and Burrell Communications Group in 1994. Industry peers presented the Mercury Award to Lord, Dentsu and Partners in 1995, the Cannes Gold Lion to Saatchi & Saatchi in 1996, and a national ADDY award to J. Walter Thompson in 1997.

Unrecognized Success

When the partnership was formed, drug use was at extraordinary levels in the United States: 23 million Americans were regular drug users in 1985. Cocaine, often portrayed as a glamorous, nonaddictive pastime, was being used by 5.7 million Americans at the time. But then cocaine started killing people—Len Bias, the University of Maryland and Boston Celtics basketball star; actor John Belushi; and others.

Partnership ads hit full force as crack cocaine arrived on the streets of urban America. Bold headlines forced the nation to take notice, and attitudes about "casual" drug use started to change.

The advertising industry's commitment to contributing outstanding creative work hit home for millions of Americans. Indeed, drug experts believe partnership ads were an important contributing factor in this country's amazing—yet unrecognized—success in the drug fight. Today, there are 10 million fewer adult drug users in this country than there were in 1985. There are 50% fewer regular users of drugs and 77% fewer cocaine users. And crime is down to 30-year lows, a trend that experts attribute in part to the decline in drug use.

Eyes off the Ball

By the early 1990s, the country had taken its focus off drug abuse as other events shaped the world. The headlines, cover stories, and exposés about drug use of the late 1980s dissipated into little—if any—news coverage. In addition, the media were forever changed by deregulation. While deregulation meant an explosion of cable channels, the increased competition resulted in a dramatic drop in exposure for public service messages.

The lack of societal attention to the drug problem has had severe consequences. Drug use among young people is, once again, alarmingly high; the number of 8th, 10th, and 12th graders who use marijuana is up by 200%, 113%, and 58% respectively since 1991, the year drug use started increasing again among kids in America. By the late 1990s, it was clear that something had to change. Not coincidentally, drug use, which had been on the decline, started to rise just as PDFA advertising began getting less and less exposure.

Up to the Challenge

Through the leadership of General Barry McCaffrey, director of the White House Office of National Drug Control Policy (ONDCP), a bipartisan commitment by members of Congress, and the continued, unflinching support of the advertising industry and the AAAA, $195 million has been appropriated by Congress for a new national antidrug media campaign, being coordinated by McCaffrey's group, the ONDCP. The bulk of this money will be used to pay for the one thing that has eluded the partnership's campaign in recent years—consistent, optimal, national media exposure.

With adolescent drug use up and public service advertising media weight down, the new paid media campaign was hatched. "This is an historic public/private partnership for the industry, and for PDFA," says Thomas A. Hedrick Jr., vice chairman of the partnership. "We will now be able to maximize the impact on our target audiences with the right messages via the right media exposure, sustained over time."

O. Burtch Drake, president and CEO of the AAAA, met with the ONDCP last September and urged the group to continue supporting the partnership. "The Partnership has a great track record, and they have access to the best creative talent in the country. . . . The Government gets its most valuable resource free of charge."

Beginning in 12 markets, the paid media campaign went national in June 1998. The White House drug office used a media-planning and -buying organization, and a consumer-tracking study was planned to measure drug-related attitudes, awareness, and usage before and after the campaign.

Advertising will continue to be created on a pro bono basis, the Screen Actors Guild has graciously agreed to continue to waive all talent payments (both reuse and session fees), and Kodak has renewed its generous commitment, which dates to PDFA's inception, to donate the film for the production of partnership spots.

The implications for this plan are far-reaching. If the campaign succeeds, the effort will go down as groundbreaking in the annals of social marketing. An entirely new type of social marketing may emerge. If it fails, reestablishing significant media support—given the current state of public service advertising—will be daunting.

The partnership is committed to reducing drug use in the United States. Effecting positive change in the drug-related attitudes of America's children, teens, and parents is the partnership's mission. The paid media campaign is an important step toward achieving that goal.

Partnership for a Drug-Free America
405 Lexington Avenue
New York, NY 10174
Telephone: (212) 922-1560   Fax: (212) 922-1570
Website: http://www.drugfreeamerica.org

The Point-of-Purchase
Advertising Institute (POPAI)

The Point-of-Purchase Advertising Institute (POPAI) is the international trade association of the Point-of-Purchase (P-O-P) advertising industry and aims to advance the evolution of P-O-P advertising as a strategic medium integrated in the marketing mix. The association is dedicated to serving its more than 1,500 members worldwide by promoting, protecting, and advancing the broader interests of the industry through research, education, trade forums, and public policy efforts. The organization is American-based and has chapters in Europe, Japan, and Australasia.

Dick Blatt, President of POPAI, made the following points in his address to the American Advertising Federation on June 19, 1997: "With over 70% of all buying decisions made instore, P-O-P advertising is the best kept secret in advertising. P-O-P is a three-dimensional medium, and serves as the final three feet of a marketing campaign."

He emphasized the medium's dual roles in integrated campaigns: (a) stimulating impulse purchases and (b) reinforcing brand decisions, at the *only* point at which the consumer, the product, and the dollars to purchase the product come together.

Blatt's address marked the first time that a general advertising audience was introduced to the industry's "brand lift index (or BLI)," developed in POPAI's landmark Consumer Buying Habits study, conducted by Meyers Research Center. The BLI reflects the impact of P-O-P materials on consumers' instore buying decisions; it is stated as the average increase in incidence of instore purchase decisions when P-O-P is present, versus when it is not. The BLI demonstrates that most product categories show *substantial* increases in store decision purchases when P-O-P supports specific brands. For example, film and photo-finishing products enjoy a BLI of 47, meaning that those products are 47 times more likely to be purchased when supported by P-O-P advertising. Although as an unmeasured medium, P-O-P cannot be described in terms of advertising *reach,* the medium's overall *effectiveness* is amply illustrated by the resultant sales data.

Awards

Five years ago, POPAI's dedicated volunteers and staff began to work toward improving the P-O-P industry's leading awards recognition contest, the Outstanding Merchandising Achievement (OMA) Awards. Through focus groups, POPAI revisited the issue of the *purpose* of the awards recognition, *what* was to be judged, by *whom,* and in what *categories* those P-O-P advertisements would be judged.

POPAI determined that the OMA Awards were meant to recognize the best in P-O-P advertising. They implemented a program whereby they selected fair and experienced judges so as to ensure the program's integrity. POPAI later added an additional step to the review process, ensuring that case histories be fully assessed and that all three-dimensional displays be reviewed in person, on the marketplace show floor.

Also, POPAI made the OMA awards an international competition. As a result of work with other POPAI chapters and task forces around the world, the OMA Awards are today the industry's only global awards contest. What has not changed is the importance of winning a POPAI Gold, Silver, or Bronze OMA. Such an achievement sets a company apart by conferring a special degree of recognition for excellence in P-O-P.

But just as the market changes, so too does POPAI continue the evolution in the OMA awards. New adjustments for the 1999 contest include the following:

- A broadened list of categories to include one for all interactive P-O-P: a category predicted to jump to $3 billion in sales by 2002.
- An enhanced definition of P-O-P segments; a category for "semipermanent" P-O-P has been added, representing material planned for use over 1 to 6 months.
- Easing the entry process by establishing a means for applying over the Internet.

Education

Now available is an interactive edition of the P-O-P advertising industry's sourcebook, the *POPAI Design Annual,* which is also available in traditional hard cover. Now the *Design Annual's* CD-ROM version makes available photography of *all* OMA Award entries, as well as strategic information culled from the case history forms. Thus, running various "sorts" through the voluminous information contained in the CD-ROM version will yield enlightening views, for example, of what is being done in various product categories. For more information contact POPAI's Information Center at (202) 530-3084.

Point-of-Purchase Advertising Institute
1660 L Street NW, 10th Floor
Washington, DC 20036
Telephone: (202) 530-3000   Fax (202) 530-3030
Website: http://www.popai.com

The Promotional Products Association International (PPAI)

Between 1993 and 1998, the promotional products industry grew by more than 112%, making it a $13.18-billion-a-year business.[1] Composed of supplier companies (product manufacturers) and distributor companies (counselors and sales force for the public), the promotional product industry continues to grow at double-digit rates each year as the popularity and awareness of promotional product marketing increases.

What Are Promotional Products?

Promotional products are useful or decorative items usually imprinted with a company's logo or message. They include ad specialties, premiums, recognition awards, business gifts, and other identification applications. Promotional product marketing dates back to 1789 when lapel buttons were given out to commemorate the presidential inauguration of George Washington. Today, the most popular category of promotional products is wearables, which are, as the name suggests, anything one can wear—T-shirts, sweatshirts, golf shirts, hats, and so on. Wearables account for approximately 28% of annual promotional product distributor sales.[2] Other product categories that round out the top five in terms of annual sales are (a) writing instruments, 11.7%; (b) glassware/ceramics, 8%; (c) calendars, 6.9%; and (d) desk/office/business accessories, 5.9%.[3]

Ad Specialties

The ad specialty fulfills three key elements:

1. It is imprinted with an advertising or promotional message.
2. The message is printed on a useful item.
3. The item is given with no obligation.

Most likely, everyone has been given an ad specialty at some time or another, and even more likely, people have been given several. For example, you will rarely find a desk drawer that does not have at least one imprinted pen or pencil. When you go to the dentist, you may leave with an imprinted toothbrush or a refrigerator magnet with the dentist's information on it. Both of these are examples of ad specialties.

Premiums

A promotional product is a premium when it is offered as an incentive to produce a specific action. For example, a promotion to buy a certain brand of tennis racket to get a free can of tennis balls would be a premium offer. In general, ad specialties are imprinted and premiums are not.

Recognition Awards

Plaques, trophies, service pins and jewelry, and other gifts that signify performance or honors can all be categorized as recognition awards.

Business Gifts

Almost half of all companies give business gifts. These are typically given by businesses to their customers and employees as a token of appreciation. These are not extravagant gifts and are not considered "buying business."

Other Identification Applications

This catch-all category includes any products used to symbolize organization members, such as embroidered patches, plaques, or caps; imprinted souvenirs, such as glassware from tourist attractions; and promotional balloons that serve as decorations for special events.

Size and Functions of the PPAI

Founded in 1904, the Promotional Products Association International (PPAI) is one of the oldest nonprofit trade associations in the United States today, established to meet the unique needs of and unite the vastly expanding promotional products industry. It represents approximately 6,500 promotional professionals—about 1,500 suppliers and 5,000 distributors.

The PPAI, formerly Specialty Advertising Association International, is an important voice in the industry, committed to creating a viable marketplace, building further credibility for the industry, establishing business standards and guidelines, enhancing professionalism, and growing the industry. The association provides industry education, including the industry's only certification program; exhibits and networking forums, including the nation's 50th largest trade show;[4] industry research and communications; industry awards and recognition programs; and products and services to help foster business success for members.

The PPAI's Mission Statement is this: "To lead a vital and growing promotional products industry and to help our members prosper in an evolving business environment."

Industry Professional Certifications

Like many professional organizations, the promotional products industry has certifications of professional achievement, indicating that recipients have attained professional standards of experience, continued education, industry knowledge, and ethical behavior. These certifications are Master Advertising Specialist (MAS) and Certified Advertising Specialist (CAS) and are earned by completing criteria from a structured curriculum and passing a certification exam. The PPAI is the only organization in the industry to meet the criteria for administering a certification program, as established by the International Association of Continuing Education and Training (IACET) and for issuing continuing education units (CEUs).

As of 1999, there are approximately 500 industry professionals with the MAS designation and 1,650 with the CAS designation. In addition, more than 21,000 people working in the promotional products industry have earned CEU credits.

Industry Awards and Recognition

Since 1957, the PPAI has recognized outstanding industry practices with the industry's only awards and recognition program. Each year, it produces awards programs for the Golden Pyramid Award Competition, Supplier Star Competition, Suppliers Golden Achievement Competition, Distinguished Service Competition, Web Award Competition, and Speaker Ambassador of the Year Competition. In addition, the PPAI maintains the Promotional Products Hall of Fame, which recognizes the industry's pioneering professionals.

Educating and Creating the Marketplace

The PPAI has implemented several programs to educate consumers on the effectiveness of promotional products, including an extensive marketing research program as well as an aggressive public relations campaign. It has had articles appear in the *Wall Street Journal, Dallas Morning News, Chicago Tribune, Adweek, Brandweek, Potentials in Marketing* magazine, *Sales & Marketing Management* magazine, *Promo* magazine, and *Incentive* magazine.

The PPAI hosts a Very Important Professor (VIP) program, designed to educate college and university professors who teach advertising, public relations, journalism, communications, and marketing about the promotional products industry and to encourage them to incorporate their knowledge into their curricula. The association also sponsors the annual National Collegiate Competition (NCC), a competition among students to develop a unique marketing plan that incorporates promotional products to meet objectives for a given case study. In addition to the VIP and NCC programs, PPAI also manages and markets a Speakers Bureau, composed of approximately 300 member volunteers, that schedules speaking engagements at colleges and universities across the United States. The VIP, NCC, and Speakers Bureau programs are designed to educate future industry professionals and/or potential promotional product buyers on the uniqueness and effectiveness of the medium.

The PPAI is composed of a Board of Directors (with 16 elected association members), 13 Special Committees (with 12 volunteer association members each), and a professional full-time staff of 60 employees.

Promotional Products Association International
3125 Skyway Circle North
Irving, Texas 75038-3526
Telephone: (972) 252-0404   Fax: (972) 258-3004
Website: http://www.ppa.org

Notes

1. 1998 Promotional Product Industry Sales Volume Estimate Study conducted by Baylor University, 1999.
2. Ibid.
3. Ibid.
4. *Trade Show Week Magazine,* 1999.

The Promotion Marketing Association (PMA)

The promotion marketing industry represents expenditures by American business of hundreds of billions of dollars each year. Promotion budgets have surpassed advertising budgets every year since 1974. Approximately two-thirds of all marketing dollars are spent on consumer and trade promotions. Promotion is the key element of any brand marketing plan, whether for packaged goods, service industries, or other segments.

Promotion is designed to stimulate an immediate product sale or ensure continued behavior—unlike advertising that creates an image around a specific brand. Sales promotion includes premiums, sampling, coupons, sweepstakes, value-added offers, refunds and rebates, games and contests, exhibits, demonstrations, continuity programs, and specialties. Promotion objectives are planned in terms of pushing or pulling products through the distribution chain by appealing to the trade or consumer audience or both.

Promotion marketing creates a unique and powerful synergy when implemented as a dynamic element in a larger marketing program. Channeled through several types of media, including radio, television, in-store, and direct mail, promotion marketing generates consumer behavior that can be measured quantitatively. A big plus when planning next year's marketing campaign!

"Buy now! And buy often!" is the marketers' battle cry and the primary goal of every promotional marketing campaign. Unlike traditional advertising, promotional marketing drives consumers to take the plunge and make an immediate purchase. Implementing the push behind the product, dealers are key players on the path to the final purchase. Promotion marketing energizes and encourages dealers to get in there and get the sale.

What Is the Promotion Marketing Association?

Established in 1911, the Promotion Marketing Association (PMA) is the premier trade association representing the $200 billion promotion marketing industry. Its 670-plus members include many *Fortune* 500 corporations, top promotion agencies, suppliers of important promotional products and services, law firms, and academics. The PMA sponsors professional development conferences and seminars, issues regular legal bulletins on promotion law, conducts industry research, and publishes books and periodicals. The PMA's annual Reggie® Awards are presented to the best promotions of the year. The association is the leading voice for companies and professionals involved in promotion marketing. The mission of the association is to encourage the highest standards of excellence in promotion marketing. As the "voice" of the industry, it represents member interests and promotes better understanding of the importance of promotion in the overall marketing mix.

Membership

More than 640 companies nationwide and from around the world constitute the PMA's membership. The association's membership is diverse, representing large and small companies, including all segments of the promotion marketing industry. Total membership (including noncompany membership) comprises the following:

- Companies or organizations engaged in promotion activities, including consumer goods and service companies, manufacturers, and retailers
- Companies that sell promotion marketing products or services such as promotion agencies and consulting firms, fulfillment organizations, and incentive marketers
- Law firms that specialize in promotion marketing law
- Individuals at colleges and universities with promotion-related curricula

PMA Key Accomplishments

Conferences

The PMA's Update, Promotion Law/Marketing, and Star Power Conferences attract more than 1,300 registrants and 100 exhibitors. Each conference offers attendees up-to-the-minute educational information and the opportunity to network with industry peers.

Educational Seminars

The PMA's Basics of Promotion Marketing Seminar curriculum was expanded to include Los Angeles; Washington, DC; Bellevue, Washington; Orlando; Minneapolis/St. Paul; Nashville; Cincinnati; St. Louis; Chicago; and New York. The course also experienced a dramatic increase in international registrants. The Basics of Promotion Marketing Seminar curriculum for 1999-2000 includes Seattle, Nashville, and San Francisco, with two sessions set for Chicago, Los Angeles, and New York City.

Specialty Councils

The *Interactive Promotions Council* in 1999 successfully organized and launched its first of a series of seminars titled "Successful Online Promotion Marketing '99."

The *Product Sampling Council* held its Trial and Conversion Conference in New York City in 1999. More than 100 people participated in a full slate of workshops and seminars.

The *Coupon Council* carried out a public relations campaign during 1999 to strengthen the awareness of this promotion tactic.

The *In-Store Council* held its 1999 annual conference in Florida. More than 100 people participated.

Chapters

The association established firm and comprehensive operating policies and procedures for all PMA chapters. The PMA welcomed the formation of Southeast (Atlanta), Seattle, and Hawaii chapters. Under development are chapters in Argentina and the United Kingdom.

Legal Activities

The PMA successfully opposed the Federal Trade Commission's Telemarketing Sales Rule proceeding. The FTC subsequently revised the proposed rule, which would have imposed severe burdens on the telemarketing industry, particularly sweepstakes programs.

The PMA legal counsel worked closely with attorneys' general offices in Connecticut, New York, and Oregon respectively, on the drafting of new prize legislation favorable to promotion marketers. It has established itself as the primary voice for the promotion marketing industry with the FTC and state attorneys general.

The PMA and the U.S. Postal Inspection Service established a Joint Industry Rebate Fraud Task Force to combat the estimated $500 billion drained from promotion marketer coffers each year. The PMA is the administrator for the new Rebate Data Center, Inc., the new entity evolved from the task force. A rebate fraud central file database will provide information to the U.S. Postal Service, who will use the data to take appropriate steps to stop the abuse.

PMA Counsel Emeritus Frank Dierson, Esq., completed work on the third edition of *Promotion Marketing Law* before his death. The book is the only comprehensive comparison extant of state, federal, and international laws affecting the promotion marketing discipline.

Promotion Marketing Association, Inc.
257 Park Avenue South, 11th Floor
New York, NY 10010
Telephone: (212) 420-1100   Fax: (212) 533-7622
Website: http://www.pmalink.org

The Radio Advertising Bureau (RAB)

The Radio Advertising Bureau (RAB), founded in 1951, is the sales and marketing arm of the radio industry with more than 5,200 member stations, networks, and sales organizations in the United States and abroad. Its purpose is to increase awareness, credibility, and salability of radio; to raise the professional standard of radio advertising; and to increase radio revenues.

The RAB offers an array of marketing services, confidential and free of charge, to advertisers and agencies interested in using radio more effectively. RAB marketing specialists work with advertisers to help them evaluate their current radio advertising strategies and "creative"—the creative content of their radio advertising—or to aid advertisers in integrating radio into their current media plans with maximum impact and efficiency.

The RAB also acts as a resource for agencies and advertisers seeking radio marketing information and statistical data, as well as examples of radio creative in hundreds of advertiser categories. RAB and other radio executives are available for speaking engagements, platform presentations, and convention appearances.

In 1992, the RAB formed the Radio Industry Executive Partnership (RIEP) of radio industry leaders, which regularly calls on major national advertisers to gauge how radio can better serve their needs.

In 1996, the RAB introduced what is called the next generation of RIEP, Building Brands with Radio (BBWR), an interactive presentation:

- It's about getting your message across in an overcrowded marketplace.
- It's about timing your message so it's in synch with your customer's buying cycle.

- It's about perfecting the balance in your media mix so you get optimum effectiveness.

Over 200 national brands and their agencies have participated in the 1-hour, interactive PowerPoint presentation. BBWR is an educational presentation that does not attempt to sell radio as an advertising medium. Instead, it explains how radio's programming is designed for maximum interactivity between its tightly targeted formats and its listeners—the advertiser's customers. This interactive relationship between programming and listeners sets up an ideal environment for the client's ads, which helps cut through the 2,500+ commercial impressions that bombard Americans daily.

BBWR also looks at the role that radio's portability plays in penetrating the workplace and delivering messages during peak working and buying hours—6 a.m. to 6 p.m.—the hours when radio dominates all other media usage.

In an effort to promote excellence in radio advertising creative, the RAB is also the administrator of the Radio Creative Fund, the ad hoc funding and advisory group of radio industry leaders that sponsors the $210,000 Radio Mercury Awards for radio advertising. The awards program, the richest in advertising, has grown to become the premier showcase for radio creative and has been credited with raising advertising agency interest in radio as a creative ad medium.

RAB members rely on the organization for sales and marketing tools and information to help them better understand and meet the needs of their various advertising clients. The RAB also runs a variety of training programs open to members and nonmembers, including its groundbreaking CRMC (Certified Radio Marketing Consultant) program, the first-ever accreditation program for media salespeople of any kind.

The RAB also hosts an annual sales and marketing conference for the radio industry, attended by nearly 2,300 radio managers and sales managers from across the Untied States and internationally. In addition, the RAB conducts regularly scheduled training programs and creates customized programs on demand for local radio associations, ad clubs, and broadcast groups in markets of every size.

Radio Advertising Bureau
261 Madison Avenue, 23rd Floor
New York, NY 10016
Telephone: (212) 681-7200   Fax: (212) 681-7223
Website: http://www.rab.com

The Second Wind
Advertising Agency Network

History

The Second Wind Advertising Agency Network is the world's largest advertising agency network, with over 600 members. The Second Wind Network is mainly made up of smaller to midsize advertising agencies, design studios, and public relations firms. Members of Second Wind benefit from access to critically needed business, research, creative information, and cost savings programs on a daily basis. It is the only advertising agency network, worldwide, specifically geared to the needs of smaller to midsize agencies. The Second Wind Advertising Agency Network was founded in 1988 by Anthony P. Mikes, an advertising executive with over 27 years' experience owning and operating advertising agencies and graphic design studios.

Membership

Second Wind addresses its potential members in the following terms:

> Membership in the Second Wind Network gives member agencies access to resources that make any smaller to mid-sized firm a more valuable asset to current and prospective clients. Belonging to the Second Wind Network means never having to reinvent the wheel. Somewhere in The Network someone has an answer or solution to the questions and problems you have on a daily basis.
>
> No matter who you are—design studio, PR firm, or advertising agency—your job is to create a unique position and identity for your client in the marketplace. To do this you need a great creative team.
>
> Unfortunately, creative genius is no longer enough to keep you and your clients ahead of the pack. The more you know about your client, their target audience, and your client's competitors, the better you will be able to create smart solutions to marketing problems. You will also find that some of the experiences network members talk to us about become the focus of newsletter articles. Agencies across the country face similar problems, and those articles help other member agencies solve or avoid those common problems. The information you need is out there, but is often very expensive and hard to find. Second Wind takes the overwhelming expense and the hassle out of getting the knowledge you need to succeed.

Publications

Second Wind advertising agency publications are unlike any other agency business publications. Any major bookstore will sell general books on better ways to run a business, but it is not possible to find anything on how to run "your" business. Smaller to midsize agencies have some very specific needs, and every Second Wind publication is written with those needs in mind.

Over the last 10 years, Second Wind has built a library of publications to help improve all facets of the agency, including account service, creative, financial, human resources, and operations. These publications offer numerous practical and procedural recommendations and templates, preventing the agency from having to reinvent the wheel . . . and help it to wheel along ahead of the competition.

Seminars

Since 1988, Second Wind has been hosting the country's best advertising agency seminars. All Second Wind seminars are designed to help smaller to midsize agencies and their employees grow. Thousands of agency executives and managers have attended Second Wind seminars and profited from the experience.

Second Wind Advertising Agency Network
120 Hobart Avenue, Suite C
PO Box 6284
Wyomissing, PA 19610-0284
Telephone: (610) 374-9093   Fax: (610) 374-9238
E-mail: info@secondwindnetwork.com
Website: http://www.secondwindnetwork.com

The State Advertising Coalition (SAC)

The State Advertising Coalition is an informal coalition consisting of the American Advertising Federation (AAF), the American Association of Advertising Agencies (AAAA), and the Association of National Advertisers (ANA). The AAF represents corporate advertisers, advertising agencies, the media, local advertising federations, and college chapters. The AAAA represents advertising agencies of all sizes. The ANA represents national and regional advertisers. (See the articles in this volume describing each of these three associations.)

The SAC provides its members an opportunity to monitor jointly legislative activity affecting advertising in the 50 state capitols. It also provides its members the means to coordinate strategy and lobbying activities.

Contact details for the SAC are available from any of its three constituent members.

The Television Bureau
of Advertising (TVB)

The Television Bureau of Advertising (TVB) represents the broadcast television industry to the advertising community. It is the only voice within the television industry that addresses the values of local spot advertising. The TVB's mission is to develop and increase advertiser dollars devoted to U.S. spot television.

Its effort is multifaceted but is concentrated into two main initiatives—national advertisers and medium-to-large retail advertisers. The TVB believes that by helping advertisers and agencies to understand consumers better, it can provide valuable insights to increasing sales and profitability. The bureau has access to some of the most sophisticated research and data resources available to the advertising industry.

The TVB has been successful with many clients. Here are some examples.

Carson Pirie Scott & Co.—Improve consumer perceptions. The retail chain Carson Pirie Scott was forced to reevaluate its business. It developed a 5-year plan to upgrade its image, departing from its association with low prices. Advertising was developed, and consumer research was carried out before and after its exposure.

Television (on seven stations), radio, and newspaper ads and newspaper inserts were all employed. Advertising awareness from television improved after the campaign, in contrast with the other media, for which it declined. Consumers' perceptions of the store improved from a number of dimensions. And sales were significantly higher in cities, where there was television advertising than in cities where there was none.

Checker Schucks Kragen CSK Auto—Boost consumer awareness and store preference. CSK Auto is one of the leading auto parts retailers in the automotive aftermarket industry. CSK developed a new advertising campaign in cooperation with TVB and ten television stations in Phoenix and Seattle. The campaign was run in these two cities, with pre- and post-research to evaluate changes engineered by the advertising.

Top-of-mind awareness of the retailer rose significantly in both cities. TV commercials were more memorable than advertisements in other media. CSK's TV advertising generated higher recall than that for other stores. Finally, store preferences and intention to shop at the store both increased measurably.

The Bon Marché—Reestablish "fashion" business. Using local market surveys, it was determined how four small specialty stores had eroded a department store's "fashion" business. The TVB explained why this had happened and how the retailer could recapture the business through an integrated merchandising and marketing program.

Burdines—Change customer perceptions. A plan was developed to exploit strategic, long-term use of TV versus tactical, short-term use of the medium. A consumer survey was set up to measure program success and convince senior management. Perceptions of a "place to shop for gifts" grew substantially in only 4 weeks.

Television Bureau of Advertising
850 Third Avenue
New York, NY 10022-6222
Telephone: (212) 486-1111   Fax: (212) 935-5631
Website: http://www.tvb.org

The Traffic Audit Bureau for Media Measurement (TAB)

The Traffic Audit Bureau (TAB) was established in 1933 as an independent, not-for-profit advertising industry organization to audit circulation of outdoor advertising displays. Its sponsors were the major advertising associations: the American Association of Advertising Agencies (AAAA), the Association of National Advertisers (ANA), and the Outdoor Advertising Association of America (OAAA). The TAB is independent and tripartite, which means its support comes from the three major industry segments—advertisers, advertising agencies, and out-of-home media companies.

Most members of the TAB Board of Directors come from the "buyers" sector (advertisers and agencies) to ensure buyer control over governing policies and auditing practices. This guarantees the main objective of audits—unbiased, third-party verification of facts.

In 1990, the TAB was renamed the Traffic Audit Bureau for Media Measurement to reflect its merger with the Out-of-Home Measurement Bureau and expansion of auditing activities. Since the consolidation, two additional industry associations have been represented on the board—the Eight-Sheet Outdoor Advertising Association and the Shelter Advertising Association.

The TAB currently audits the circulation of 30-sheet posters, 8-Sheet posters, bulletins, and shelter advertising displays. The bureau is actively seeking to expand services to other out-of-home forms not audited at present.

The TAB's Mission

The primary purpose of the TAB is to authenticate circulation data for out-of-home media. It seeks to inform and educate the advertising community regarding the quantitative and qualitative values of all forms of out-of-home media—accommodating new forms, as developed, without compromising standards of integrity. In specific instances, the TAB also audits visibility values and certifies advertising placement.

Advertisers require undisputed quantitative data for media decisions. Recommendations must be based on unassailable facts, and audits performed by the TAB as an objective third party satisfy this requirement.

Audits assure advertisers that they are getting what they pay for. Audits impose a discipline on users of audited data and lead to greater professionalism in the buying and selling of out-of-home advertising. Audits train buyers to turn to reliable facts for evaluating media proposals. Sellers have greater conviction and confidence when their sales proposals are based on audited information. Audits help to educate advertising practitioners on media values and how to use them effectively.

The TAB audits circulation of out-of-home displays and their visibility values where designated. Factors developed by the TAB are used to accurately convert official (mechanical/electronic) and manual vehicular counts to people aged 18 and over. (This is comparable to data presented by other media.) Circulation is defined as advertising opportunities or impressions, the same as other media. Industry-approved scientific standards covering approach distances and visibility to traffic are used to qualify advertising exposure.

Circulation is secured from two sources: (a) official traffic counts from government agencies and (b) manual counts by plant operators in accordance with set procedures. During the audit, official sources are scrutinized by the TAB auditors, and recounts of manual counts are taken. Field inspection is conducted on a statistically reliable sampling of the locations to verify plant inventory, assignment of circulation counts, and the visibility of each display to traffic.

The most important fact for the market, the *average daily effective circulation (DEC)*, is calculated by dividing the total market circulation by the number of displays. DEC means the daily number of potential impressions for a display and is derived from mathematical factors that make the vehicular traffic directional, converts it to people, and adjusts it to the period of exposure (12, 18, or 24 hours).

Following the audit of the market, *plant operator statements* are produced and distributed to advertisers and advertising agency members as well as to the plant operators. These audit statements include information on population, average DEC, county coverage, visibility, and audit history. The TAB also produces an annual *Summary of Audited Markets* book containing the key audit data for all currently audited 30-sheet and 8-sheet posters, bulletins, and shelter advertising in member markets.

Separately, the TAB provides verification of advertising placement. On a system-wide basis, using a statistical sample of locations, a report is created showing the percentage of displays placed correctly according to contract specifications. Such reports are released to advertiser and agency members as well as to the media companies involved.

Audited Data

The use of audited data can create business opportunities. For the advertiser or advertising agency, the TAB audit furnishes information vital to planning—market facts critical to location selection, advertising exposure, coverage, and so on.

Audits can offer sales opportunities for out-of-home media companies. Other media salespeople use media facts to buttress sales arguments. Print media use audited data from the Audit Bureau of Circulations (ABC) and Business Publications Audit of Circulation (BPA). Broadcast media rely on Nielsen and Arbitron for data to use in sales presentations. Using audited facts in selling makes presentations more professional, more credible, and more useful for comparison with competitive media.

Salespeople often use audited data to show media planners how their medium can work in conjunction with other media. Marketing information based on audited data is used to demonstrate delivery of advertising impressions to target groups, ethnic markets, and other segments. The TAB has recently published adjustment factors for other demographic breakdowns in addition to the 18 and over age group. Cost per thousand and cost per point of GRP, reach and frequency data, and the like are all based on audited circulation. Audits offer essential information for conclusive buying decisions.

The TAB circulation data are available from individual member plant operators (media owners) for local/regional markets.

Other TAB Services

- *Summary of Audited Markets*—This annual publication contains current audited data for painted bulletins, 30-sheet posters, 8-sheet posters, and bus shelter advertising.
- Plant Operator Statements—Audit statements by market are distributed to members as issued.
- TAB Annual Meeting Conference—Annual all-industry conferences present pertinent issues and programs of high-profile interest to both buyers and sellers of out-of-home advertising.
- *Planning for Out-of-Home Media*—This 150-page handbook covers basic information and planning statistics on buying and selling out-of-home advertising.
- *Factsletters*—This TAB newsletter reviews current activities of the TAB and industry trends and insights.
- Special seminars—These seminars are conducted by the TAB staff and available to advertiser and agency media people and plant sales staffs; special seminars are conducted on request.

Traffic Audit Bureau for Media Measurement
420 Lexington Avenue, Suite 2520
New York, NY 10170
Telephone: (212) 972-8075   Fax: (212) 972-8928
Website: http://www.tabonline.com

The World Federation of Advertisers (WFA)

The World Federation of Advertisers (WFA) is the only worldwide professional body to exclusively represent the collective voice of commercial and industrial companies engaged in the marketing of products and services that span a wide spectrum of business sectors. The WFA's membership comprises several thousand businesses operating at national, regional, and global levels.

The WFA defends the common interests of its national associations of advertisers, corporate members, and corresponding members throughout the world and, in so doing, promotes the free circulation of goods and services, including a company's intrinsic right to commercial communications.

Objectives

The WFA's primary objective is to safeguard an advertiser's inherent right to un-impeded marketing and commercial communications throughout the world—with particular emphasis on developments in free trade areas and other economic blocs. The federation defends the industry from excessive legislative intervention and unacceptable restrictions on all advertising and marketing-related practices.

The WFA makes it its business to anticipate problem areas before they arise and to take the lead in defending and, whenever possible, extending the freedom of commercial communications. To this end, the WFA counsels and influences supranational organizations and legislative bodies both directly and indirectly. Furthermore, the WFA supports its member associations in dealing with domestic governmental bodies, whenever the freedom of commercial communications—the economic lifeblood of the free trading world—is questioned or threatened.

WFA aims to do the following:

- Achieve recognition by governments and the business world of the fundamental importance of marketing communications to the economy and consumer choice
- Encourage a constructive and workable legislative practice among members
- Promote excellence of marketing communications practice among its members
- Stimulate maximum effectiveness and commercial openness of communication agencies and consultancies

Strategies

The WFA seeks every opportunity to promote the economic benefits of advertising on behalf of its members and industry at large. Over recent years, advertising has come under serious attack from various sources, under many different guises. One of the main challenges facing advertisers today is to raise the profile of advertising and to highlight the vital economic role it has to play in the world of free trade. Directly, and indirectly through its members, the WFA actively promotes the economic arguments in favor of free commercial communications. This is achieved through various channels and different public platforms:

- Lobbying and other representational activity with appropriate governmental and institutional bodies, to influence the various legislative processes affecting advertising
- Public presentations and guest appearances at major trade fairs, conferences, seminars, think-tanks, and so on
- Active participation in expert working groups on key advertising-related issues
- Dissemination of position papers and publications
- Targeted public relations and press relations
- Sponsoring of key advertising events and studies
- The forging of strategic alliances with other supranational or cross-industry organizations

This list is by no means exhaustive, but it illustrates the different levels of activity undertaken by the WFA at worldwide, national, and regional levels on behalf of its members.

International Affiliations

The WFA actively contributes to the work of international bodies in the field of advertising communications and human rights, such as: the United Nations (UN), the International Chamber of Commerce (ICC), the Council of Europe, the EU Commission, and European Parliament. The WFA also enjoys nongovernmental organization (NGO) status within the Codex Alimentarius (Joint World Health/Food & Agriculture Organization), the World Intellectual Property Organization (WIPO), and the UN Educational, Scientific and Cultural Organization (UNESCO) and has developed a close working relationship with the World Trade Organization (WTO), formerly GATT (General Agreement on Tariffs and Trade), and the World Health Organization (WHO).

The WFA: The Organization

The federation, as such, was established in 1953 as the International Union of Advertiser Associations (Union Internationale des Associations d'Annonceurs (UIAA). Today, for historical reasons, the membership of the WFA comprises both national associations of advertisers in some 41 countries and several corporate members—some of the world's leading multinationals. Indirectly, through its national association membership, and directly, through its corporate members, the WFA "family" represents over $320 billion of annual advertising investment, roughly 85% of the world's total media advertising expenditure. To this can be added other advertising-related expenditures that cannot be quantified in precise economic terms—sales promotion, sponsorship, product information, and direct marketing. When we add to this list the various corresponding members with whom the WFA enjoys a close working relationship, the federation's membership takes on a global dimension—from the perspective of both geographic and sectorial coverage.

The WFA—The Structure

In 1994, the WFA streamlined its organizational structure by establishing an Executive Committee which, under the chairmanship of its president, decides and executes the federation's long-term policy and goal setting. The WFA's structure relies on two main pillars: The Directors' Forum (TDF) and the International Working Group (IWG). The former comprises the WFA's national association members from around the world and provides an ideal platform in which the various association heads can meet to exchange news and views on advertising-related issues, review WFA policy matters, and make recommendations to the Executive Committee, which comprises representatives from both the TDF and IWG. The latter represents the interests of the WFA's corporate membership and is composed of senior executives designated by the companies concerned. The IWG provides a unique forum for major international companies to come together to discuss and formulate policy on cross-industry issues affecting advertising throughout the world.

The president is appointed by the General Assembly for a 2-year term of office. That person is aided by a deputy president (representing the IWG members). A vice president, representing the national associations, is elected by the General Assembly following a proposal from representatives of the TDF. The everyday running and implementation of WFA policy is overseen by the WFA's managing director, based at the federation's permanent secretariat in Brussels, Belgium.

The WFA has several working groups: the Media Committee, the European Committee, the Latin American Committee, and the Advertising and Children Committee.

WFA's Membership Worldwide

The WFA has members in 41 countries: Argentina, Australia, Belgium, Brazil, Canada, Chile, Colombia, Czech Republic, Denmark, Finland, France, Germany, Greece, Iceland, India, Indonesia, Ireland, Israel, Italy, Japan, Korea, Lebanon, Morocco, New Zealand, Norway, Pakistan, Paraguay, Peru, Portugal, Russia, South Africa, Spain, Sweden, Switzerland, the Netherlands, Turkey, the United Kingdom, the United States, Uruguay, Venezuela, and Zimbabwe.

The WFA has also over 25 multinational advertisers from the world top 50 as corporate members.

World Federation of Advertisers
18-24 Rue des Colonies
B-1000 Brussels
Belgium
Telephone: +32 (2) 502-5740   Fax: +32 (2) 502-5666
E-mail: info@wfa.be
Website: http://www.wfa.be

The Yellow Pages Publishers Association (YPPA)

The Yellow Pages Publishers Association was established in 1988 with the merger of the American Association of Yellow Pages Publishers (AAYPP) and the National Yellow Pages Service Association (NYPSA). These two vital groups were brought together to better serve the Yellow Pages industry, which is the fifth-largest advertising medium.

YPPA is composed of publisher members who publish and distribute Yellow Pages directories throughout North America and annually generate $12 billion in advertising revenue. Its membership also includes international publishers from nearly every corner of the globe. In addition, the association represents certified marketing representatives (CMRs)—Yellow Pages advertising agencies—who sell national and international Yellow Pages advertising. The association's associate members represent suppliers to the industry, from paper manufacturers to software developers.

The mission of the YPPA is to support its members in growing their Yellow Pages businesses, while maximizing attractive business opportunities in complementary markets. The association develops a number of programs and services and is a central resource for the improvement of the industry as a whole.

Through the YPPA's order transmission system, CMRs are able to place national Yellow Pages advertising for clients into over 6,000 directories on a one-contact, one-bill basis. The YPPA produces *YPPA—Rates & Data,* an electronic and print publication that includes the advertising sizes, rates, closing dates and publishing dates, and other information pertinent to preparing national Yellow Pages orders for the over 6,000 directories.

The association develops a variety of materials on subjects such as Yellow Pages co-op advertising, effective ad design, and how to track return on investment from Yellow Pages advertising. In addition, the association commissions research on how consumers use the Yellow Pages when looking for products and services. Brochures based on this research are developed for the benefit of sales reps and advertisers.

The YPPA works to monitor and shape public policy through the surveillance of legislation on the federal and state level. Hundreds of bills are tracked and, where appropriate, the association disseminates notices and alerts to its membership.

The association oversees the industry's national ad campaign, which features actor/comedian Jon Lovitz as "The Man Who Wrote the Yellow Pages." Its aim is to increase usage of the medium by repositioning the Yellow Pages as an idea source on everything from home improvement to personal growth rather than just a place to look up phone numbers.

Link, the association's newsletter, is a communications vehicle for both internal and external audiences. *YPPA—News Link,* an annotated industry-focused news page, is available on the YPPA's home page at http://www.yppa.org.

The association's "Bogus" Yellow Pages program represents an industrywide, long-term commitment to countering the fraudulent practice of "bogus" Yellow Pages invoices. Each year, advertisers lose millions of dollars to "bogus" Yellow Pages billing schemes. Often bearing the famous (but never trademarked) "walking fingers" logo, these misleading and fraudulent Yellow Pages solicitations look like bills—and they routinely get paid by many unsuspecting advertisers nationwide.

YPPA publisher members strongly support the Partnership for a Drug-Free America, as well as the Ad Council. Over the past 9 years, they have collectively donated nearly $450 million in directory advertising space to these causes.

Yellow Pages Publishers Association Headquarters
3773 Cherry Creek North Drive, Suite 920
Denver, CO 80209
Telephone: (303) 333-9772   Fax: (303) 320-6999
Website: http://www.yppa.org

Yellow Pages Publishers Association Operations Office
820 Kirts Blvd., Suite 100
Troy, MI 48084
Telephone: (248) 244-6200   Fax: (248) 244-0700

Advertising Publications

Admap[1]

Admap is an influential British-based monthly marketing and advertising journal. When it was first founded in 1964, *Admap* strongly reflected the media research preoccupations of the times. Particularly in the United Kingdom, the inquisitive and intellectual nature of a new breed of media planner was reshaping all of marketing thinking, from target setting to advertising effectiveness. This much more solid conceptual basis for understanding consumers' identity and behavior tended to expose the inadequacy of existing hierarchical models in explaining purely creative effects—advertisements themselves, excluding consideration of their size, target group penetration, frequency distribution, and so on.

This in turn led to the new concept of account planning, with its emphasis on advertisement testing and long-term tracking. By the 1970s, *Admap* had begun to treat the entire marketing and communications process as one continuum, whose effects and methods all deserved—even if they did not always get—the same rigorous understanding as the media studies that had marked the journal's starting point.

Admap has two unusual characteristics. One is that it combines much of the objectivity and seriousness of an academic journal with the greater focus on use and the accessibility of a more practical magazine directed at the profession. Retaining the intellectual rigor of the academic journals in its peer group, but without their obscurity, *Admap* aims to focus on the operational aspects of new ideas and knowledge: application and context, not just abstract concepts and specialized methodology. Its other characteristic is that it treats the many individual disciplines that make up the large subjects of "marketing" and "communications" in an interrelated way rather than in isolation.

Its main contents are serious papers on important issues, often at an academic level of stringency but with a strong emphasis on practical new information, ideas, and methodologies. These are written mainly by practicing experts rather than academics and are sometimes refereed. However *Admap* is not a refereed journal. The length of these articles, often published in groups of three or four so as to examine the same topic from contrasting viewpoints, can be a deterrent to the more hurried reader. But *Admap*'s material typically has a very long shelf life, and many large businesses retain complete sets of the journal as an essential reference. For most subscribers, it is seen as a unique authority and working tool. A (subscription) archive of *Admap,* together with extensive other material, is available on the Internet at http://www.WARC.com

While some papers deal with local U.K. topics, of little interest to non-British readers, *Admap*'s subject matter ranges from management and marketing (the formation of strategy, distribution, branding, target setting, and segmentation) through advertising and other elements of the marketing mix (including ad testing, tracking, monitoring, planning, and media selection) to the media industry (audience measurement, editorial and program quality effects, and media finances). As the journal's circulation becomes increasingly international, the content carried has a more international flavor than in the past.

This broad continuum of topics can make the journal seem somewhat eclectic; however, the aim is that each topic should be treated with sufficient depth to be of value to experts—so as partly to fulfill the role of a specialist journal—while being accessible enough to inform those in adjacent disciplines. The emphasis is therefore on context, and on the general lessons and knowledge provided by new methodologies and ideas, rather than on the methodologies themselves.

Admap has influenced the evolution of best practice in many areas over the years. These include the following:

- The adoption of single industry-wide media research bodies in most developed countries and the standards and methodologies used (Peoplemeters, etc.)
- The concept of "single-source data" to relate media consumption directly to buying behavior at the individual level
- The development of increasingly reliable and robust econometric models and their widespread application
- The development of "data fusion" to simulate single-source information, by ascribing the characteristics measured by one large continuous survey to similar individuals in another survey (e.g., of buying behavior), by way of attributes common to both surveys (e.g., demographics, media consumption)
- Advertising theory: "how it works" and, more specifically, theoretical and practical models of the different ways it can work; the isolation of short- and long-term marketing effects of advertising
- Account planning
- The concept that consumers *use* advertisements rather than being simply stimulated by them, and the consequence of this for advertising research

Admap also conducts many important advertising conferences and seminars in the United Kingdom.

Admap
NTC Publications
Farm Road
Henley-on-Thames
Oxfordshire RG9 1EJ
United Kingdom
Telephone: +44 (149) 141-1000   Fax +44 (149) 157-1188
E-mail: email@admap.co.uk

Note

1. This article is largely based on discussions with the late editor of *Admap*, Nicholas Staveley, and the current editor, Roderick White.

Advertising Age

A *dvertising Age,* often referred to as *Ad Age,* is an international and domestic journal published by Crain Communications in Chicago. It is considered important by marketing, advertising, and media professionals who want to advance their careers and understand the total business environment.

The weekly publication is the leader in its field in the United States. It not only covers advertising news by reporting on new advertising campaigns, client changes, media news, account action and people moves, but also analyzes and defines the markets. *Ad Age* covers every aspect of the marketing, advertising, and media industries worldwide. Each issue includes much hard-hitting, late-breaking, exclusive news. Full of features, special issues, international news, and departments, *Ad Age* gives readers the insight they need to work at the top of their fields.

The Features Department produces special reports, including the Salary Survey, the 100 Leading National Advertisers, the Marketing 100, and the highly requested Agency Report, which has been published for more than half a century.

Departments include Bob Garfield's Ad Review column, James Brady's Brady's Bunch, Account Action, and many more. And leading the way into the superhighway of advertising is *Advertising Age's* own Interactive Media and Marketing—a weekly section headed by Brad Johnson that explains the interactive side of advertising as it is being created.

In addition to the weekly tabloid publication with a readership of more than 310,000, *Advertising Age* also publishes the *Ad Age Daily* for fax transmission every afternoon except Friday and has a Website (see address below). Global marketing news and information is available on e-mail via *Advertising Age's* Daily World Wire. *Advertising Age* also does custom publishing and markets videotape training programs for marketing, advertising, and media professionals.

Every year, *Advertising Age* publishes standardized data of great importance to the advertising industry. In May, it releases detailed estimates of advertising volumes in different media for the preceding year. These "industry standard" data are compiled by Robert Coen of McCann-Erickson.

Advertising Age
Crain Communications, Regional Offices
711 Third Avenue
New York, NY 10017-4036
Telephone: (212) 210-0100   Fax: (212) 210-0200

740 North Rush Street
Chicago, IL 60611-2590
Telephone: (312) 649-5200

6500 Wilshire Blvd., Suite 2300
Los Angeles, CA 90048-4947
Telephone: (323) 651-3710
E-mail: Editorial information: edit@adage.com
          General site information: webinfo@adage.com
          Marketing information: mktg@adage.com
          Advertising & sponsorship info: adv@adage.com
          Subscription information: subs@adage.com
Website: http://www.adage.com

Adweek Magazines

A*dweek,* based in New York, is one of the two major trade publications directed at the advertising industry. (The other is the Chicago-based *Advertising Age.*) *Adweek* began publication in 1960.

Adweek has six regional editions to provide information and comment from regional perspectives. These editions cover the six major regions: New England, East, Southeast, Midwest, Southwest, and West.

Because of growing specialization within the advertising industry, *Adweek* is one of three interlocking journals. While *Adweek* has a general coverage and emphasis, *Mediaweek* covers news about the media industry and is an up-to-date source of information for media planners, buyers, and supervisors, in agencies, independent media organizations, and client companies. *Brandweek* has a focus on client organizations and is devoted to the fortunes of the 2,000 major brands in the United States—all those with advertising budgets above $3 million.

The 1998 circulation figures for the three magazines were as follows:

Adweek	40,441
Mediaweek	21,380
Brandweek	24,063
Total	85,884

Of the paid (or qualified) circulation, more than half went to agencies and less than half was purchased by client organizations.

Adweek's subscribers comprise senior executives (40% of the total), vice presidents (25%), and more junior people (35%). *Mediaweek's* subscribers cover most of the media professionals in the 350 largest American advertising agencies. *Brandweek's* readership concentrates on marketing and media staff in the manufacturing companies that produce the 2,000 leading advertised brands in the United States.

Adweek Service Center
PO Box 1973
Danbury, CT 06813-9844
Editorial Department telephone: (212) 536-1423   Fax: (212) 536-1416
Website: http://www.adweek.com

American Demographics (AD)

A*merican Demographics*, first published in January 1979, was founded by Peter Francese, author of *Capturing Customers* and *Marketing Know-How* and creator of the *Wall Street Journal's* "People Patterns" column. Its first mission was to bring to light the work of demographers and the importance of the field for business leaders and marketers. Dow Jones, Inc. owned the magazine until March 1997, and many articles in the *Wall Street Journal* credited *AD* as the source of statistics on a wide range of topics.

Following its purchase by Cowles Business Media in March 1997, the magazine's editorial focus was sharpened to spotlight emerging consumer trends and issues based on population shifts and demographic changes across the American landscape. The magazine helps marketers and business leaders to identify, acquire, communicate with, and retain customers, by examining strategies and tactics. On the strategic side, the magazine looks at economic and cultural data to discuss how to evaluate markets, who the customers are, where they are, and what they value, want, and do. For tactical implementation, editorial coverage deals with technology and competition: which channels reach the customer, what drives purchase behavior, what builds loyalty, and which tools and applications work best with each customer group.

Typical monthly editorial coverage includes trends in health care, retirement, migration patterns, ethnic markets, media habits, database marketing, and Internet usage. Regular columns such as "Top Lines," "Media Channels," and "Databasics" focus on the latest market research reports and how they relate to the changing American population. Feature story topics look at American lifestyle trends and influences, such as the quiet phenomena of second-family fathers, the hidden market of single mothers, analyses of government data on consumer spending habits, the growing retail emphasis on the back-to-school shopping season, and the pervasive influence on American culture from the fast-growing Latino youth population.

The magazine's 35,000-plus paid circulation encompasses a broad range of disciplines—from brand marketers to urban planners and from financial services marketers and business school students to advertising and media executives. Readers also include entrepreneurs and small-business owners eager to find the next big trend and build a business on it.

American Demographics
PO Box 4274
Stamford, CT 06907
Telephone: (203) 358-9900   Fax: (203) 358-5833
E-mail: Editors@demographics.com
Website: http://www.demographics.com

Campaign

Campaign is the leading British trade press journal in the advertising field. It has been in existence for 30 years. With a current total weekly circulation of 15,775 (14,050 in the United Kingdom and 1,725 in other countries), the journal provides a reasonably comprehensive coverage of the advertising field in Britain. This tends to be concentrated in London and the Southeast of England.

Although there are three competing titles in the field, *Campaign* has a larger readership than all three combined. *Campaign* is read weekly by 80% of executives who decide where advertising money is to be spent, and virtually universally by advertising agencies. In addition, it is read every week by nearly half the United Kingdom's top-spending clients.

The editorial style is lively and topical.

Campaign
174 Hammersmith Road
London W6 7JP
United Kingdom
Telephone +44 (0)20 7413-4570   Fax: +44 (0)20 8267-4914
Website for *Campaign* on-line: http://www.campaignlive.com

Commercial Communications

Commercial Communications, the journal of advertising and marketing policy and practice in the European Community, is published by *asi* and sponsored by Directorate General XV (DG XV). The sponsoring DG is responsible for the Internal Market and Financial Services.

The Internal Market was established at the end of 1992. This process largely focused on the free circulation of goods and came about from an analysis of the increased efficiencies that could be achieved from economies of scale in the areas of production and distribution. Marketing communications did not feature in the review that was launched in 1985, but it was generally recognized that branding strategies are becoming crucial in advanced markets typified by ever-more sophisticated and demanding consumers.

With the development of cross-border television and the advent of on-line digital broadband communications, the opportunities for reception and use of cross-border commercial communications in Europe were increasing. It therefore became important to assess the extent to which there are any regulatory barriers affecting these activities and, if so, what might be done to tackle them.

To help address these problems, *asi* proposed to the European Commission the *Commercial Communications* journal. This proposal followed a 3-day conference that the company had organized to allow industry and consumer groups to voice their concerns directly to the European Commission and, equally, to allow the commission to articulate some of the issues to which it had to respond. The initiative was based on the principle that the formulation of good policy should be based on sound knowledge and understanding. The success of this series of interchanges resulted in the continuance of the dialogue through the journal.

This was for a number of reasons. First, it was considered necessary because commercial communications cross every sector of the economy and are aimed at all consumers. The activity has such a wide remit that it would be impossible for the commission to contact directly all the various trade, media, and consumer associations (and their members) that would have an interest in this policy work. A broad and open communications channel is therefore necessary for the commission to be able to address all these constituents.

Second, the market is changing rapidly. The findings of the commission's policy documents will therefore have to be updated through constant contacts with the relevant market players. The *Commercial Communications* journal seeks to contribute to this exercise.

The publication reflects the issues being discussed within the European Union (EU) and provides a forum where all sides can put forward their points of view. It was clear from a questionnaire published in one of the early issues that significant barriers to trade still exist in the Internal Market. Some of the respondents give an insight into some areas of difficulty. Consider the advertising of alcohol:

> The advertising and marketing of alcoholic drinks is controlled to a greater or lesser degree throughout the EU, either by legislation or self-regulatory code. Problems arise from widely differing national policies in relation to both media and creativity. These make cross-border campaigns legally hazardous, or else reduce them to the standards of the "most restrictive" country.

Or take the extent to which advertising should be directed to children:

> The regulations controlling the content of TV advertising to children are different in all Member States. These differences are amplified by further differences in national laws having a general bearing on advertising and by the existence of statutory or voluntary code-based control systems which also differ.

It appears that various sales promotions represented further problems: "Restrictions on the value of free gift items with a product ... are a major disadvantage to products which have limited advertising budgets. This affects cross-border activity in that value-added packs can be used in some countries but not transferred." And, again: "The rules which govern the level of incentives or rewards which one can offer a consumer to try a brand prohibit investment in brand development."

Last, two respondents highlighted difficulties associated with sponsorship in Europe:

> A considerable problem is the fragmentation of governance, with commercial communications in general (and sponsorship in particular) being considered by a diverse number of government departments in the EC and in Member States. This means that no central responsibility or decision is taken, and information is difficult to establish, particularly for interested parties.

And, then: "Rules (are) so strict that they limit the creative scope for European campaigns."

It is thus clear that if manufacturers or service providers attempt to establish their brand in a number of countries in the EU, they will find a number of varying restrictions on how their products may be marketed. Indeed, in certain categories and in certain countries, the restrictions are such as to effectively block market entry. The *Commercial Communications* journal provides a record of Europe's attempts to reconcile these difficulties while providing the opportunity to identify new problems as they arise. Crucially, it provides a forum for interested parties to debate these matters.

Although the core circulation of the publication is in Europe, special issues that relate to global problems are occasionally produced and circulated more widely to broaden the debate. A good example is the development of e-commerce.

While the publication necessarily carries much material relating to the regulatory framework in which commercial communications are (or might be) conducted, *Commercial Communications* also features articles of interest to the marketing practitioner. These may relate to research studies of note or case history material reflecting industry "best practice." The involvement of marketing practitioners in the debate on any regulatory framework is essential to the journal's purpose. The structure of such a framework is too important to be left to regulators and corporate lawyers.

The journal is published in three languages: English, French, and German. It has a controlled circulation of some 5,000 individuals. It is sent to (a) the Directors-General of each of the European Commission's Directorates, (b) about 100 members of the European Parliament who have an interest in the subject, (c) individuals within the administration of the Member States of the EU who brief their ministers on regulatory issues, (d) a number of trade associations, (e) the CEOs of European advertising agencies and television and print media owners, and (f) CEOs and marketing directors of companies engaged in cross-border commercial communications activity.

The editorial director of *Commercial Communications* is Mike Sainsbury. He has formerly published *MediaWorld, Media International,* and *Admap.* He also conceived and established MediaTel, an on-line media information service, in 1981. Its extensive database is accessed over the Internet by nearly all the major media-buying companies, media owners, and media analysts in the United Kingdom.

Commercial Communications Headquarters
111 Whitchurch Road
Tavistock PL19 9BQ
United Kingdom
Telephone: +44 (182) 261-8628   Fax: +44 (182) 261-8629
E-mail: asi@dial.pipex.com

The Integrated Marketing Communication Research Journal

T*he Integrated Marketing Communication Research Journal* is published by the graduate Integrated Marketing Communication (IMC) program at the University of Colorado. The *IMC Journal* publishes work by faculty, students, alumni, and friends of the program. The articles seek to inform the professional community of research, trends, and theories about IMC and integrated marketing. The articles report on original research. However, they are written for a professional audience with the goal of translating research and theory building for people who are grappling with the development of IMC practice.

Articles include major research projects conducted by several of the university's IMC classes; one was a study of relationships for packaged goods products, and another is a 2-year tracking study of interactivity that monitors how well dialogue is being managed through 800 numbers, Websites, and published e-mail addresses.

International articles include a piece on the communication aspect of relationship marketing by a team headed by Christian Gronroos, an internationally known scholar from Finland; one on a stakeholder audit by a team of New Zealand researchers headed by Brian Murphy; and a research report on the intersections between public relations and marketing by an Austrian doctoral candidate, Thomas Hunter.

Faculty articles have included a piece on cross-function teams by Professors Brett Robbs and Larry Weisberg, an article on the IM Audit by Professors Tom Duncan and Sandra Moriarty, a report on the development of an IMC scale by Wayne Henderson at Texas Tech, and articles on the accounting challenges of integrated communication and on lessons learned from leading total-quality corporations, by then professor and now consultant, Anders Gronstedt.

IMC student articles include pieces on multitier branding, cyber-relationships and brand building, knowledge branding, experiential marketing and events, technology-enabled relationship marketing, privacy, sports sponsorships, strategic alliances, integrated marketing and IPOs (initial public offerings), interactivity cues on television, customer defections, and brand personality.

For those wishing to submit an article, selection is made through a blind review process. Deadline for submission is December 1, and authors will be notified of acceptance or rejection in March. Articles should be no longer than 12 to 15 pages (double-spaced, typed-manuscript format), including footnotes and graphics. Five copies should be submitted. One copy should have a full title page with contact information; the other four copies should not have a title page with any type of author identification.

Send submissions to the following address:

Professor Sandra E. Moriarty
Journalism and Mass Communication
Campus Box 287
University of Colorado
Boulder, CO 80309-0287
Telephone: (303) 492-1451   Fax: (303) 492-0969
Website: http://www.colorado.edu/Journalism/sjmcgrad/imc

Interactive Marketing (United Kingdom)

Interactive Marketing is a new magazine published by the (British) Institute of Direct Marketing.

The journal, which will be published quarterly, is focused on the following objectives:

- To identify, describe, and assess the strategies and processes of interactive marketing, through the publication of refereed papers and case studies
- To foster an understanding of the organization—systems, people, and processes—required for effective interactive marketing
- To encourage best-practice interactive marketing
- To address, in rigorous, detailed, and evidence-based fashion, the major and current issues facing the modern marketer
- To present studies, measurement, empirical evidence, and research into the success (and failure) of interactive marketing strategies and applications
- To provide a forum for presenting challenging and coherent new models that describe the interactive marketing process
- To build a valuable resource of abstracts summarizing the best writing in traditional and electronic media

The journal is directed by an editorial board of 29 senior and experienced executives in professional organizations, 18 from the United Kingdom and 11 from other countries.

Interactive Marketing
Henry Stewart Publications
Museum House
25 Museum Street
London WC1A 1JT
United Kingdom
Telephone: +44 (0)20 7323-2916, ext. 109   Fax: +44 (0)20 7323-2918
E-mail: ed@hspublications.co.uk
Website: http://www.henrystewart.co.uk/Journals/IM

The International Journal of Advertising (IJOA)

The *International Journal of Advertising (IJOA)* is a quarterly "reviewed" journal. Its remit is "to cover all aspects of marketing communications from the academic, practitioner and public policy perspectives." Its editors interpret this as an intention to build bridges between those who practice or regulate marketing communications and those who teach or research them. The publishers, NTC Publications Ltd., in the United Kingdom, have reinforced this policy by usually appointing a professor at a leading university or business school as editor-in-chief and a practitioner as editor.

The subject matter is therefore wide ranging and includes public relations, sales promotion, direct advertising, sponsorship, and interactive media in addition to the conventional channels of communication of media advertising. In addition to classic branded packaged consumer goods, articles look at campaigns aimed by or at business, government, and "not-for-profit" sectors. *IJOA* is interested in topics such as the roles, behavior, and interaction of advertisers/

sponsors, agencies, the media, and target audiences; the economic, social, and regulatory environment; and research and measurement of the effectiveness of campaigns. The journal prefers studies with international application to the domestic issues of a single country.

Submissions within remit are welcomed from both practitioners and academics from a wide range of disciplines, subject to blind peer review. On occasion, it has published the views of experts in other disciplines—for example, lawyers, historians, and anthropologists. The members of the editorial advisory board who assist the editors with the reviewing include respected experts from universities and commerce and are supplemented on occasion by appropriate specialists.

IJOA appears in February, May, August, and November, and most issues cover varied topics. Recent articles include the following:

- "Does Advertising Affect Market Size?" (Ambler, Broadbent, and Feldwick)
- "Perceptions of the Media in Three Different Cultures" (Chan and Allmon)
- "The Influence of Advertising on the Pattern of Food Consumption" (Duffy)
- "Incorporating Generic or Brand Advertising Effects into the Rotterdam Demand System" (Brown and Lee)
- "Effects of Tobacco Advertising Restrictions" (Hoek)
- "Blasphemy, Indecency and English Advertising" (Miller)
- "Will Older Models Turn Off Shoppers?" (Greco, Swayne, and Johnson)

IJOA also publishes occasional special issues on a single topic, under the guidance of an expert guest editor—for example, "Advertising in the People's Republic of China" (November 1997), "Commercial Sponsorship" (February 1998), "Advertising Effectiveness" (November 1998), and "Food Advertising" (scheduled for 2000). In 1998, the publishers started to sponsor an annual Best Paper Prize with an award of $2,000 for the best paper submitted on a specific topic of widespread interest in the business, particularly where recent serious published work is lacking. The first topic was "food advertising," and the second was "What does advertising really do for brands?"

Subscriptions to institutions for 1999 are £159 p.a. for the United Kingdom and Europe, $264 for North America, and £167 for the rest of the world (individual subscribers can claim substantial discounts on these rates).

International Journal of Advertising (IJOA)
NTC Publications, Ltd.
Farm Road
Henley-on-Thames
Oxfordshire, RG9 1EJ
United Kingdom
Telephone: +44 (149) 141-1000   Fax: +44 (149) 157-1188
E-mail: ijoa@ntc.co.uk

Journal of Marketing Communications (JMC)

Philip Kitchen

The *Journal of Marketing Communications* was launched in January 1995. The rationale behind the proposal at that time was the sense of a major gap in the marketplace where so few journals at that time sought to address marketing communications in the broadest sense. The journal has three associate editors, drawn from America and Canada (Professor Don Schultz at Northwestern), Europe (Professor W. Fred van Raaij at Erasmus Universiteit in the Netherlands), and the Pacific Rim (Professor David R. Corkindale at the University of South Australia). Review board members are likewise drawn from a mix of these major areas of world trade.

Every paper is rigorously double-blind refereed, and generally, *JMC* publishes four articles per issue.

JMC was and is devoted to publishing research papers and information concerning all aspects of marketing communications and promotion management. It is also seen as a channel for discussing emergent and emerging issues affecting marketing communications, wherever and whenever they occur. *JMC* is also concerned with the behavioral foundations of marketing communications and promotion management.

Issues that *JMC* covers include the following:

- Marketing communications—communications via any or all of the marketing mix elements
- The way(s) marketing mix elements are operationalized and interrelated for communication purposes in marketing plans
- Promotional management—including the bedrock subjects of advertising, sales promotion, personal selling, and marketing public relations but also the emerging areas of sponsorship, relationship marketing, the Internet, database marketing, and integrated marketing communications (IMC)
- The process of developing effective communications via specific case studies
- Behavioral foundations of marketing communications and promotion management, including semiotics, creativity, consumer behavior, attitudes and persuasion, source and message factors, diffusion of innovation, and adoption
- Effects of changing environmental circumstances on marketing communications and promotional strategy—altered budgetary allocations, messages, media infrastructure, and globalization
- Exploration of the trends leading toward integrated marketing communications, marketing public relations, and relationship marketing
- Examples of sound innovative or teaching practice in relation to marketing communications and promotional management
- The interface between corporate communications and marketing communications and their public relations equivalents

Contributing Authors

The mix of papers accepted, not necessarily submitted, reflects *JMC's* aim to be represented in each of the major economic areas:

Regions	Percentage
United States/Canada	47
Pacific Rim	21
Europe	31
Elsewhere	1

Countries of authors who have published in *JMC* include Australia, Bahrain, Belgium, Brazil, Canada, Greece, Hong Kong, Ireland, Korea, Malaysia, Netherlands, New Zealand, Singapore, Taiwan, the United Kingdom, and the United States.

Conferences

In the year following the launch of *JMC*, a new conference was introduced (1996) to try to meld and further synergize the views and opinions of marketing communications and corporate communications practitioners and academics. This International Conference on Corporate and Marketing Communications is held in April each year. A further development took place in 1998 with the launch of the Global Institute for Corporate and Marketing Communications at the University of Strathclyde in the United Kingdom. It aims to build a research network of like-minded individuals throughout the world and to build synergy between the two communication disciplines.

Journal of Marketing Communications
Professor Philip Kitchen, Editor
Martin Naughton Chair in Business Strategy
Queen's School of Management
Lanyon Building
Queen's University
Belfast BT7 1NN
Northern Ireland
Telephone: +44 (0)28 9027-3782   Fax: +44 (0)28 9024-8372
E-mail: p.kitchen@qub.ac.uk

Market Leader

Market Leader is the journal of the Marketing Society in Britain. It is published by NTC Publications Ltd. and goes free to all members. The Marketing Society is the premier organization in the United Kingdom for senior marketing professionals and general managers of marketing-oriented companies. The society has approximately 3,500 members, and its mission is to "champion marketing excellence." Its core activity is to organize a nationwide series of conferences, seminars, and workshops where key business leaders address the topical issues of the day.

Market Leader was launched in the spring of 1998 as a quarterly journal. It is designed exclusively for marketing directors, board directors, and other senior managers who need to keep abreast of new ideas and thinking in marketing and business. Although the remit of the journal is to cover business issues in the widest sense, it is the only journal of its type that concentrates primarily on key strategic marketing issues.

Contributors to *Market Leader* are of the highest caliber. Authors are chosen for their leadership in their field of expertise and are drawn from the ranks of business leaders at blue-chip companies, management and marketing consultants, and business schools. *Market Leader* regularly features the most respected thinkers on marketing issues in the world.

Every issue of *Market Leader* contains practical ideas and new thinking about key marketing and business issues. For example:

- An in-depth feature providing differing perspectives on a vital business topic such as brand equity, strategies for growth, and innovation
- State-of-the-art "how-to" advice in important areas such as competitor profiling and market segmentation
- Case studies that reveal the marketing strategies of leading international companies such as Volkswagen, Merrill Lynch, and Intel
- A question-and-answer session with a business leader from a top company such as Unilever, Coca-Cola, and Nestlé
- Management summaries of the most useful and thought-provoking articles published in leading international business magazines and journals such as the *Harvard Business Review, McKinsey Quarterly,* and *Sloan Management Review*

In addition, each issue carries regular columns from leading marketing writers and international perspectives from the United States and elsewhere.

The following articles have appeared in recent issues of *Market Leader:*

- An analysis by PIMS ("profit impact of market strategy") of the marketing strategy used by 1,000 companies in Britain during periods of recession, concluding that companies that increase their marketing activities during recession are more successful than ones that cut back
- An extensive interview with Niall FitzGerald, chairman of Unilever, on his vision for this international giant
- How Michael Dell has revolutionized the computer industry with his direct-selling model and how he built the innovative culture required to maintain the company's success
- Professor Rosabeth Moss Kanter talks to *Market Leader* about her latest insights in the management of innovation
- "How to find the Holy Grail," an article by a leading analyst at McKinsey & Company detailing the most effective strategies for growth
- An article by PriceWaterhouseCoopers on the convergence of industries worldwide and the implications of this phenomenon for business strategy

Market Leader can be obtained on subscription.

Market Leader
NTC Publications, Ltd.
Farm Road
Henley-on-Thames
Oxfordshire, RG9 1EJ
United Kingdom
Telephone: +44 (149) 141-1000   Fax: +44 (149) 157-1188
E-mail: market_leader@ntc.co.uk

Advertising Organizations That Publish Journals: United States

In addition to the publications listed individually, a number of significant journals are published by various advertising organizations in the United States and abroad. These organizations are described in this volume. The journals themselves are best understood in the context of their parent organizations. In this and the next article, the journals marked with an asterisk (*) are of particular importance.

- The Advertising Research Foundation
  Journal of Advertising Research
- The American Academy Of Advertising
  Journal of Advertising
- The American Advertising Federation
  American Advertising

- The American Association of Advertising Agencies
  Agency
- The American Marketing Association
  Marketing Management
  *Journal of Marketing
  *Journal of Marketing Research
- The Direct Marketing Educational Foundation
  Journal of Interactive Marketing
- The Marketing Science Institute
  Insights From MSI
- The Media Research Club of Chicago
  MRCC Review
- The National Advertising Division/National Advertising Review Board
  *NAD Case Reports
- The National Newspaper Association
  Publishers' Auxiliary
- One Club for Art and Copy
  One

Advertising Organizations That Publish Journals: International

- The European Association of Advertising Agencies
  The Ad Business
- The European Society for Marketing and Opinion Research
  *Marketing and Research Today
- Genootschap Voor Reklame
  GVR Info
- The History of Advertising Trust Archive
  HATNEWS
- The International Advertising Association
  IAA World News
- The International Federation of Periodical Publishers
  Magazine World

- The Market Research Society (United Kingdom)
  Journal of the Market Research Society
- The Market Research Society of Australia
  Australasian Journal of Market Research

Postlude

The Founding Fathers

Philip Jones

A dvertising is the product of the human intellect and imagination. It is there-fore not surprising that the business has been built by talented individuals and not by the discovery of mechanisms, systems, and procedures. Scale econ-omies and production efficiencies have never been important in advertising, in contrast to other types of business, such as manufacturing or financial services.

The trade journal *Advertising Age* emphasized the importance of talented individuals in its 1999 special issue titled *The Advertising Century*. In this are described the careers of 100 recognized figures whose combined endeavors made the business what it has become.[1] While not denying the contribution of any of these people, it must be admitted that some are rather more significant than others. This article concentrates on the hard-core pioneers—the Founding Fathers, as it were. Their stories are not only intrinsically interesting, but they also have a direct bearing on the advertising organizations with which they were associated—most of which remain important to this day.

These 10 figures are all American, with the single exception of David Ogilvy, who nevertheless spent virtually his entire professional career in the

United States. All 10 are men; women did not emerge into positions of leadership in the advertising industry until well into the second half of the 20th century. The Founding Fathers comprise three managers and seven creative men—a balance that is appropriate, given the nature of the advertising profession. The 10 figures were chosen for the following reasons:

- *Wayland Ayer* established the foundation of agency practice as it was carried out during the century of steady and almost continuous growth from 1875 to 1975. The agency business, as established by Ayer, was "full-service"; agencies were concerned with all aspects of advertising and were compensated by a uniform rate of media commission.

- *Albert Lasker*—the most powerful figure ever produced by the advertising industry—together with his closest creative collaborator, *Claude Hopkins,* established hard-selling advertising as a dynamic force for building brands. During the first two decades of the 20th century, business leaders began to recognize advertising as a very important activity, and the Lord & Thomas agency, run by Lasker, was to a large extent responsible for this.

- *Stanley Resor,* with his creative *alter ego, James Webb Young,* boosted the professionalism and stature of the advertising enterprise. They began to use research, to study the working of advertising in psychological and behavioral terms, and they made advertising an international activity. Under the guidance of Resor and Young, J. Walter Thompson was the leading player on the world advertising stage from the late 1920s to the late 1950s.

- *Stirling Getchell* and *Raymond Rubicam* were rainmakers: the most dynamic creative leaders of the advertising business during the troubled 1930s. This was an important decade, because during its course, advertising began to take its modern form, departing from its original direct-response heritage and also expanding into the audiovisual media.

- Three inspiring creative leaders, *Leo Burnett, William Bernbach,* and *David Ogilvy,* had a greater impact on the business than any of their contemporaries during the decades of advertising's most explosive growth and evolution, the 30 years that followed the end of World War II. After the golden era dominated by these three figures, economic uncertainties ushered in the age of the agency financiers who to a large degree control the business today.

F. Wayland Ayer (1848–1923)

F. Wayland Ayer was born in 1848 to solid New England pioneer stock. His father, Nathan Wheeler Ayer, was an important influence on his life and encouraged Ayer to become a teacher. This he did for a short time before drifting into advertising sales for religious publications. In 1869, at the age of just 21, he pooled all his savings with a loan from his father and started his own company in Philadelphia, which he called NW Ayer and Son (in an effort to hide his youth and inexperience). From such humble beginnings, he built what was to become, in his lifetime, the largest advertising agency in the world, and he was to become quite probably the industry's wealthiest practitioner.

Ayer created an agency in his own image: conservative, trustworthy, blue-blooded, and slightly old-fashioned. He specialized initially in the newspaper end of the business, and it was here that he made perhaps his largest contribution to the industry. Drawing on his experience in advertising sales, he revolutionized the billing process. The standard procedure of the day was that the agency would buy the space for an advertisement and then charge the client as much as he was willing to pay. Ayer devised the scheme whereby the client would pay for the actual amount of the space plus an additional percentage commission, which normally worked out to between 12.5% and 15% of the gross cost of the space, which paid for the creative development of the advertisement. Ayer's new system of compensation soon became popular with both agencies and clients because both parties could better control and budget their advertising revenues and expenses. Although it remained the industry norm for many years, recently more and more agencies are billing on a fee basis, normally computed by the number of hours worked by the agency personnel.

Ayer was also a great believer in research and empirical data gathering long before this was fashionable, and to this end, he published the *American Newspaper Annual and Directory,* which was to become a standard reference in the business.

In the early stages of his agency's life, Ayer would accept any client that could pay his commissions, but he soon built an enviable list of accounts, including Cadillac and H. J. Heinz.

In later life, he gave himself over to more philanthropic concerns and became very involved in the Baptist church and its various charitable arms. He was also on the boards of several financial institutions, most notably the Merchant's National Bank, and he founded a hugely productive dairy.

On the 50th anniversary of NW Ayer and Son, in 1919, ex-President Taft said, "We are honoring a man who made advertising a science, and who has robbed it of its many evil tendencies, and who has the right to be proud of the record he has made." He stands as one of the giants of the industry.

Claude C. Hopkins (1866–1932)

Claude Hopkins, along with William Bernbach and David Ogilvy, is probably one of the three most influential copywriters ever to have penned an advertisement. He was raised in a strict Baptist family and as a teenager became a lay preacher, an experience that certainly affected his copy style in later life. He soon tired, however, of the restrictions that this existence imposed. He got a job as a bookkeeper before moving to the Bissell Carpet Sweeper Company where he learned the art of the hard sell, which was also to serve him well.

After a series of other jobs, Hopkins was hired in 1908 by Albert Lasker as a copywriter. Lasker was in the process of turning Lord & Thomas (later to become Foote, Cone & Belding) into his own personal empire, which he ruled as a near dictatorship until his retirement in 1942. Lasker had employed John E. Kennedy in 1904 as his senior copywriter. Kennedy converted Lasker to his philosophy of hard-hitting, sales-oriented advertising, and when the former left the company, Lasker needed a replacement. Hopkins was the inspired choice, and the two made a formidable team up to Hopkins's retirement in 1922.

Like Kennedy, Hopkins believed that an advertisement should sell the product it was endorsing. He always maintained that "brilliant writing has no place in advertising"; he preferred dense but simple copy that explained why the consumer should buy the product. He felt that art work only detracted from the primary aim: an increase in sales.

Hopkins set out to prove that advertising was not, as many up to this point had believed, a gimmick or fad, but a legitimate means of increasing sales and thus profits for his clients. His intention was to document this relationship with empirical data, and in the process, he helped make the business, with its new scientific base, respectable.

He struck on the idea of using mail order advertisements with which he would enclose a coupon that could be redeemed by the customer. For the first time for many clients, they could see exactly how many people were responding to an advertisement and adapt their strategy accordingly.

He was also the first to take advantage of comprehensive market surveys, most notably with the Van Camp's Pork and Beans account. Hopkins dispatched numerous canvassers to go door-to-door and interview housewives to ascertain their preferences concerning the client's product. He would then decide on the best strategy for selling the goods, depending on what the surveys discovered.

Hopkins also made a point of understanding the product he was trying to sell. He toured the plants where they were manufactured and tried to incorporate the knowledge he attained from this experience into his advertisements. On one legendary occasion, he was being shown around the Schlitz brewery and was much impressed by the machines they used to clean their bottles with steam. He based his advertisements on this fact, never claiming that Schlitz alone used this process; indeed, virtually every competing company did also. Yet the idea stuck with the public that Schlitz was innovative and hygienic: a perception that sold lots of beer. Hopkins's campaign became a classic example of preemptive advertising.

Hopkins was an extremely hard-working but retiring man with an eccentric appearance and a pronounced lisp. Despite this, he became enormously rich. He also wrote one of the great treatises on the business, *Scientific Advertising*. David Ogilvy has claimed that "nobody should be allowed to have anything to do with advertising until he has read this book seven times."

He was a man ahead of his times. He understood that advertising is a science long before anyone else did, and he remains one of the industry's most influential figures.

Stanley Resor (1879–1964)

Stanley Resor is one of the most important figures in the history of the advertising business. He was born in 1879 and graduated from Yale in 1901. His first job was to sell Bibles before being hired in 1904 by Procter & Collier, the house agency of Procter & Gamble in Cincinnati. From there, he moved to J. Walter Thompson (JWT) in 1908.

While still at JWT in Cincinnati, Resor had employed a young female copywriter named Helen Lansdowne. When he relocated with the company to New York in 1912, she followed him, and in 1917, they married. The couple was to have a fruitful professional relationship, a happy private life, and she was a significant contributor to his success. It was said that it was only possible to understand JWT when it was seen as an extension of Mr. and Mrs. Resor's drawing room.

J. Walter Thompson himself had acquired the Carlton & Smith agency, which had been founded in 1864. He built it into the largest agency in the world, but by 1916, the time Resor decided to buy JWT, with its 177 employees, 5 offices, and 300 clients, Thompson himself had lost his grip on the business. Resor and several partners paid $500,000 for the company, the majority of which he had to borrow, and he ran the organization until his retirement in 1960.

Resor immediately set about stamping his particular style on JWT. He brought in new faces, many of them from Cincinnati, most notably James Webb Young and Henry Stanton, both of whom were to become valued long-term colleagues. He also changed the emphasis of the company, deciding to concentrate on a few large accounts rather than on many small ones, and he set about slashing the client list from 300 to around 80.

He was very much an old-fashioned gentleman: unfailingly polite, considerate, scholarly, and dignified. He engendered immense loyalty from his employees by treating them fairly and letting them get on with their own jobs. Unlike many of the men who have run large agencies, he was not an autocratic figure but liked to manage by consensus, and he chose to surround himself with equally congenial personalities. He distrusted the turbulent maverick individualists who were to become a fashionable part of the creative departments of many companies. He did, though, have a penchant for academics, a throwback to his time at Yale, and he hired many of them. Under Resor's tenure *Fortune* dubbed JWT "the University of Advertising" because of its highly educated staff, well-developed research department, and extensive training programs.

JWT under Resor's control also became a conservative institution, more concerned with the account end of the business than with dramatic creativity. His favorite mode of advertising was the celebrity endorsement or "testimonial," which he used again and again, most notably for Pond's Cold Cream and Lux Toilet Soap.

It is interesting that a man who was as conservative as Resor should be responsible for one of the major social changes in the business. Probably influenced by his wife, he was the first advertising executive to make a regular habit of hiring women to work for him. Considering that, traditionally, so much of advertising is aimed at a female audience, it seems curious today that there was a time when the industry was peopled almost exclusively by men. Resor was the first to identify this contradiction and make a conscious effort to address it.

Perhaps his most lasting impact, though, was a result of his global vision. He was the first advertising figure to see the business on a worldwide scale. Starting in 1927, he opened branch offices in Europe, the Far East, South America, and Australia. By the time he retired, JWT was in 24 countries, with annual foreign billings of $150,000,000, and was one of the two or three agencies well equipped to tackle the challenges of a global economy.

Resor eventually retired in 1960. The major criticism leveled against him is that he remained at the helm for too long. He was over 80 at this point and, like Thompson before him, had lost some of his edge. Even so, his impact was almost entirely positive, and he remains one of the really significant figures in advertising's brief history.

Albert D. Lasker (1880–1952)

Albert Lasker was born in 1880, the son of German Jewish immigrants in Texas, and got his first job working as a writer for the *Galveston Morning News*. At the age of 18, he landed a job in Chicago working for Lord & Thomas, at that time the third-largest advertising agency in the world, and which had been founded in 1893. Initially, his role was menial, but he soon discovered a talent for attracting new business, and within a few short years he bought the company.

In his book *The Mirror Makers,* Stephen Fox describes the early years of the 20th century, a very prosperous era in advertising, as "The Age of Lasker." He strode the business like a colossus, and by the sheer power of his personality made Lord & Thomas the biggest and most influential agency in the world—and himself the unquestionable king of the industry.

A key moment in Lasker's early career came in 1904 when John E. Kennedy walked into the building where Lord & Thomas had their offices. He promised to be able to show Lasker what real advertising was. Lasker hired him. Kennedy always referred to advertising as "salesmanship in print," and Lord & Thomas became renowned for the quality and persuasiveness of its copy. Hard facts were considered more important than any aesthetic concerns, and for many years, Lasker wouldn't deign even to hire an art director. He also abhorred research, considering it only an expensive way of corroborating his own intuition. Kennedy stayed with Lasker for only a few years. His place as senior copywriter was taken by Claude C. Hopkins.

Lasker was a distinctively authoritarian figure, even a dictatorial one. David Ogilvy has described him as "overbearing, intolerant and arrogant . . . bad-tempered, demanding and inconsiderate." He did, however, hire talented people, and he paid them well but expected immediate results. He could be ruthless and irascible and would periodically fire large numbers of employees, or even resign accounts, on a whim. Yet this abrasiveness was offset by the quite remarkable vibrancy and exuberance of his personality, which inspired great loyalty from the people around him. He also had the most unusual ability of being able to immerse himself in the minutiae of a campaign without ever losing sight of the overall concept. All this, coupled with his willingness to work enormous hours, made him a formidable presence.

Lasker had many interests outside the advertising business. He was active in Republican Party politics, as well as being involved in many philanthropic concerns, mostly dealing with medical research. He enjoyed poker games with his male friends and played an enthusiastic, if unskilled, game of golf, even building an 18-hole golf course at his country estate. He also put together an extraordinary collection of paintings that many a museum would envy.

He retired, characteristically on impulse, in 1942 and had virtually nothing more to do with the business until he died in 1952. In 1942, he sold his share of the organization to three of his lieutenants, Emerson Foote, Fairfax Cone, and Don Belding on the proviso that they rename the company. And so the agency became Foote, Cone & Belding (now True North Communications).

It is unlikely that anyone will ever again be so dominant or leave such a legacy to the industry as Albert Lasker.

James Webb Young (1886–1973) and the Ways in Which Advertising Works

James Webb Young (always known as Jim Young) is the practitioner who had the greatest single influence during the 20th century on the advertising education of men and women in the business. Much of this comes from his small but influential corpus of published work; his influence thereby continues.[2]

Young was born in 1886 and grew up in Cincinnati. He left school at the age of 12 but spent the rest of his life educating himself by reading, thinking, and careful observation. This was how he developed the wide range of interests that he saw as the key to an advertising education. As described in his monograph *A Technique for Producing Ideas,* Young argues that the broader a person's knowledge and the greater his or her curiosity, the more fertile is that person's capacity for detecting interrelationships, which is the magical process at the heart of idea generation.

After he left school, Young had a variety of jobs, most successfully as advertising manager for a religious publisher, where he learned his skills as a mail order copywriter. Young joined Stanley Resor at the Cincinnati office of J. Walter Thompson (JWT) in 1912. He was to follow Resor to New York City in 1917.

For the next decade, Young and Helen Lansdowne Resor were the most influential creative figures in JWT. They both had a huge role in establishing the pattern of JWT advertising, which was characterized by long persuasive copy and stylish visuals. As a result, much of JWT's success can be attributed to them. Young also played a major part in opening JWT offices overseas.

In 1928, Young left the agency (albeit not permanently). He traveled widely and also embarked on a number of successful business ventures, including magazine publishing and the marketing of apples and hand-woven neckties from New Mexico: enterprises for which he wrote the advertising copy himself. He also carried out a number of assignments for the advertising industry and for the U.S. government.

From 1941 to 1964, he worked regularly for JWT as Senior Consultant. His wartime experience with the agency formed the foundation for his *Diary of an Ad Man*. In 1951-52, he served as consultant on mass communications for the newly organized Ford Foundation.

Young was a remarkable teacher. During the early 1930s, he spent 5 years as professor of business history and advertising at the University of Chicago. His two most important books, *How to Become an Advertising Man* and *A Technique for Producing Ideas* grew out of his university teaching. These slim volumes have been in continuous use as educational tools at JWT and many other agencies. Always interested in education, Young bequeathed money to help endow the graduate program in advertising at the University of Illinois.

The simplest and wisest commonsense description of the ways in which advertising works was written by Young in his book *How to Become an Advertising Man*.

Young emphasized the importance of advertising knowledge: knowledge of messages, of message carriers (i.e., media), and of trade channels. He always believed that knowledge and understanding are necessary conditions for successful advertising practice, and he thought that the best way to study advertising was by examining, classifying, and evaluating advertisements themselves. As mentioned, he was convinced that successful advertising practitioners were men and women with a broad range of interests, because it was only by people having broad interests that fresh, unorthodox ideas—which are in reality rearrangements of existing ideas—can develop and ripen. The wider the range of interests, the more unusual the juxtaposition that gives birth to new ideas.

Young saw advertising as working in five ways. Most advertisements work in more than one of these, although virtually every advertisement will concentrate for its effect on one specific way:

1. *By familiarizing:* making something better known. In Young's eyes, this represents the basic and underlying *value* created by advertising.

2. *By reminding:* a process sometimes strong enough to pay off on its own.

3. *By spreading news:* not just news of general interest but also news of specific product-related importance.

4. *By overcoming inertias:* that is, when the advertising campaign is endeavoring to alter or even slightly modify behavior. Overcoming inertia means change. However, for many large brands, advertising works as a reinforcement of existing buying behavior—that is, as a resistance to change. Inertia, in the sense of continuity of habit, works positively for such brands. This idea of maintaining (as opposed to overcoming) inertia is something that Young did not explore.

5. *By adding values not in the product:* the most challenging field for advertising creativity.

The greatest contribution made by this analysis to our understanding of advertising is the way Young articulates the notion of psychological added values. These have come to be accepted as the main features distinguishing a brand from an unbranded product. Young laid the foundation for the theory that a brand is a construct of two elements—competitive functional performance plus added values, the latter created to a large degree by advertising.

Raymond Rubicam (1892–1978)

Raymond Rubicam was born in 1892 to a large family. He had little formal education and spent most of his teens and early 20s doing a series of odd jobs before being hired to write copy for the Philadelphia agency F. Wallis Armstrong. He soon tired of the autocratic and conservative atmosphere at this company and in 1919 moved to NW Ayer where he blossomed and was involved with the legendary work being done for Steinway & Sons, the makers of pianos.

Being a free spirit, he very quickly began to feel the pull of being his own boss. To this end, he decided to set up his own shop in 1923 with a colleague from NW Ayer, John Orr Young. Thus was born Young & Rubicam, which was to become one of the giants of the industry. The two founders were well matched, Young being responsible for client services while Rubicam dealt with the creative product. Despite such modest beginnings and being initially underfunded, the partnership soon flourished.

Rubicam realized instinctively the importance of research in creating successful advertising campaigns. He employed a brilliant young journalism academic called George Gallup in 1932 to start one of the first and most important in-house research departments in any agency. Gallup, with Rubicam's support and active encouragement, developed techniques to ascertain the amount of information from an advertisement that a sample group remembered, and what portions they felt positive about. This, of course, is invaluable information for both agencies and their clients to assess how effective an advertisement has been. Gallup kept up his association with Young & Rubicam until 1947, in the process giving his employers an enormous edge over their competition.

Like Bill Bernbach, who was largely responsible for the creative frenzy that occurred in American advertising in the 1950s and 1960s, Rubicam built an environment in his agency where talented people could prosper. He hired Vaughn Flannery, one of the great art directors. He continually supported his creative staff in the regular wrangles that beset most agencies between the creative and the account people. He figured, correctly, that the client could forgive much in terms of compromised service if the final product was outstanding. He was also quite willing to resign an account if the client annoyed him or tried to intimidate his employees. He would refuse to accept a new client that he felt he couldn't service properly and would advise existing clients to hire other agencies if Young & Rubicam couldn't give them the level of performance they deserved.

Rubicam could be brutally honest, to the point of rudeness, but was also capable of enormous generosity. He was a conspicuous workaholic who demanded a similar commitment from those around him, and which he invariably received.

He retired in 1944 and moved to Arizona, although he kept himself busy with consulting jobs and real estate investments. He left behind one of the largest and most respected agencies in the world, and his influence is still felt by the successive generations of Young & Rubicam employees.

Footnote by the Editor

Raymond Rubicam was included in this volume among the 10 figures of major importance to the development of the advertising business at the personal insistence of David Ogilvy.

Leo Burnett (1892–1971)

Leo Burnett was born in Michigan in the last decade of the 19th century and graduated from the University of Michigan. After a short stint working for several small-town midwestern newspapers he moved to Detroit to write copy for Cadillac. From there, he moved to Indianapolis for Homer McKee Advertising and finally, in 1930, aged almost 40, to the mecca of middle America, Chicago, to work for Erwin Wasey & Company.

Then, as now, New York was the city to which all American advertising roads led. Young executives, having made a name for themselves in the smaller markets, would have to head east to scale the next step on the ladder. Burnett thought differently: He perceived an opportunity to create an agency in Chicago that spoke the language and shared the honest values of the great majority of American citizens who didn't live and work in New York skyscrapers. To this end, in 1935, he opened his own shop, with eight employees (all creative) and one client. At the time of his death, 36 years later, it was the fifth-largest agency in the world.

What set Leo Burnett Company apart from its rivals were the qualities that set the man himself apart. Burnett believed in what he referred to as "sod-busting corniness." He created advertising that spoke in plain and simple tones to the American people, reflecting and tapping into the basic core values that they held. He was never much interested in building an enormous agency with an ever-increasing list of clients but, rather, preferred to concentrate on a few valued (and high-profile) accounts. He believed in fostering a special relationship not only between his agency and its clients but also between those clients and their customers, the consumers of their brands.

To achieve this, he searched for the "inherent drama" in a brand and created a succession of "product characters" that the buying public recognized and with whom they identified. Most notable among these were the Jolly Green Giant, the Pillsbury Doughboy, Tony the Tiger, and the Marlboro Man. The latter was probably his crowning professional achievement and is largely responsible for turning a small brand into the biggest-selling cigarette in the world today. The success of these campaigns in turn led quite naturally to a remarkably close and long-term agency-client partnership.

Burnett's work credo was simple. He lived by the twin pillars of hard work and research. He was unstinting in his personal work habits, and he both expected and received a similar level of commitment from his employees. He managed to elicit an almost fanatical sense of loyalty from his people, and even today, almost three decades after his death, he is revered in his company. Employees are still trained in the Leo Burnett style of advertising, and senior positions are normally always filled from within the agency. Burnett had a mistrust of traditional forms of market research. He was more interested in ascertaining whether an advertisement was liked by the public. He thought that if he could manage to create a feeling of warmth between the public and the product, then the former would buy the latter. An increase in the client's sales meant more to him than any industry awards.

There is a school of thought that says that Burnett's methods are old-fashioned and out-of-date. There may be some truth in this; audiences are certainly more sophisticated than they were, but he left an indelible mark on the business, and his agency remains one of the most powerful in the United States and abroad. One reason is that—unusually—it long remained privately owned, which means that the management of the company has traditionally been focused on the advertising enterprise rather than on profit growth.

J. Stirling Getchell (1899–1940)

One of the greatest copywriters in the history of the advertising business, Stirling Getchell was born in New York in 1899 and was still at school in 1917 when America joined World War I. He enlisted in the Army Air Service and was discharged in 1919.

Then started a peripatetic apprenticeship in the art of writing advertising. During the next 10 years, he worked for numerous agencies, including Lord & Thomas and J. Walter Thompson, and earned a reputation as a brilliant copywriter. Yet he seemed unable to find a niche for himself. By the time the Great Depression descended on the country, Getchell was unemployed and unable to persuade anyone to hire him, the result of having trodden on rather too many toes over the course of the previous decade. In 1931, desperate, he decided, with partner John V. Tarleton, to set up his own company, J. Stirling Getchell, Inc.

The company's big break came a year later. Getchell had landed the advertising for DeSoto, a division of the Chrysler Corporation, and he managed to persuade Byron Foy, President of DeSoto, to let him try a new angle for an advertisement for the new Plymouth, also a separate division of Chrysler. Chrysler was at the time the smallest of the three Detroit automobile giants, and Getchell struck on the idea of running an advertisement with a photograph of the owner of the company, Walter P. Chrysler, inviting the car-buying public to "Look at All Three."

This advertisement helped create the idea that the head of Chrysler was a real human being, an honest, straightforward salesman who believed so strongly in his product that he felt the consumer should compare all the alternatives, because he was confident that his car was better. Despite the fact that the advertisement ran only once and that Getchell was paid only for his expenses, it remains one of the most famous and effective advertisements ever run and represents a technique still used to this day.

Getchell was a believer in the value of research, and he hired Dr. Ernest Dichter, an eccentric Austrian psychologist who used Freudian principles to develop much of his "motivational research" theory under Getchell's guidance.

Getchell also pioneered the use of large candid photographs in press advertising: a technique of presentation that subsequently became the norm.

Getchell's agency became the creative standard by which others were measured throughout the 1930s. Other accounts he worked on included Mobil Gas and Mobil Oil; Airtemp, Inc.; and Devoe & Reynolds Company, Inc.

In 10 years, the agency became one of the 10 largest in the world, but it is for that one Plymouth advertisement that Getchell will always be remembered. He died tragically in 1940 at the age of 41.

William Bernbach (1911–1982)

Bill Bernbach was born in Brooklyn in 1911. After majoring in English at New York University, he went to work for Schenley. There he met Grover Whalen who became an early mentor, and when Whalen left Schenley to coordinate the New York World's Fair in 1939, Bernbach went with him. When this was finished, he moved to Weintraub where he remained until America joined World War II, at which point he joined the Army.

After the war, he picked up his career at Grey, where he became Creative Head while still only in his mid-30s, In 1949, along with a colleague from Grey, Ned Doyle, and the independent owner of a small agency, Maxwell Dane, he founded his own company, Doyle Dane Bernbach. From the outset, each partner had a clear-cut role in the enterprise: Dane was the businessman who managed the financial end of the operation, Doyle ran the client service branch, and Bernbach was the creative inspiration. Despite modest beginnings (the company had an initial investment of just $1,200 and first year billings of $500,000), Doyle Dane Bernbach soon made an enormous impact on the industry, in large part due to Bernbach. The company became renowned for being on the creative edge, incorporating a fresh, innovative, and humorous approach to their advertisements. By the time of Bernbach's death, the agency was the 16th largest in the world.

In the era of the company's greatest growth, the 1950s, Doyle Dane Bernbach specialized in taking small accounts that were overshadowed in their respective fields by larger rivals and giving them a unique image that enabled them to make large inroads into their competitors' market share: Notable examples include Polaroid Cameras and El Al. This strategy continued into the 1960s when they acquired the Avis Car Rental Service and Volkswagen accounts. The latter provided a particularly striking example of Bernbach's philosophy. America was still the land of gas-guzzling automobiles, and Volkswagen was fighting a losing battle trying to sell their small, foreign—and to the general public—unattractive cars. Bernbach capitalized on the product's uniqueness and with a series of simple advertisements with the message "Think Small" managed to persuade a disillusioned generation of Americans that they were purchasing a totem.

At a time of great creative energy in the industry as a whole, Bernbach was able to keep his agency one step ahead of the competition. He did this by employing the most talented people available, many of whom were temperamentally unsuited to a career in the still quite rigid world of corporate America, and he gave them their creative freedom. He took the then unusual step of pairing copywriters and art directors in teams, working in the same office. He would then act as a firm but kind guiding hand, coordinating, cajoling, and inspiring his protégés. This made for an exciting, inspiring, and happy work environment, if sometimes a frenetic one, and his employees were fanatically loyal to him.

Like many creative people, Bernbach had great faith in his own intuition and a parallel distrust of research, which he felt could only lead to uninteresting advertising. He felt that, above all else, an advertisement should be vibrant, original, and fun, and more than any other individual he realized that a commercial could be an art form in its own right.

In the 1970s, there was a backlash against the free-thinking creative explosion of the previous decade. Doyle Dane Bernbach suffered as a result and began to lose clients. Things stabilized in the mid-1970s, but the company never returned to its previous glory days. Bernbach died of leukemia in 1982, and the downward spiral continued until 1986 when the company was forced into a three-party merger with Batten, Barton, Durstine & Osborn and Needham Harper Worldwide to form the Omnicom Group, Inc.

Despite this decline, Bernbach remains, perhaps, the single most important creative figure in the history of the business.

David Ogilvy (1911–1999)

This series of handbooks is dedicated to David Ogilvy. He is the last of the Founding Fathers, and it is unlikely that the business will throw up in the future any comparable figures to add to this list.

Ogilvy lived in France in his retirement and for a number of years was no longer directly involved in the advertising business. His achievements, however, lived after him, particularly in the vigor of his offspring, Ogilvy & Mather.

Ogilvy is the only one of the 10 seminal figures who was not born in the United States, although his professional career was built there. Born in 1911, he was a Scot and was educated at a distinguished Scottish boarding school, Fettes College (which Tony Blair later attended) and at Oxford University, where Ogilvy did not complete his degree.

During the depression of the 1930s, he had a variety of jobs, including one as junior chef in a leading Paris restaurant. In retrospect, he regarded all his early working experience as indirect preparation for his eventual career in the advertising business. During the late 1930s, he gravitated toward advertising and got a job in the old-established London agency Mather & Crowther. With their encouragement, he traveled to the United States in 1938 and decided to build his career in that country.

He spent a number of years working in market research under George Gallup, but he also did other things before he opened the doors of his own agency in 1948. In the beginning, he had few clients and slim financial resources. However, his agency, which was eventually named Ogilvy & Mather, became a national force in the advertising industry within 10 years, and it was one of the leading agencies in the world within 20.

David Ogilvy made four extraordinary contributions to the advertising business.

1. He was one of the most important creative figures in the history of advertising. As a writer of advertisements, he was almost unique (Claude Hopkins was his only rival) in that his creative work was embedded in a knowledge of consumers derived from research. Ogilvy was a full-time researcher before he started writing advertisements, and he remained passionately concerned with the mystery of how advertising actually works. His greatest talent was in writing print advertisements that were characterized by an unusual combination of strong salesmanship and elegant presentation.

2. He was one of the outstanding agency leaders. This was the result of a combination of commanding creative talent and a strong and persuasive personality. Paradoxically, he was not interested in agency management, and he always delegated this function at Ogilvy & Mather.

3. He was a visionary about advertising in certain important respects. He was well-known for articulating the long-term importance of brand values. He pioneered the move away from the commission system toward agency compensation based on payment for time-of-staff. However, he did not have much success in this, because of a lack of interest among clients and resistance from competitive agencies. Ogilvy & Mather was one of the first agencies to be publicly owned: a move Ogilvy admitted in hindsight to have been a mistake. It made it possible for the agency to be acquired in 1988 by the British communications conglomerate WPP.

4. David Ogilvy wrote four books about advertising: the only one of the 10 major figures to bequeath such a legacy.[3] The first of these books, *Confessions of an Advertising Man,* a best-seller published in 1963, is one of the handful of works on advertising that have had lasting value.

David Ogilvy died on July 21, 1999, as this book was going to press.

Notes

1. "The Legends," *Advertising Age*, Special Issue, "The Advertising Century," 1999, 50-78.
2. James Webb Young, *The Diary of an Ad Man* (Chicago: NTC Business Books, 1990). James Webb Young, *How To Become an Advertising Man* (Chicago: Crain Books, 1963 and 1979). James Webb Young, *A Technique for Producing Ideas (Chicago: Crain Communications, 1940 and 1972).*
3. David Ogilvy, *Confessions of an Advertising Man* (New York: Atheneum, 1963 and 1984). David Ogilvy, *An Autobiography* (New York: John Wiley, 1997). David Ogilvy, *Ogilvy on Advertising* (New York: Crown, 1983). David Ogilvy, *The Unpublished David Ogilvy* (New York: Ogilvy & Mather, 1986).

Background Reading

Among works consulted for this article are the following:

Advertising Age, Centennial Issue for J. Walter Thompson, December 7, 1964.
Derdak, Thomas, *International Directory of Company Histories* (Chicago: St. James Press, 1988).
Edwards, Larry, "Auto Advertising 'Hall of Fame' an Exclusive Club," *Advertising Age,* January 8, 1996, S40.
Elliot, Stuart, "The Media Business: Advertising; Leo Burnett Still Celebrates the Principles of its Founder," *New York Times,* November 6, 1991.
Fox, Stephen, *The Mirror Makers* (New York: William Morrow, 1984).
"J. Walter Thompson, Advertising Leadership, 1964–1989," *Advertising Age,* Special Supplement, November 27, 1989.
Lasker, Albert, *The Lasker Story* (Chicago: Advertising Publications, 1963).
"The Legends," *Advertising Age.* Special Issue, "The Advertising Century," 1999, 50-78.
Marchand, Roland, *Advertising the American Dream: Making Way for Modernity, 1920–1940* (Berkeley: University of California Press, 1985).
Mayer, Martin, *Madison Avenue USA* (New York: Harper Bros, 1958).
The New York Times Biographical Edition (New York: Arno, 1974).
Ogilvy, David, *An Autobiography* (New York: John Wiley, 1997).
Ogilvy, David, *Confessions of an Advertising Man* (New York: Atheneum, 1963, 1984).
Ogilvy, David, *Ogilvy on Advertising* (New York: Crown, 1983).
Ogilvy, David, *The Unpublished David Ogilvy* (New York: Ogilvy & Mather, 1986).
Siano, Jerry, "In for Repairs: Ayer's Image," *New York Times,* June 10, 1990.
Watkins, Julian Lewis, *The 100 Greatest Advertisements* (Toronto: Coles, 1980).

About the Contributors

Paula A. Alex, who began her professional career in 1968 at Olin Corporation, in new business and market research, joined the Advertising Educational Foundation (AEF) in 1985 as Vice President, became Executive Vice President in 1988, and was named Managing Director and Board Member in 1991. She came to the AEF with a strong background in business and advertising. In 1976, she joined SSC&B Lintas, making a change from corporate life to the world of advertising. At SSC&B, she worked on new business and broke into account management on the Lipton Tea account. She spent 7 years on Noxell's Cover Girl, which included new product development and international advertising. That was followed with 3 years at Laurence, Charles and Free, where she managed Del Laboratories' Sally Hansen and Heublein's Valbon wine introduction. During her tenure at the AEF, she established and implemented programs addressing the social and economic roles of advertising. These programs are steadily growing at college and university campuses across the country. In addition, under her guidance, the scope of AEF activities has broadened to include educational video production and a major Website expansion. She attended Connecticut College, received a diploma in French civilization from the Sorbonne, and completed her B.A. in French at American University in Washington, D.C., where she studied at the Graduate School of International

Studies. In addition, she has a certificate in business management from the New York University Graduate School of Business. She is a member of Advertising Women of New York and the American Academy of Advertising.

David Barr is Director General of the Market Research Society (MRS) in the United Kingdom. He has spent almost his entire career in the creation and marketing of information products and services. Having held executive and management positions with Xerox Publishing Group, the British Tourist Authority, and Reed Elsevier plc, he took up the position at MRS in July 1997 with a brief to strengthen MRS and its membership services and to broaden its international appeal.

Andrew Brown has been Director General of the Advertising Association (United Kingdom) since May 1993. He joined J. Walter Thompson, London, in 1965 and spent most of the subsequent 28 years in account management, with a 4-year stint in account planning. He was an agency Board Director for 10 years, and his account responsibilities included Rowntree Mackintosh, Teacher's Whisky, Rolex, the Anglo American Corporation of South Africa, Warner Lambert Healthcare, and Gallagher Tobacco. Internal management responsibilities included training and the account management department. He served on the Institute of Practitioners in Advertising (IPA) training committee for 12 years and was a member of the IPA Council from 1991 to 1993. He was Chairman of the CAM Education Foundation from 1994 to 1996 and was awarded a CAM Fellowship in March 1996. Since 1993, he has been a director of the Advertising Standards Board of Finance (ASBOF) and was appointed Chairman of the Committee of Advertising Practice (CAP) for an initial 2-year period commencing January 1, 1999.

Diane Foxhill Carothers was raised in suburban Philadelphia and moved to Illinois in 1959 when her husband joined the University of Illinois faculty. She later returned to college, received a B.A. and an M.L.S. from the University of Illinois, and became a library faculty member. In 1991, she compiled *Radio Broadcasting From 1920 to 1990: An Annotated Bibliography*. As Communications Librarian, she was responsible for the processing, indexing, microfilming, and administration of the D'Arcy Collection. Microfilming was underwritten by the National Endowment for the Arts. She also helped acquire the

Woodward Collection. She belonged to the American Academy of Advertising and was one of the Book Review Editors of *Journalism and Mass Communications Quarterly.* She retired as Communications Librarian and Associate Professor Emerita of Library Administration in 1995.

Helga Diamond has been the research and communications manager with the Advertising Federation of Australia (AFA) since 1995, where she researches and writes information material for the industry, for submissions, and for media and promotional releases. She also runs the AFA educational program, looks after associate members, and is responsible for publishing and marketing the AFA Effective Advertising Books. She holds a diploma in business administration from Cologne University and has a marketing background in the food industry with Unilever in Australia and Dr. Oetker in Germany.

Tessa Gooding is a member of the Institute of Public Relations and joined the Institute of Practitioners in Advertising (IPA) in London in 1990 from the Public Affairs Department of ESSO UK. She is responsible for the management side of the IPA's communication and marketing program and, in particular, the IPA's press relations program.

John Philip Jones is a British-born American academic and a graduate of Cambridge University (B.A. with honors and M.A. in economics). He spent 27 years in the advertising agency business, including 25 years with J. Walter Thompson in Britain, Holland, and Scandinavia, managing the advertising for a wide range of major brands of repeat-purchase packaged goods. In 1981, he joined the faculty of the Newhouse School of Public Communications, Syracuse University, where he is now a tenured full Professor and former Chairman of the Advertising Department. He is also Adjunct Professor at the Royal Melbourne Institute of Technology, Australia. His published works include eight books and more than 70 journal articles. He specializes in the measurement of advertising effects and is an active consultant to many advertisers and advertising agencies in the United States and overseas. He has been the recipient of a number of professional awards.

Philip Jones was born in London in 1963 and grew up in an advertising household. After living in Holland and Denmark as a small child, he was educated at

Stowe School in England and received a B.S. from Syracuse University in 1986. He lives in New York City with his wife and daughter. He is the Director of Research and Fulfillment and also a Copy Editor for the Social Register. His professional specialty is biographical research, and he has published several articles in the *Social Register Observer.*

Robert L. King, Executive Secretary of the American Academy of Advertising (AAA), is Professor of Marketing and Director of International Business Studies, Emeritus, in the E. Claiborne Robins School of Business of the University of Richmond in Richmond, Virginia. Previously, he served as Professor of Marketing, Head of the Department of Business Administration, and Associate Dean of the Graduate School at Virginia Polytechnic Institute and State University, as well as holding appointments at The Citadel, and the University of South Carolina. Besides being Executive Secretary of the AAA, he has held the offices of President of the Southern Marketing Association and Vice President for Finance, Treasurer, and Chairman of the Board of Governors of the Academy of Marketing Science, among others. In 1991, he was named "Senior Fellow" of the Academy of Marketing Science. He is the author or editor of approximately 90 books, articles, monographs, and published papers in the marketing academic literature. He lectures worldwide and has visited more than 30 countries during recent years. He is a graduate of the University of Georgia, where he received a bachelor of business administration degree. He also holds graduate degrees of master of arts and doctor of philosophy in business administration from Michigan State University. In 1992, he was awarded the degree of Doctor Honoris Causa by the Oskar Lange Academy of Economics in recognition of his research of Polish marketing structures and procedures and for his contributions to Polish-American educational cooperation.

Philip Kitchen is the Martin Naughton Professor of Business Strategy, specializing in marketing, at the Queen's University Business School, Belfast in Northern Ireland. There, he teaches and carries out research in marketing management, marketing communications, corporate communications, promotion management, and international communications management. He is Founding Director of the Executive MBA (1998) program. Before Queen's, he was Senior Lecturer in Marketing, and Founder and Director of the Research Centre for Corporate and Marketing Communications within the Department of Marketing at Strathclyde University. Prior to university life, he worked as a regional manager for a national firm in the United Kingdom before entering higher education as a mature student. A graduate of the CNAA (B.A. with honors), initially, he received master's degrees in marketing from UMIST (MSc) and Manchester Business School (MBSc), respectively, and his Ph.D. from Keele University. Since 1984, he has been active in teaching and research in the communications domain. He is Founding Editor of the *Journal of Marketing Communications.* He is editor of *Public Relations: Principles and Practice* (1997) and *Marketing Communications: Principles and Practice* (1999). He is coauthoring *IMC: A Multinational Approach* (1999) with Don Schultz of Northwestern University. He is a regular contributor to leading practitioner and academic conferences in Europe, the Pacific Rim, and the United States and Canada. He has written numerous articles that have appeared in all the leading communications publications, both in Europe and worldwide.

Elizabeth Lascoutx, Director of the Children's Advertising Review Unit (CARU), began her career there as its staff attorney in January 1991. In May 1994, she became the Acting Director until her promotion to Director in 1995. She was named a vice president of the Council of Better Business Bureaus in February 1997. She led CARU's comprehensive revisiting of its *Self-Regulatory Guidelines for Children's Advertising* in 1996 to include the new on-line media. One of her major successes on behalf of CARU was the conception and implementation of the informal inquiry procedure in mid-1991; this innovation reduced the time taken to modify inappropriate advertising to children from 60 to 15 days. Under her leadership, CARU continues to be a strong voice in children's advertising, as evidenced by her participation at the Federal Trade Commission's Public Workshop on Consumer Information Privacy in June 1997 and the Department of Commerce's Public Meeting on Internet Privacy in June 1998. CARU's progressive accomplishments monitoring national children's advertising earned an invitation to participate in the White House ceremony on July 1, 1997, when President Clinton announced his administration's Framework for Global Electronic Commerce, which supported self-regulation of the new media. In March 1999, she was honored with the first annual "Cyberangel of the Year" awarded by Cyberangels, the largest on-line education and safety organization. In April 1999, she was named to the U.S. National Action Committee of UNESCO's worldwide Internet safety project, Innocence in Danger. A graduate of Barnard College and Fordham University School of Law, she worked for 2 years as a partner in a general practice law office after receiving her J.D. in 1977. She was a sole practitioner in general law from 1980 to 1991, concentrating for the last 3 of those years on custody and divorce mediation. Her mediation experience has proven to be particularly valuable in working with advertisers to resolve conflicts with CARU's guidelines under the informal inquiry procedure.

Rana Said is a graduate of Valparaiso University, Indiana and received her M.S. in advertising from the S.I. Newhouse School of Public Communications, Syracuse University. She is currently Associate Account Director at Memac/Ogilvy & Mather, Dubai, United Arab Emirates, handling the Nestlé milk/nutrition account. In the early 1990s, she held the position of Advertising Instructor at Syracuse University, teaching the principles of advertising, and has been instructing at the American University in Dubai, specializing in integrated marketing communications and marketing research. She participated in a research project devoted to "environmental/economic factors influencing buying behavior," which was published in *Adweek* in 1991.

John G. Sinclair joined the Institute of Canadian Advertising (ICA) in 1990. He was appointed President in 1992, served for 4 years in that position, and has been a part-time consultant to ICA since then. He was born in Toronto, attended the University of Toronto, and joined the advertising agency industry in 1958. He served in contact management and administration in McKim Advertising, Toronto (now part of BBDO Canada), and Case Associates Advertising (a related company) until joining ICA in 1990. His advertising experience encompassed packaged goods, automotive, financial services, and government accounts.

Jan Slater, Ph.D., is Assistant Professor of Advertising in the E. W. Scripps School of Journalism at Ohio University in Athens, Ohio. Prior to her appointment at Ohio University, she was Assistant Professor and coordinator of the advertising major at Xavier University in Cincinnati, Ohio, and before that an Instructor in Advertising at the S. I. Newhouse School of Public Communications at Syracuse University, as well as at the University of Nebraska in Omaha. In addition to her 10 years of teaching experience, she has 20 years' experience in the advertising industry, having worked in both private industry and advertising agencies. Until 1990, she owned her own agency, J. Slater &

Associates in Omaha, Nebraska. Dr. Slater earned her B.A. from Hastings College, Hastings, Nebraska; an M.S. in advertising from the University of Illinois, Urbana—Champaign; and a Ph.D. in mass communications from Syracuse University.

Jim Spaeth is President of the Advertising Research Foundation (ARF). He is a past member of the ARF Board of Trustees. He previously served as Vice Chair of the ARF's Media Communications Council and as a member of the Video Electronic Research Council, Copy Research Council, and the Research Quality Council. Before joining the ARF, he was Executive Vice President— Ventures, at ASI Market Research, Inc., where he was responsible for ASI's Research Services for New Interactive Media, including Nielsen ASI Direct, a joint venture with Nielsen Media Research to provide Infomercial and long-term advertising research services; and ANYwhere Online, a joint venture of ASI, Nielsen Media Research, and Yankelovich Partners to provide research services for interactive on-line media, as well as interactive television. He was also responsible for the development of new services at ASI, including Brand Equity Measurement Services, Advertising Tracking, and Consumer Response Modeling. He started his career at Young & Rubicam as Vice President, Associate Director of Communication Information Services. He next spent 4 years with SAMI/Burke, first as Vice President, Marketing, and later in the BASES Group as Vice President, Advertising Decisions. Next, he was with Viewfacts, Inc., the research operations division of PEAC Media Research, Inc., Toronto, which measures consumer response to advertising, programming, and other creative material; Scan Canada, a single-source split-cable electronic test market facility in Canada; and Viewtel, an electronic consumer panel and survey system. He has a B.A. in mathematics and philosophy from Fordham University and an M.S. in econometrics from the Polytechnic Institute of New York.

Laurie J. Spar, Vice President, Academic & Industry Relations, Direct Marketing Educational Foundation (DMEF), has supervisory responsibility for the planning, promotion, and administration of all DMEF programs for students and professors. A frequent speaker to college groups, she has also written about DMEF activities and direct marketing education for various trade publications. She serves as educational liaison to regional direct marketing clubs, associations, and related business organizations, as well as to the Direct Marketing Association's Special Interest Councils. Named by Women in Direct Marketing International as its 1991 Direct Marketing Woman of the Year, she is a past member of its Board of Directors. She is also an adviser to the Educational Committee of Direct Marketing Day in New York and is a recipient of the Direct Marketing Club of New York's 1997 Mal Dunn Leadership Award. She also served on the advisory board and as speaker for the Direct Marketing Training Program, the Service Fund of NOW-NYC.

Henning von Vieregge served as a reserve Lieutenant in the Federal German Army before studying political science, sociology, and constitutional law at the universities of Bonn and Cologne. After more than 20 years in the fields of scientific research, journalism, and advertising, he became Spokesman and Director of the Federal Employers' Association. In May 1994, he was made Managing Director of GWA, the German Association of Advertising Agencies, and was promoted to Director General in 1995. He has for many years been involved in the Lutheran Church (Lutheran Academy Arnoldshain).

Printed in the United States
By Bookmasters